A HISTORY OF THE
EXMOUTH LIFEBOATS

A HISTORY OF THE
EXMOUTH LIFEBOATS

Across the Bar

ALAN SALSBURY

HALSGROVE

First published in Great Britain in 2010

British Library Cataloguing-in-Publication Data
A CIP record for this title is available from the British Library

ISBN 978 0 85704 073 2

HALSGROVE
Halsgrove House,
Ryelands Industrial Estate,
Bagley Road, Wellington, Somerset TA21 9PZ
Tel: 01823 653777   Fax: 01823 216796
email: sales@halsgrove.com

Part of the Halsgrove group of companies
Information on all Halsgrove titles is available at: www.halsgrove.com

Printed and bound in Great Britain by SRP Ltd, Exeter

Contents

Dedication
To the bravery and selfless dedication of the crews of
the Royal National Lifeboat Institution's Exmouth Station, past, present
and those yet to come.

Acknowledgements
I would like to thank and express my appreciation, not only to the RNLI, but to
all those who have assisted with facts, personal accounts and images which comprise this
publication. I extend my special thanks to Melanie and Tim Mock for putting up with my
endless questions, and for their assistance, knowledge, guidance and tireless efforts
in assisting me in the collation of this book.

Foreword

This book is an illustrated history of the Royal Lifeboat Institution, Exmouth Station. It tells us a lot about the bravery of the crews, and of the lives saved, bringing to life all that is best in the lifeboat service and giving a vivid insight into the boats and their service, from the very first boat launched in 1803, costing only £150, to the present day £2.5M Mersey Class all-weather lifeboat.

It is a great pleasure to be writing the foreword to Alan Salsbury's book *A History of the Exmouth Lifeboats - Across the Bar*. As a boat owner and a member of the Royal Yacht Squadron, of which several past members have been Chairman of the RNLI, it gives me a deep interest in the work of the lifeboats, especially those which have served the town of Exmouth.

From the early days of the first lifeboats, it has been a privilege for my family to have been involved with Exmouth and its lifeboats. The Royal National Lifeboat Institution, supported by the newly formed local committee, in launching their first Exmouth lifeboat, the *Victoria*, established a further landmark in the history of the town.

In this very interesting book, Alan Salsbury brings to life the first launch, on Monday 5 September 1859 when local dignitaries, about to embark upon a trial trip, witnessed the lifeboat being brought 'out of her house' and launched into the estuary. These dignitaries included Lady Rolle and various gentlemen, as well as the lifeboat crew.

I recommend this excellent book to those who read it, both locally and nationally, and dedicate it to the work of the RNLI and to the lifeboat in its new home.

Lord Clinton
Heanton Satchville
2010

Introduction

The town of Exmouth, as we know it today, takes its origin from a medieval fishing village that once stood at the mouth of the River Exe. It is the oldest resort town in Devon and for three centuries, from the time that resorts were known as 'watering places,' men and women have visited the town in search of health and contentment.

With the growth and development of the town, Exmouth became established as an important port, standing as guardian to the River Exe and gateway to the ports of Exeter and Topsham. Throughout the years, many unsuspecting vessels, both commercial and pleasure, have fallen victim of the infamous Exmouth Bar which guards the entrance to the River Exe, or strayed from the narrow navigation channel onto the waiting sandbank known as the Pole Sands. The Exe Estuary is not alone in witnessing maritime disasters, for the coastline between Exmouth and Lyme Regis has also seen its fair share of shipwrecks.

In later years, with a greater emphasis being placed upon leisure-time, the tourist trade enjoyed by Exmouth, together with her neighbouring resorts of Sidmouth, Branscombe, Seaton an Axmouth, has seen an increase in water-based recreation, often providing an individuals' first contact with the sea. It is unfortunate that in seeking recreation, some people have little or no regard for their own safety or the safety of others. Likewise they show little or no respect for their surroundings. It is often a salutary lesson learned that, although she may reflect moods: enticing, romantic, volatile, unforgiving and dangerous, she will not suffer fools gladly; after all, she is The Sea!

There will be a time when even the most experienced seafarer, professional or amateur, will encounter difficulty at sea. In many cases the circumstances warranting assistance will be beyond the individual's immediate control, many are of their own making. It is in such circumstances that, whatever the need and with out judgement of the individual, the unquestionable bravery and dedication of the men and women of the Royal National Lifeboat Institution is at hand.

In 2003 the Exmouth Lifeboat Station celebrated its bicentennial year. Whilst it is not possible to chronicle every launch of every lifeboat, during the 207 years of the station's history, this book attempts to record some of the acts of heroism and bravery of the crew of the Royal National Lifeboat Institution's, Exmouth Station.

Alan Salsbury
Devon 2010

'THE BANE of lifeboatmen is the cowboy
who comes down and puts his boat in the water
without knowing if he's going North, South, East
or West. His engine stops when he's in 30-fathoms
of water with a 10-fathom anchor line.'

Maurice "Mar" Mellish
2nd Coxswain Exmouth Lifeboat,
upon his retirement.

1
The Birth of the Exmouth Lifeboat

During the year 2003, the Royal National Lifeboat Institution's lifeboat stations at Exmouth, Plymouth, Penzance (Penlee) and Guernsey (St Peter Port), celebrated their 200th anniversary. The need for a lifeboat to be placed at these strategic stations was identified long before the creation of the Royal National Lifeboat Institution, so where did it all start?

The latter part of the 18th century, and the early years of the 19th century, saw a considerable interest in the development of a purpose built lifeboat. In 1789 a major sea tragedy occurred when, in a storm, the collier, *Adventure*, ran aground on the River Tyne, to attempt a rescue mission in such weather conditions would have meant almost certain death for the rescuers. Several thousand onlookers are reported to have watched in horror, as all the crew of the stricken vessel drowned. The tragedy so struck the members of a Gentlemen's Club in South Shields, that they sponsored a competition to provide a design for a Lifeboat, offering a reward of two guineas. William Wouldhave, the Parish Clerk of South Shields, drew up the winning design. The design, modified by the judges, was given to Henry Greathead from which he constructed the first purpose built lifeboat, *The Original*. The boat was launched on Saturday, 30 January 1790; she was 30-feet in length and was propelled by twelve oars. Her high-rise design, at the bow and stern, provided cases that contained 7cwt. of cork buoyancy, the hull was lined with cork and a cork rail provided additional buoyancy. *The Original* served for 40 years on the River Tyne, whilst thirty other vessels, built to the same specifications, were placed throughout Britain.

Locally, the 'stone-boats' that served the Maer limekilns with limestone and culm, continued to be numbered amongst the perennial casualties. These sailing vessels were obliged to approach close to the shore in order that the limestone could be thrown overboard and collected from the beach at low tide. Exmouth suffered the effects of a particularly severe storm, in July 1802, which

Left: The '*Original*' (later named *Zetland*) a North Country Class lifeboat built to the design of Henry Greathead.

Below: Greathead's plans for the '*Original*'

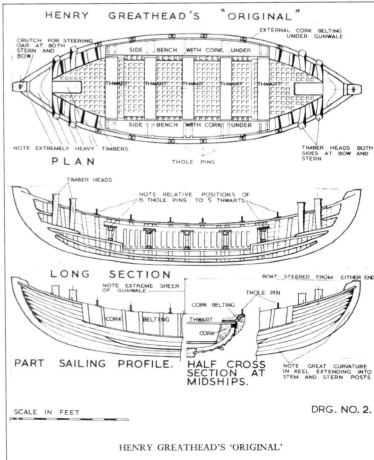

HENRY GREATHEAD'S "ORIGINAL"

EXTERNAL CORK BELTING UNDER GUNWALE

CRUTCH FOR STEERING OAR AT BOTH STERN AND BOW

SIDE BENCH WITH CORK UNDER

SIDE BENCH WITH CORK UNDER

NOTE EXTREMELY HEAVY TIMBERS

PLAN

THOLE PINS

TIMBER HEADS BOTH SIDES AT BOW AND STERN

TIMBER HEADS

NOTE RELATIVE POSITIONS OF 6 THOLE PINS TO 5 THWARTS

LONG SECTION

BOAT STEERED FROM EITHER END

NOTE EXTREME SHEER OF GUNWALE

THOLE PIN

CORK BELTING

CORK BELTING

THWART

CORK

PART SAILING PROFILE.

HALF CROSS SECTION AT MIDSHIPS.

NOTE GREAT CURVATURE IN KEEL EXTENDING INTO STEM AND STERN POSTS

SCALE IN FEET

DRG. NO. 2.

HENRY GREATHEAD'S 'ORIGINAL'

resulted in loss of three lives, the sinking of a 'stone-boat' on the Bar, and the loss of two fishing vessels. This tragic loss led to a public subscription for a lifeboat, the local press, Trewman's *Exeter Flying Post* of 23 September 1802, reporting that:

A Humane Public is solicited to subscribe towards the purchase and maintenance of a LIFE BOAT, to be kept at Exmouth, for the purpose of saving the Lives of Mariners in Danger of being shipwrecked in the Vicinity of the Harbour and other places. The sum necessary for the purpose is about £200.

Contributions are received at Exeter by (?) MILFORD Esq. and at Exmouth by the Rev. Ken MARKER.

Subscriptions:

The Commissioners of Lloyds	*£50*
Rt. Hon. Lord Rolle	*£30*
Milford	*5.5*
W. T. Hall and others	*5.5*
E. Devett	*5.5*
John Cholwich	*5.5*
Edward Cosforth	*5.5*
T. H. Lee	*2.2*
Rev. Marker	*1.1*
Mr. Black	*1.1*
Mr. Heathcote	*1.1*
Rev. Mr. Jenkins	*1.1*
And others	
Total Raised approx.	*£134.17s.0d*
Total Cost of Boat approx.	*£150.0s.0d*

By December 1802 the Fund had realised £140, the majority of which was defrayed by Lord Rolle of Bicton. From this subscription, together with a donation of £50 from the Lloyd's Corporation, a lifeboat, of the Greathead design, was purchased and placed in the Port of Exmouth. Once again it was *Trewman's Exeter Flying Post* that, on Thursday 29 September 1803, reported the occasion:

The inhabitants of Exmouth and its Vicinity were on Saturday left highly grateful with the arrival of the Lifeboat, purchased by subscription, of which the Rt. Hon. Lord Rolle was the principal promoter, for the laudable purpose of preserving the lives of those who may suffer shipwreck. She is lying near the

Passage House, Exmouth, where numbers of spectators daily arrive to gratify their curiosity with a view of this curious boat.

It was reported that this first lifeboat cost approximately £150.

Lord and Lady Louisa Rolle, formerly Louisa Barbara Trefusis, were great philanthropists laying and shaping the town of Exmouth that we know it today.

Upon the death of Lord Rolle, certain parts of his estate were inherited by the Hon. Mark George Kerr Trefusis, second son of the nineteenth Lord Clinton.

In 1852, by Royal License, the Hon. Mark Trefusis assumed the title and armorial bearings of Rolle. Upon his death in 1907 his estate and title passed to his nephew Charles, the 21st Baron Clinton, and subsequently to his great grandson Gerald Neville Mark Fane Trefusis, the present Lord Clinton.

Even with the introduction of Exmouth's first lifeboat for many years to come rescues were undertaken, and assistance given to vessels in distress in the waters off, and adjacent to the River Exe, by the port's Pilot cutters and local boatmen. In October 1806 the brig *Pursuit*, of Shields, was severely damaged when she struck the Bar, whilst inbound with a cargo of coal. The privateer, *Thornborough* of Plymouth, together with her crew of four, was lost on Monday 2 November 1806. That very same day, the cutter *Mermaid* of Guernsey was found drifting in the channel of the River Exe; the whereabouts of the crew was never established. In 1807 the *Fox* was lost when her Captain apparently mistook Exmouth for Bridport and on 26 November 1810 the *Widdecombe* inward bound from Dartmouth to Exeter, became a total wreck on the Maer Rocks. Further lives were lost on Monday 16 November 1812 when the *Brothers*, of Cardiff, ran onto Orcombe Point. With the wreck of the *Brothers*, six lives were lost; the survivors were rescued having spent the night clinging to the rigging.

During one particularly violent storm, in 1814, the heavy seas and rising tide undermined the lifeboat house completely washing it away. The fate of the lifeboat is not known. It is however known that the 'North Country' lifeboat did not find favour with lifeboat crews, other than on the east coast of England, the handling, shape and size of the craft being totally alien to the men of the West Country.

At some point, following the storm of 1814, the Exmouth lifeboat station lapsed into disuse until a new boat was sent to the station, and a new boathouse was constructed, in 1859.

On 20 February 1817 the *Moon* bound from Teignmouth to Topsham with a cargo of clay pipes, foundered, and was also smashed to pieces, under Orcombe Point.

It is unfortunate that enquiries made, both locally and with the British Library's Newspaper Library at Collingdale, London, have failed to locate contemporary account of these tragedies as newspaper records, for the town of Exmouth, do not appear to exist prior to July 1869, albeit short references may be located in the newspapers of adjoining towns. One factor, however, is common to all these tragedies; nowhere in the brief accounts of these incidents is reference made to the use, or indeed the existence, of an Exmouth lifeboat. Indeed, to date, no records have been traced to indicate that Exmouth's 'North Country' lifeboat was ever launched to provide a service for the saving of life at sea.

At this time in our history, many lifeboats were independently operated. A man with great foresight, Colonel Sir William Hillary, a member of the Douglas lifeboat crew, Isle of Mann, readily identified the need for a co-ordinated approach to saving life at sea, and the requirement of a national regulating body.

In 1823 Sir William Hillary published his paper '*An Appeal to the British Nation on the Humanity and Policy of Forming a National Institution for the Preservation of Lives and Property from Shipwreck*', in which he highlighted the short falls, which he perceived, in the existing provision of lifeboat cover and outlined his recommendations for a national lifeboat service. His paper found wide spread support and sympathy for victims of shipwreck. On 4 March 1824, at a meeting in the City of London Tavern, the National Institution for the Preservation of Life from Shipwreck (NIPLS) was formed. King George IV became Patron of the Institution, The Prime Minister, Lord Liverpool, the President and Thomas Wilson M.P., the Secretary. Hillary's Institution sought to alleviate the nation's loss and misery caused by shipwreck. Sir William Hillary became the holder of no less than three RNLI Gold Medals, the Life-boatman's' equivalent

of the Victoria Cross. Not surprisingly, Hillary's family motto was '*With courage, nothing is impossible.*'

Initially the Institution received annual Government funding but this soon fell by the wayside. Subsequent to 1827, HM Customs, or Revenue, were primarily responsible for rescuing and saving lives of shipwrecked mariners. The boats used by the Revenue were not of a specific design but were of a model, and colour, that reflected, and blended in with, those used in the local community, thus proving advantageous for the detection of Revenue evasion.

In these formative years of the RNLI there was not an active lifeboat at Exmouth, nevertheless the Institution continued to recognise bravery shown by individuals in rescuing and preserving life from shipwreck. The Institution acknowledged such acts of bravery by the presentation of Gold or Silver Medals, and subsequently, in 1917, Bronze Medals.

The Institution awarded five such Silver Medals in respect of Exmouth rescues as follows:

In 1831 a Silver Medal was awarded to the Chief Officer of Coastguard, Lieutenant John Sargeant R.N. for the rescue, on Monday 6 December 1830, of the crew of the brig *Unity*. The vessel was driven ashore, near Exmouth, during a violent storm. The use of the 'Manby' rocket apparatus failed when the line broke. Lieutenant Sargeant went into the surf, taking with him a rope and, with the assistance of two of his crew and several local inhabitants succeeded in saving the crew of seven from the brig.

Thomas Pincombe, a local pilot, was awarded a Silver Medal following his attempt to rescue the crew of the brig *Mary*, which was wrecked at Exmouth on 5 January 1851. Pincombe's efforts were however thwarted when his boat capsized and he was himself thrown into the sea.

Following the wreck of the schooner *John Grónsünd*, of Svendborg, on Thursday 4 January 1894, the Institution awarded three Silver Medals. The awards were made to John Bradford, Uriah Bradford and George Prowse who, at great personal risk, launched a small boat into a full south easterly gale and heavy seas to save the lives of the schooner's crew of six; the vessel having been driven onto the Pole Sands. *(see Joseph Somes.)*

On 3 January 1854 the 73ton schooner *Friends*, of Exeter, laden with coal and on passage from

Hartlepool, anchored off Exmouth to ride out north-easterly storm force 10 winds. Unable to enter the River Exe unaided, the Master of the *Friends* burned distress signals in an attempt to attract assistance from the river pilots; assistance was not forthcoming. The Master of the *Friends* set a new course to seek the shelter of Torbay but in so doing struck either the 'bottom' or a submerged object and was force to beach the vessel between the Langstone Rock and Dawlish. Although the crew of five reached the safety of land, the *Friends* was a total loss.

The *John Grónsünd*, of Svendborg - Silver Medal rescue by Bradford, Bradford and Prowse, 1894.
Courtesy of the Bill Sleeman Collection

2
The Victoria
June 1859 – April 1867

Type: Peake - Self Righting   Propulsion: Pulling / Sail   Oars: 6   Crew: 8
Length: 30' 0"   Beam: 6' 3"   Displacement: 1T 5Cwt
Built: 1858   Builder: Forrestt, Limehouse.
Services: 2   Lives Saved: 0   Coxswain: Edward Tupman

With a continuing number of shipwrecks being witnessed in the waters adjoining Exmouth, the Committee of Management of the RNLI, at a meeting on Thursday 5 February 1857, considered a letter that had been received from Lieutenant J. D. Agassiz R.N. a resident of Exmouth. In his letter Lt. Agassiz expressed his considered need for a lifeboat to be placed at Exmouth. The necessary inquiries were made by the Institution and, subsequent to the intervention of Lady Rolle of Bicton, in October 1858, offering to provide the full cost of such a vessel, the second lifeboat to be placed at Exmouth arrived 'on station' in June of 1859.

Prior to the arrival of the new lifeboat, which was to be the first Exmouth Lifeboat to be operated under the Authority of the Royal National Lifeboat Institution, the contemporary press reported, on 9 December 1858, upon the formation of a Local Branch Committee:

'An effective branch of the Royal National Lifeboat Institution is being formed at Exmouth. Admiral Sir Fairfax Moresley K.C.B., has consented to become the chairman of the local committee and Lieutenant Agassiz R.N. their honorary secretary. An estimate for the building of a substantial and attractive Life Boat House has been given by the parent Society and orders have been given to proceed with the house forthwith; it is expected to be ready in about six weeks from this time. The Life Boat and her transporting carriage will be on station as soon as the house is ready for

their reception. The local committee have issued an appeal for public support in which they state that although Lady Rolle munificently offered to contribute £250 towards the undertaking, the amount will not defray much more than the cost of the Life Boat and carriage.

It will therefore be necessary to provide funds for the erection of the boat-house, and annually from £20-£30 towards the future maintenance of the establishment. We trust that the appeal will be liberally responded to. Agreeable to the rules of the institution coxswain, at a salary of £8 a year and a volunteer crew for going off to wrecks and for periodically exercising her will be appointed.'

To the obvious delight of the newly appointed Committee, the following announcement also appeared in the local press:

'Our members are probably aware that the Royal National Lifeboat Institution is about to send a new Life Boat and carriage to Exmouth, the cost of which together with that of a substantial Life Boat House, Lady Rolle has munificently promised to defray. We are glad to understand the Hon. Mark Rolle has also, with his went liberality, promised to lease at a moderate rent, a piece of ground on which the Life Boat House is being built and to give in addition a very liberal subscription of £10 a year to the general object of the Royal National Lifeboat Institution.

The launch of the *Victoria* Illustrated London News

The Society now has eighty-one boats under its management. The boats saved last year the lives of 110 of our fellow creatures from a watery grave.'

Lady Rolle in fact donated the sum of £375, meeting the entire cost of the lifeboat and boathouse. A further sum of £60 was raised, by public subscription, allowing the purchase of the lease of the land upon which the boathouse was to be built. The lifeboat, which cost £140.1s.0d, carried a crew 8 and rowed 6; the launching carriage cost an additional £51.12s.6d. The boat was 30-feet in length and had a beam of 6' 3". She had self-righting properties and was built, in 1858, by Forrestt of Limehouse.

The Exmouth boathouse was built to the design and specifications of the Institution's Honorary Architect, C. H. Cooke, and set out in an Instruction issued by Richard Lewis, Secretary of the Royal National Lifeboat Institution, which read:

Royal National Life-boat Institution
Exmouth Life-Boat House
INSTRUCTIONS

The local Life-boat Committee are requested, as soon as possible, to select the most suitable site for the Life-Boat House, having reference to convenience, and for conveyance of the Life-boat upon her Carriage by land along the coast; and to procure and forward to the Central-Office in London, estimates from two or more parties for building the House. The dimensions should be, for Double-banked boats or Single-banked boats

Length (inside measurement)
40 feet   40 feet

Width (inside measurement)
17 feet   14 feet
Width of doors
14 feet   12 feet
Height of doors
12 feet   10 feet

There should be large folding-doors of the above dimensions on the side facing the water, and if it will be an advantage to be able to take the Boat out on the Carriage in the rear of the House, when about to proceed by land along the coast, doors of the same dimensions should also be placed at that end, otherwise, a small door at the rear will suffice.

The materials had better be brick or stone, whichever is most economical; and the roof should be slated. A boarding or flooring about six feet in length should be placed for the purpose of forming a loft at the level of the wall-plate of roof at the rear end of the house, on which to keep spare gear, &c., and a batten with wooden pegs for hanging up the Life-belts should be fixed at a convenient height along the side walls.

The floor should be paved with bricks or stones, or floored with wood as may be thought best. If the boats be provided with a carriage, ways of timber or large stones will be required to be placed at the requisite distance apart for the wheels to run on.

There should be two windows to admit light, and openings above the doorway at each gable to secure ventilation.

The words "LIFE-BOAT, supported by Voluntary Contributions," to be painted at one end of Doors of Boat House. As it will be desirable to have the Boat on her station as soon as practicable, it will be well to lose as little time as possible in getting a House prepared for her reception.

The boathouse, built fronting onto the beach, close to the Coastguard Station, at a cost of £184.19s.7d. It was officially inaugurated on Friday 3 September 1859.

The following quotation is taken from the publication 'All the Year Round' by Charles Dickens, 1860:

'I came by accident upon the lifeboat house. It was a neat stone building, with some show of architecture in it, with a verandah due east and west, sheltering forms on which pilots and others might sit under during foul weather. I have been told that at this town, boathouse and boat were the gift of a lady of fortune, and it was evident that she was one who did not give two fingers.'

Records of an official Ceremony of Inauguration of the new lifeboat have not been found, albeit it is known that the boat was named *Victoria*. The Coxswain of the new lifeboat was Edward Tupman.

A party of dignitaries and officials, including Lady Rolle and the Secretary of the Royal National Lifeboat Institution, inspected the boat and took to the water in her, on Monday 5 September 1859. The following account is to be found in the Illustrated London Times of 24 September 1859:

'The usually quiet little town of Exmouth, Devon, was thrown into some excitement on Monday, the 5th inst., when it had become generally known that Lady Rolle and some of her friends, accompanied by the secretary of the Royal National Lifeboat Institution and some gentlemen of the place, had decided on taking a trial-trip in the new life-boat recently sent here by that society. Accordingly, at about eleven o'clock, the life-boat was brought on her carriage out of her house and launched from it, having on board at the time Lady Rolle, the Countess of Antrim, Lady Helen McDonell, Miss Parlby, the Rev. J. Hall Parlby, Lieut. Agassiz, R.N., and several other gentlemen, with the boat's crew. This operation which is sometimes so difficult of accomplishment with some life-boat carriages, was in this instance quickly performed, in consequence of the ingenious but simple mechanism of the life-

boat carriage. Indeed, the whole work of launching, from the time the boat and carriage, drawn only by her crew and a few extra hands, were taken from the house to the beach, which is very soft and sandy, did not occupy ten minutes. Nothing could have been more satisfactory, and loud were the expressions of approbation of the proceedings, and of the singular energy and intelligence which the National Life-boat Institution had brought to bear on its sacred and humane objects.

The life-boat afterwards proceeded, with Lady Rolle and her party, in gallant style outside the bar. The boat's behaviour whilst ploughing through the seas elicited the admiration of every one on board. She was afterwards brought alongside a vessel, and there, with the aid of tackling, she was, after some difficulty, capsized, but she instantly righted herself, from a peculiarity in her construction, and self-ejected the water she had shipped in a few seconds. This operation again excited the loud applause of the people on board, and on shore, as such an effect was doubtless quite novel to many persons at Exmouth. Some successful experiments were also made with the cork life-belts, which each man of the crews of the society's life- boats is now always

Edward Tupman, Coxswain 1859–1880.

required to wear before going afloat in the boat. One of the crew fearlessly plunged into the sea with his belt on, and, after performing various exploits, readily regained the shore.

The life-boat is a beautiful craft. She is 30 feet long, 6½ broad, and was built by Forrestt, of Limehouse, after the plan of the boats now adopted by the Institution. The life-boat house is a commodious and handsome building.

There is probably, not a more complete life-boat station on any coast of the United Kingdom than that at Exmouth. The entrance to this port is very dangerous, being surrounded with sandbanks and hidden rocks, and some dreadful wrecks have occurred here.'

After once again extolling the generosity of Lady Rolle, and her munificent donation, the article offered the following information:

'A life-boat establishment is not an ordinary affair. Here often the hope of the shipwrecked seaman when struggling with deathlike grasp to some frail piece of his once-noble ship is concentrated. In the dark hour of the tempestuous night the minute-gun at sea is heard from the sinking ship. At its sound the people from far and near make with all haste for the life-boat house. The well-known report of the signal-gun has already brought the crew of the life-boat to the station. She is quickly launched. With brawny arms and stout hearts they valiantly contend with the raging surf, which runs, as they say, mountains high; but, with a resolute will, they are determined, with God's blessing, to reach the stranded vessel or perish in their perilous undertaking. At last the ship is reached; the crew are saved, and are soon on shore. The life-boat is carefully housed in readiness for another hazardous expedition, should her services be again required. This is no imaginary description. What we have related took place even last week at Southwold, Wick, and Bridlington; and previously at many other life-boat stations. We are told that the National Life-boat Institution has now eighty-five life-boat establishments in connection with it, on which it has expended upwards of £28,000. More than eleven thousand shipwrecked persons have been rescued from a watery grave since its first establishment, for saving whom it has been

voted upwards of £10,000, besides gold and silver medals and other honorary distinctions. Let the reader enquire at out sea port towns and fishing villages, and he will not fail to hear many a wife and mother expressing their gratitude for the preservation from drowning of either a husband or son. Indeed, only a few days ago we heard from the lips of a pilot in Shaldon expressions of heartfelt gratitude that his life and that of his "poor boy," as he feelingly called him, had been saved some time since during a gale of wind, and in the night, from inevitable death, on Teignmouth bar, by one of the lifeboats of the institution. There are many noble and valuable societies in this country, but we believe that there is none so deserving of public support than the National Life-boat Institution, judging exclusively from the plain and stirring facts which it frequently places before us. Even at its last monthly meeting on the 1st. inst. we have been informed that payments amounting to about £900 for new life-boats and carriages could not be discharged without infringement upon its funded capital. Surely the few facts which we have here stated relating to this valuable society will call forth from the British public such prompt and liberal aid as will enable it to persevere in its course of usefulness on a scale somewhat adequate to its great an national importance.'

Trewman's *Exeter Flying Post* did not see fit to report upon the inauguration of the *Victoria* but the issue of Thursday 8 September 1859 did comment upon a *'recent inspection of the lifeboat,'* the article leading one to assume that the inauguration and inspection probably took place on the same day:

'The new life-boat on this station was visited a few days ago by an officer from the National Lifeboat Institution. He expressed his entire approval of the excellent order in which he found the boat, transporting carriage, and boat-house, with their gear. We feel persuaded that there is not in connection with the above named valuable society a more thoroughly-organised life-boat station than that at Exmouth. The coxswain and seamen of the place speak in the highest terms of the qualities of the life-boat, which possesses the valuable qualities of self-ejecting instantaneously

any water she may ship, and of self-righting in the event of any untoward accident capsizing her. The cost of the life-boat establishment was the munificent gift of Lady Rolle to the National Life-boat Institution; but its thorough organisation is the work of Lieut. Agassiz, R.N., who, being a thoroughly practical sailor, has, in conjunction with Mr Hawkins, chief officer of the coastguard at Exmouth, devoted much attention to this philanthropic work. We trust it will receive the liberal support of the inhabitants of this place, for about £20 a-year is needed to meet the coxswain's salary and the crew's payment for exercising every quarter the boat.'

The *Victoria* underwent her quarterly exercise in December 1859 and receive a glowing report in the local press:

'This lifeboat, which belongs to the Royal National Lifeboat Institution, and is the munificent gift of Lady Rolle, had her quarterly exercise a few days ago. There being a strong south-east breeze blowing, there was sufficient sea on the bar to test her seaworthy qualities. The boat was launched in the usual manner about two o'clock, and the crew having their lifebelts on, pulled away gallantly through the roughest of the water out over the bar; and after rowing about for some time, she was brought to anchor in the worst part of the broken water, over which she rode most buoyantly. She was afterwards tried under sail and in going over the bar a sea broke into the boat, and filled her, when it was instantly self-ejected, and she passed on as though nothing had happened, whereas an ordinary boat must have foundered. She behaved admirably both pulling and under sail, and the crew have the utmost confidence in her safety. Colonel Browne, of the 87th Regiment, accompanied the crew, and expressed himself highly delighted with the admirable adaptation of the boat to the purpose for which she is intended.'

It is worthy of note that The Pilots Handbook of 1863 included the following entry in respect of the River Exe:

'As the entrance is not lighted, it cannot be run for with safety at night. It is at all times difficult of access, unapproachable in a heavy sea, and must on no account be depended on for refuge. From the entrance, which has a long shallow bar, the channel is narrow and winding and ought not to be attempted without a pilot.'

The coxswain and crew of the *Victoria* fulfilled their commitment to the Local Committee of the Institution by keeping the lifeboat in a state of readiness and putting her through her paces during the quarterly exercises. However, a full six years passed before the lifeboat was called upon to perform a duty, but even then the crew and boat were not put to the test.

It was on Wednesday 14 March 1866 that the brig *Congo* got into difficulty off Budleigh Salterton. Distress signals summoned the crew of the *Victoria* to assemble and ready her for service, but before the lifeboat could be launched the crew were informed that their services were not required.

Just over two months later, on Monday 21 May, the *Victoria* was launched into a full south-easterly gale, to go to the assistance of the French lugger, the *St. Luc*, which had run ashore on the Monster Sands at Dawlish. As in many early lifeboat services, at great personal risk, the crew battled very heavy seas as the boat struggled through severe weather conditions to reach the casualty, only for their assistance to be refused by the master of the French vessel. Wet, cold and exhausted, the crew of the *Victoria* returned to Exmouth without providing a service.

The *Victoria* was launched into the teeth of a south-easterly gale, and heavy rolling seas, on Saturday 5 January 1867 when she went to the assistance of the brigantine *Julia*, of Exeter, belonging to Mr J. Norrie, of Exmouth, under the command of Captain Canham, which had run aground, off Exmouth, striking the south-east corner of the notorious Pole Sands. The 148-ton vessel was carrying 240-ton of Newcastle coal destined for the merchant P. Varwell of Exeter. There was '*a considerable undue delay*' in launching the lifeboat, caused primarily by the adverse weather conditions, the launch finally being made by dragging the lifeboat seawards by the use of ropes. The crew of the *Victoria* made several gallant attempts to reach the brigantine but the racing seas and tide drove the lifeboat up river, thwarting their rescue efforts. Within 30 minutes, the *Julia* was reduced to wreckage with six of her crew of seven losing their lives in sight of the spectators that had gathered on the shore. The sole survivor of this tragedy was a seaman, Adam Stewart of Aberdeen who clinging to wreckage, was washed ashore. Of those who lost their lives, only the body of Captain Canham was recovered, being found between Lympstone and Exeter by the cutter *HMS Nimble*.

This tragic loss of life, combined with the apparent inability of the lifeboat to provide effective service, led to local criticism of both the lifeboat and her crew. The accusations were countered in the Exmouth Lifeboat Station Minutes, dated 15 January 1867:

'In compliance with a request from Capt. Ward. R.N., Inspector of Royal National Lifeboats, the under mentioned members of the local committee of this Branch assembled to enquire into reports stated in the local paper relative to the inefficiency of this Lifeboat and Station of her house.

Capt. Ward R.N. - Inspector of Lifeboats
Capt. Agassiz - Chairman
Capt. T. J. Phillips R.N.
R. Barnes R.N. - Commanding Nimble *Cruiser*
Wm. Hawkins R.N. Chief Officer Ct.Gd. Hon. Sec.

The other members being unable to attend through sickness and absence from the Town.

1st. After having fully considered the relative advantages and disadvantages of the Lifeboat House with that recommended near the Royal Naval Reserve battery. Resolved unanimously that the position of the present house is best.

2nd. Resolved that a ten-oared double banked lifeboat would be beneficial in place of the present six-oared single banked boat, provided a sufficient number of men could be inrolled to man the ten-oared boat proposed, and that the coxswain be directed to ascertain amongst the local boatmen, whether a sufficient number could be obtained for this service when required.

3rd. That we are of the opinion that the men who manned the lifeboat on the 5th January used their utmost exertions to reach the wrecked vessel "JULIA" of Exeter but in consequence of the violent gale that was blowing, together with the rapid tide, and the short time that the vessel held together, it would have been impossible for any lifeboat to have reached her in time to be of service.

4th. That the committee desire to acknowledge their thanks to W. Hawkins for his valuable and zealous services on the above occasion.

5th. That the Hon. Secretary be requested to summon the local committee quarterly to transact the necessary business of the Branch.

Criticism of the lifeboat was once more brought to the fore following the capsizing of the *Victoria*, whilst on exercise, on Tuesday 26 March 1867. The *Victoria's* self-righting properties proved effective and her crew of nine successfully regained the safety of the lifeboat. The local committee reviewed this incident at a meeting on 4 April1867; an extract from the minutes states:

'In consequence of the accident which took place on the aforementioned date by the lifeboat capsizing, the local committee met to enquire into the circumstances. We are of the opinion that there was no want of skill on the part of the coxswain or exertion of the crew, that the Coxswains objective was to keep the boat to windward to perform which he was under the necessity of dispensing with the drogue, had it been used it would have brought the boat to far leeward for her sails to assist her in regaining her station. That the behaviour of the lifeboat on this occasion, was such as to give the greatest confidence to her crew as to the self-righting qualities and a safe boat. That three of the crew by the accident damaged their clothes and two lost their caps. Recommended to the Parent Institution to make good these losses and to make also an extra payment to each of the crew as they may deem fit.'

Signed Fairfax Moresby, Chairman
Edwin L. Rich (Rear Admiral)
J. D. Agassiz (Comd. R.N.)
Thos Phillips - Inspecting Coastguard

Fortunately no lives were lost on this occasion but the incident amply illustrated the need for a more substantial vessel, one that could pull a greater number of oars, to meet the requirements of local conditions.

Following representations and careful deliberations, the R.N.L.I. pledged to equip the Exmouth Station with a larger lifeboat.

3
The Victoria
(Second of Name)
April 1867 – 1884

Type: Self Righting   Propulsion: Pulling   Oars: 10   Crew: 12
Length: 32' 0"   Beam: 7' 6"   Displacement: 2T 0Cwt
Built: 1867   Builder: Forrestt, Limehouse.
Services: 12   Lives Saved: 15
Coxswains: Edward George Tupman (1867-80), Edward Knight (1880-84).

Following the criticisms, concerns and representations, that had been expressed in respect of the lifeboat i.e. *'that she was not deemed heavy enough for making her way out of the passage in a gale,'* the *Victoria*, was replaced in April 1867 when a new 32-foot replacement boat was sent to the station. Overall, this boat was 2 feet greater in length and 15 inches greater in breadth. She was nearly twice the weight of her predecessor and could pull an additional four oars. The crew of the lifeboat was also increased from 8 to 10. Like her predecessor the new lifeboat, which cost £253.11s.0d., was also a gift from Lady Rolle and was likewise to carry the name *Victoria*.

The arrival of the new lifeboat was chronicled in *Trewman's Exeter Flying Post* newspaper of Wednesday 24 April 1867:

'The Royal National Lifeboat Institution last week sent one of its single banked lifeboats to Exmouth. The lifeboat is thirty feet long, and rows six oars. She is on Mr Peek's design, and was built by the Messrs. Forrestt, of Limehouse. She combines all the latest improvement that have been made in the boats of the institution. She will row fast in a seaway, if filled by a sea she will clear herself of water in twenty-five seconds, and she would instantly self-right if upset. A harbour trial of the lifeboat was made at Limehouse a few days before her departure for her station, when her peculiar and remarkable qualities were fully and satisfactorily developed. She is diagonally built of well-seasoned pine, which is the construction now adopted by the institution. The cost of the lifeboat station has been munificently presented to the institution by Lady Rolle. The lifeboat possessed all the qualities which it is desirable that a lifeboat should possess, viz., great lateral stability, speed against a heavy sea, facility for launching and for taking the shore, immediate self-discharge of any water breaking into her, the important advantage of self-righting if upset, the strength and stowage room for a number of passengers. The lifeboat carriage, which is in Capt. Ward's plan, is admirably suitable to its requirements. The boat on her carriage can thus be made available for a considerable distance on the adjacent coast. A substantial and somewhat ornamental boat-house has also been built for the boat and the carriage. There have also been forwarded with the lifeboat life-jackets for her crew, and every kind of useful store, many of which are of great value in cases of shipwreck. These life-jackets the crew are compelled to wear every time they go afloat in the lifeboat, for the institution is equally solicitous for the lives of the brave men who now so readily man its lifeboat as for those whom the violence of the storm has unhappily cast away on our shores. Accordingly, we find that notwithstanding that the lifeboats of the society have been manned by about 3,000 persons during the past year, not a single life was lost from them. The society has now

eighty-two lifeboats, and lifeboat establishments, which are so many beacons of mercy and tokens of our philanthropy on our sea-girt isle. When we state that each of these lifeboats involves an expense of nearly £30 a-year – to pay the coxswain's salary, and the crews for exercising them and to keep them in thorough working order, it will at once be seen that a large permanent annual incomes indispensable to maintain in an effective state, independent of the amount required to replace lifeboats, which from various causes have become useless. On our own coasts the National Lifeboat Institution has lifeboats at the following places:- Teignmouth, Penzance, Sennen Cove, Padstow, Bude Haven, Appledore (two boats), and Braunton.'

The *Victoria* had not long to wait before being called upon to prove her worth. She was launch into a severe gale, on Monday 15 July 1867, to go to the aid of the brig *Ranger*, of Newcastle, which was reported to be in distress, off the coast of Budleigh Salterton. The crew of the lifeboat were engaged in a titanic struggle, against both wind and sea, as they attempted to cross the Exmouth Bar and on more than one occasion the lifeboat took considerable amounts water. By the time that the *Victoria* had gained the comparative safety of the open sea, four of her oars had been broken. The valiant crew continued to fight their way into the teeth of the gale, as they made their way along the coast to Budleigh Salterton, a distance of approximately 2.5 nautical miles. Before the *Victoria* had reached the *Ranger*, the brig had run ashore, her crew having been rescued by the local rocket apparatus team. Leaving the wreck of the *Ranger* behind them, the crew of the *Victoria* struck out for home with little to show for their efforts.

One of the most difficult decisions to be made by a lifeboat Coxswain must be that of selecting a crew to accompany him on any particular call-out. This is as true today as it was in days gone by. The matter was reflected in the minutes of the Local Committee on Tuesday 3 January 1871, in which it is recorded that some dissatisfaction had been expressed at the mode of selection of the crew for the Quarterly Exercises. The following resolution was accepted:

'That all seafaring men who present themselves,

being in every other respect suitable, shall have a chance of Drawing in a Lottery, 1st for the boat crew & 2nd for the shore or launching and hauling up party, the former to be paid the proper Institution fee of 4/- each – the latter 1/6 each – but no person shall be allowed to go in the Lifeboat for the Quarterly Exercise who would not go if required for Service.'

During the late afternoon of Sunday 5 February 1871, the barque *Teviotdale**, of North Shields, was under tow by the Exmouth tug, the *Haswell*, having left Dartmouth, the previous afternoon, bound for Exmouth. The vessel, under the command of Captain Inch, was laden with a cargo of Indian corn, which was destined for the warehouses of Mr Lang, of Exeter. Between 1700-1800 hours, the vessels were at a point approximately 1 mile out of Exmouth, near the Mear Rocks, when the wind shifted dramatically to the West. With the change in wind direction, and fighting against a strong ebbing tide, the *Haswell* fought to keep the *Teviotdale* in clear water. The strain upon the towrope proved too great and it parted, leaving the barque to drift onto the sands. The *Victoria* was launched and immediately made her way to the stricken barque. The lifeboat's offer of assistance was rejected, the crew of the *Teviotdale* refusing to leave their ship. The following morning, assisted by the Pilots the barque was refloated, having sustained minimal damage.

This rescue is the first to be recorded on the Service Boards of the Exmouth Lifeboat Station, the inscription simply reads:

'1871 Feb. 5. Barque Teviotdale of North Shields, stood by.'

*Note: *Freemans Exmouth Journal*, of Saturday 11 February 1871, recorded the name of the casualty as the *Cheviotdale* and her port of registration as being *South Shields*.

Exmouth was being subjected to west-north-westerly gale force winds, on the night of Thursday 5 December 1872, as the schooner *Flora*, of Exeter, prepared to enter the River Exe. The vessel was negotiating the entrance channel when the wind suddenly veered to the west, driving the vessel towards the Pole Sands. In endeavouring to regain open water, she missed stays and started to drift ashore. The *Flora* let go both anchors in an attempt to prevent the vessel from being driven onto the sands. The skipper of the *Flora* realized the potential danger of his situation and order distress signals to be burned. The signals were spotted and both the *Victoria* and the pilot boat were launched.

With the assistance of both the pilots and the lifeboat crew, the *Flora*'s sails were raised; one anchor weighed, the other slipped, and on a rising tide the schooner floated free from the sands and reached the safety of the open sea. The following morning the schooner was taken into Exmouth Harbour, where subsequently the condition of the vessel was described as being '*considerably strained but not seriously damaged.*' In saving the *Flora*, the lifeboat also saved her crew of six. This rescue was infact the first on which the Exmouth lifeboat was credited with the saving of lives.

As previously noted, at this time a large number of vessels were registered in the Port of Exeter and the sub-ports Exmouth and Topsham. One of the most important shipbuilding and ship-owning families of the River Exe was the Holman family of Exmouth. It was a vessel, belonging to this family, to which the *Victoria* was requested to render assistance as the town celebrated the New Year of 1873. The New Year celebrations took place as Exmouth was subjected to severe gales, heavy rain and treacherous seas that lash the town for most of the first week of January. It was on the morning of Friday 3 January 1873 that Holman's barque, the, *Mary Ann Holman* of Topsham, Perriam Master, and valued at four thousand pounds, was seen to be in difficulty approximately one and a half miles from the Exmouth Preventive Station. The barque had been returning from Plymouth to Topsham dock, where she was to undergo necessary repairs. In gale force conditions, the vessel, which was in ballast, was making her way over the Bar when she was driven to leeward. The vessel's anchors were set and had they failed to hold, she would have found herself in a very perilous position indeed.

On this particular day the prevailing adverse weather conditions were accompanied by a very dense fog, which shrouded the vessel's critical state until breakfast-time. To many, the first indication to be given of the potential danger, in which the *Mary Ann Holman* rested, was the firing of the gun at the Coastguard Preventive Station. The lifeboat, *Victoria*, was immediately launched and a steam-tug also put to sea. Notwithstanding the gale force wind, which was blowing from the west-northwest,

and the torrential rain, hundreds of people are reported to have left their breakfast tables and headed to the beach, and surrounding areas, to render any assistance they could. The crew of the *Victoria* approached the barque and for two hours showed great skill and seamanship in keeping the lifeboat in a position from which they could immediately take off the crew of the *Mary Ann Holman*, should the necessity have arisen. The *Exmouth Journal* reported that:

'*...not a little anxiousness was manifested for the safety of a plucky couple of sailors who put off in an open cockle-shell boat to give their assistance on board, if such were needed.*'

The barques' anchors held and the crew of the steam-tug were successful in establishing a towline but, unfortunately, before the tow could commence, the line parted. The barques' anchors continued to hold and the tug re-established the tow. Again the towrope parted. The *Mary Ann Holman* dragged her anchors and ultimately drifted onto the shore near Rodney Steps. Commander Quigley, of the Coastguard Station, had ordered his lifesaving team to set up their rocket apparatus at a point close to Rodney Steps, from where they were successful in establishing a lifeline and bringing two men, Holman and Thomson, who were apparently the occupants of the open cockle-shell boat, ashore. The Captain and crew of the *Mary Ann Holman* declined to leave their vessel, the Captain requesting that the lifesaving apparatus team should remain nearby until nightfall. Every effort was made to refloat the barque but she was gradually driven further up the beach until the receding tide left her stranded thus enabling her crew to walk ashore. The condition of the *Mary Ann Holman* was described as '*Much shaken – her keel having been carried away by the force of the gale she encountered.*' These efforts to refloat the vessel proved unsuccessful; infact the Exmouth Journal of 11 January reported that the vessel '*remains hard and fast in her perilous position.*'

The circumstances surrounding this rescue were discussed at a special meeting of the Local Committee held on 21 January 1873, as the lifeboat Coxswains were absent at the time of the Service. The 'inconvenience' had resulted from both Coxswains being engaged on duty as Pilots

Above: The second *Victoria* and Boathouse.
Courtesy of the Bill Sleeman Collection

Left: Edwin Knight, Coxswain 1880–1897.

Below: Wreck of the *Julia*. A photograph of water colour painting by George Whitaker dated 1868.
Courtesy of the Bill Sleeman Collection

and no suitable deputy was available. It was resolved *'that the Coast Guard authorities be requested to permit one of their men to fill the position of 2nd Coxswain.'* It was felt that, from his knowledge of the Port, George Gibbons, Chief Boatman of Coast Guard was best suited for the position. He was subsequently appointed.

The distress gun of the lifeboat house sounded on Wednesday 25 February 1874 to warn the lifeboat-men and town that a vessel was in danger. A large number of people soon gathered, and made their way to the beach, to watch a French galliot, running before the wind, just outside the Exmouth Bar. In crossing the Bar, the vessel, the *Marie Elizabeth*, of Havre, was seen to touch the bank on two or three occasions, before becoming stranded on the sandbank. The galliot, which was laden with hides, was bound for Teignmouth where she was to await orders. The galliot first got into difficulty near the Pole Sands and her Captain, realising that he was unable to make Teignmouth, made for the port of Exmouth. Upon entering the mouth of the River Exe he found himself surrounded by breakers; he put his helm up and boldly steered for the shore, hoping that the tide was sufficiently high to carry him over the Bar and into safer water. Had the *Marie Elizabeth* arrived at the Bar about an hour earlier, she could very well have been carried over the sand-bank, however there was only sufficient water to carry her onto the highest part of the Bar where she was to become stranded, broadside on to the sea.

The *Victoria* was launched and reached the casualty, which was being pounded by the breakers, within ten minutes. Timing their approaches to the Frenchman, the lifeboat crew closed the vessel and, as the sea allowed, one at a time, the crew of four jumped from the galliot into the safety of the lifeboat; all were taken safely ashore. During the afternoon a coastguardsman was put onboard the galliot to take charge of the vessel. Although the crew were unable to save their personal effects, a large quantity of the vessel's cargo was subsequently saved.

The launch of a pulling and sailing lifeboat having been authorised, moving her from the boathouse to the launch was apparently not always as straightforward as one might expect. It was not unusual for a team of horses to be employed to convey the lifeboat and carriage several miles in order that the boat could be launch in favourable

conditions. Such were the circumstances surrounding the launch on the *Victoria* on Friday 29 March 1878.

The rescue started to unfold when a lookout at 'High Peake', (High Peak Fort, a coastal Iron Age fortification near Sidmouth), reported sighting a distress signal being flown by a fishing smack. The casualty was identified as the Portsmouth vessel, the *Lady of the Lake*.

Upon the initial sighting of the distressed vessel, the Sidmouth lifeboat, the *Rimington* had been launched into a strong east-north-easterly gale that was accompanied by driving snow. The Sidmouth lifeboat located three crewmembers from the *Lady of the Lake* who, in a small boat, were drifting towards the coast, just outside a line of heavy breakers on a lee shore. The lifeboat crew successfully took the fishermen onboard the lifeboat and the *Rimington* continued her sojourn towards the smack. Having located the fishing boat, the lifeboat crew were surprised that the skipper of the smack refused to leave his vessel. As, in the horrendous sea and weather conditions that prevailed, it was not possible for the *Rimington* to return to Sidmouth, Coxswain Henry Conant headed his boat for Exmouth, where she landed the survivors from the *Lady of the Lake*.

The gale force winds, and accompanying snow, continued unabated throughout the day. That same evening the *Lady of the Lake* was once again seen to burn distress signals. This time it was Coxswain Tupman and the crew of the *Victoria* that were to launch. As the force and direction of the wind were not favourable to a launch at Exmouth the Victoria was hauled on her carriage, by a team of horses, through the narrow, twisting Devon lanes to Budleigh Salterton from where she was launched. Battling through the gales force winds and heavy seas, the lifeboat-men of Exmouth reached the fishing smack and succeeded in taking off her injured Captain, later reuniting him safely with his own crew in Exmouth.

An excerpt from the Exmouth Lifeboat Local Committee minute book, dated 7th February 1880, records:

'Ed. Tupman the coxswain attended and tendered his resignation in consequence of a hurt, which was accepted by the committee with regret to loose his valuable services and was requested to send in the same in writing,

and it was resolved by the committee to send a statement of his services to the Institution with a view that some recognition of the same be made for his 20 years attention to his duties.

Tupman was then asked if he could recommend a suitable man as his successor, when he named E. Knight who formerly held the appointment of Second Coxswain.'

At a Special Meeting held in March 1880, the Chairman of the Local Committee, C. Prettijohn, presented a binocular glass and a cheque for £10 to Ed Tupman as an acknowledgement from the parent Institution of his valuable services as Coxswain of the lifeboat.

On 4 March 1880, Edward Knight succeeded Edward Tupman as Coxswain of the Exmouth Lifeboat.

The *Victoria* was launched at just after 12.00 hours on Monday 13 December 1880, following the arrival at the Exmouth lifeboat station of a horseman who, having ridden from Budleigh Salterton, brought news of a fishing boat in distress 3 miles east of Exmouth. The lifeboat soon reached the casualty, which, it was reported, was in danger of being driven on to nearby rocks. With a towrope established between the two vessels, the lifeboat recovered the fishing boat, and her crew of four, to Exmouth.

The first detailed Service Return to be discovered at the Exmouth Station relates to the launch of the *Victoria* on Wednesday 1 November 1882.

It was at about 13.00 hours that the Exmouth Lifeboat Station received a telegram, from Budleigh Salterton, to the effect that a schooner, flying a signal of distress, was in difficulty off Ladrum Bay, and requested the assistance of the Exmouth lifeboat. The crew were immediately summoned and at 13.30 hours the *Victoria* was launched under the command of Coxswain Edward Knight. The lifeboat put out into a south-westerly gale that was accompanied by heavy rain and a very heavy sea, which was then breaking over the bar. The crew of the *Victoria* battle against the elements until they reached the given location of the schooner, only to find that the vessel and apparently disappeared. Coxswain Knight immediately commenced a search for the vessel, which proved fruitless. Shortly before dusk, as the lifeboat crew prepared to beach their boat, the *Victoria* was struck by a very heavy sea, resulting in her capsize, and her entire crew were thrown into the icy sea. The *Victoria* quickly self-righted and expelled the water that she had shipped. Thankfully every member of her crew regained the safety of the lifeboat.

Coxswain Knight abandoned his search for the distressed vessel, which proved to have been the *Lady Elizabeth* of Poole, sailing light from Exmouth to Portland, with a crew of three. She had infact been driven ashore approximately 1 mile East of the Weston Coast Guard Station, her crew being rescued by the Beer Rocket Apparatus Team. Having been continuously rowing to windward, the crew of the *Victoria* struck out for their homeport. Cold, wet and being without food for 9½ hours, the *Victoria* returned to her station at 23.00 hours.

During the *Victoria*'s capsize four oars were lost together with ancillary equipment albeit the boat herself was undamaged. Bowman John Spiller sustained cuts to his nose and face, a badly contused arm and a badly bruised hand. Lifeboatman Joseph Hayman sustained a contused arm.

In the Service Return for this incident, the Station Honorary Secretary recorded:

'Notwithstanding this accident the men have confidence in the boat and would go in her again should circumstances require it.'

The circumstances surrounding the capsizing of the lifeboat were considered by the Local Committee who concluded:

'...having examined the coxswain and made every possible inquiry, are of the opinion that the life-boat was capsized by an unusually heavy sea on the port quarter while nearing the shore, with the intention of beaching on a small opening between the rocks on Ladrum Bay; that the accident was unavoidable and that the coxswain and crew behaved most gallantly in extricating their boat from a most dangerous position.'

This proved to be the last launch undertaken by the *Victoria* in her capacity as the Exmouth lifeboat.

4
The Joseph Somes
11 February 1884 – 17 November 1903

Type: Self Righting   Official Number: 41
Propulsion: Pulling - Sailing   Oars: 10   Crew: 13
Length: 34' 0"   Beam: 7' 6"   Displacement: 3T 0Cwt   Builder: Woolfe, Shadwell.
Launches: 11   Lives Saved: 7
Coxswain: Edward Knight, (1884-97), Henry Christopher Squire (1897-1903)

On Monday 11 February 1884, the R.N.L.I. sent a new lifeboat to the Exmouth Station. The boat was a gift from Mrs. Joseph Somes of North Devon, given in memory of her late husband. Somewhat belatedly the following short report of the arrival of the lifeboat appeared in *The Bideford Weekly Gazette* of Tuesday 4 November 1884:

MRS SOMES AND LIFEBOAT WORK. –
The Lifeboat Journal states that during the past year a new life-boat has been placed at the Exmouth Station. The cost of this boat had been defrayed out of the generous gift of Mrs. Somes of Annery House, Bideford, who has given £3,000 to the Institution to defray the cost of a Life-boat and its permanent maintenance, in memory of her late husband, formerly M.P. for Dartmouth. The boat is accordingly named The Joseph Somes; *it is 34 feet long, 7½ feet wide, and rows ten oars, double banked. It reached the station in February last and has since been tried in rough weather and pronounced everything that can be desired.*

Since 1887, a unique Official Number (O.N.) has identified each lifeboat in the Institution's fleet. The *Joseph Somes* was the first Exmouth lifeboat to be allocated such identification, her Official Number being O.N.41; but how did these numbers originate?

What has become regarded as probably the very worst lifeboat disaster in the annals of the Royal National Lifeboat Institution, occurred on Thursday 9 December 1886 when the lifeboats of St Annes, Southport and Lytham launched, off the Lancashire coast, to go to the assistance of the Hamburg trading Barque, the *Mexico*, from Liverpool to Guayaquil. Tragically, on that fateful night, both the St. Annes lifeboat, the *Laura Janet* and the Southport lifeboat, the *Eliza Fernley* were lost, together with the lives of twenty-seven brave and courageous lifeboat-men.

Following this disaster, the Royal National Lifeboat Institution invited George Lennox Watson, a well-known yacht designer of Glasgow, to become the Consulting Naval Architect to the Institution, his task being to take a hard, in-depth look at lifeboat design. At the time that Watson concentrated upon the future design of lifeboats, the Institution's Chief Inspector, Captain the Hon. H. W. Chetwynd R.N., was instrumental in compiling a list of the Institution's lifeboats, each vessel was to subsequently undergo evaluation and testing to a far more exacting standard than had previously been applied.

At the time of this undertaking, the R.N.L.I. had lifeboats at 290 stations, and a further 20 to 30 boats in reserve, all of which were to be surveyed, tested, modified and, if necessary, re-tested before being certified as being fit for service. Details of the test certificates were entered into a large ledger with numbered pages, the page number providing a unique Official Number for the lifeboat to which that page referred. The Official Number would thereafter remain with that individual lifeboat throughout her service with the Institution.

The sequential numbering system was achieved as the Inspector travelled from station to station but in no way reflected the age of the individual lifeboat, indeed some of the more modern lifeboats were allocated comparatively low Official Numbers. The last vessel of the 'old fleet' to be surveyed was O.N.317, the *Springwell* of the Harwich station. Although built in 1881 the *Springwell* was not allocated her O.N. until 1892. Upon the completion of issuing O.N's. to the existing fleet, new lifeboats were allocated chronological numbers as they were built, which gave an indication of the age of the vessel. The exceptions were boats that were taken over from other authorities when an O.N. was allocated in the year that the boat came under the authority of the R.N.L.I. The system of allocating Official Numbers continues to this day.

The *Joseph Somes* remained on station, at Exmouth, for just over 5½ years before she was called upon to provide an active service. She was launched on Monday 7 October 1889 following the receipt of an urgent telegram, from the Coast Guard at Dawlish, reporting the sighting of a vessel flying a distress signal. Coxswain Knight assembled his crew of twelve and upon the agreement of the Hon. Secretary, Mr Moresby, the Chief Officer of Coast Guards, and one member of the Local Committee, the lifeboat was launched at 12.00 hours. In a west-north-westerly gale and very rough seas, the *Joseph Somes* proceeded to the casualty, which was lying about a mile and a half off Langstone Head. The casualty was the fishing cutter *Topsy* of Torquay, which was laden with an estimated catch of 3000 to 4000 herring. The *Topsy*, Master - James Paine, Owner - Daniel Skinner, had left her homeport of Torquay at 14.00 hours on Sunday 6 October in fair conditions. A southwesterly wind blew 'moderate' for the first part of the night but by 0200 hours on Monday, it had increased to gale force and blew from the northwest. At 05.00 hours the *Topsy* raised her nets and got under weigh at daybreak. The cutter filled with water on three occasions and pumping had to be continuously employed. The *Topsy*'s exhausted crew of three finally anchored and hoisted a distress signal.

The *Joseph Somes* reached the distressed vessel at about 13.00 hours and by skilful manoeuvring of the lifeboat, in a full gale, Coxswain Knight managed to place members of his crew onboard the *Topsy* to establish a tow and assist in raising the anchor. Under main lugsail and oars the *Joseph Somes* towed the *Topsy* into Exmouth '*in an admirable manner.*' The lifeboat crew regained the shore at 14.30 hours.

A strong southwesterly gale force wind, accompanied by heavy driving rain, unexpectedly sprung up on the morning of Tuesday 20 May 1890, stranding about 20 vessels of the Exmouth fishing fleet outside the Bar. As at about 12.00 hours one of the fleet was observed in obvious distress, the lifeboat was launched, at the direction of the Hon. Secretary, and immediately made her way to assist the casualty. Unfortunately before the Joseph Somes could reach the small craft, she was pooped by the heavy sea and sank, her crew being picked up by another boat. With the

The *Joseph Somes* – second of name.

wind increasing in velocity and the sea state deteriorating on a falling tide, Coxswain Edward Knight took the lifeboat out to the Bar in order to render any assistance necessary in assisting the fishing fleet in to port. The Service Report records:

'*One fishing boat coming in was twice struck by the heavy seas and but for the assurance given the man by the immediate proximity of the Life Boat (100 yards) would certainly have been lost but stimulated to renewed exertion got in accompanied by the Life Boat about 2.30PM.*'

A telegram was received from Budleigh Salterton indicating that further vessels required the assistance of the lifeboat but this request was subsequently cancelled.

As members of the fishing fleet continued to run for the Bar, Coxswain Knight and his crew put out for a second time, returning to station at 16.30 hours being assured that all boats and crews were safe.

A further 19 months passed before the Coxswain Knight and the crew of the *Joseph Somes* were required to provide further service, the service being to the sloop, the *Mater Dei* of Dunkirk. Wednesday 9 December 1891 dawned to witness a Force 5 wind, blowing from the southwest, and a moderate sea. It was at 13.00 hours, on a falling tide, that the 64ton French registered sloop, started to cross the Pole Sands. By 13.30 hours the vessel, which was on passage to Exeter with a cargo of potatoes, in endeavouring to reach the Eastern entrance to the Exe, had drifted onto the Sands and was firmly aground. Several boats approached the sloop and offered assistance but the Master of the vessel, Master Gouris, rejected all help.

Throughout the afternoon the lifeboat crew kept a weather eye on the sloop as conditions deteriorated. By 19.30 hours barometric pressure had fallen drastically, the wind had increased and, with on a rising tide, heavy seas were breaking over the Pole Sands. Storm signals were hoisted, the lifeboat crew assembled and at 20.00 hours the *Joseph Somes* was launched. Battling into the teeth of a full gale and huge seas, which were now breaking over and swamping the *Mater Dei*, it took Coxswain Knight and his crew one-and-a-half hours to reach the stricken vessel. In atrocious conditions, Coxswain Knight anchored the lifeboat

to windward of the sloop and veered down onto her. On this occasion Master Gouris was only too pleased to accept the assistance of the lifeboat crew, the *Joseph Somes* successfully taking off the crew of three men and a boy. The crew of the *Mater Dei* were landed safely at Exmouth at 22.30 hours.

The Return of Service records, '*It is blowing hard now (10 Decr. noon) but little chance of saving the vessel as she seems full of water.*'

Coxswain Knight, and the crew of the *Joseph Somes*, returned to the Pole Sands on the evening of Saturday 16 December 1893; it was a fine moonlit night with smooth water inside the sands, albeit there was a moderate ground swell outside the sands, which was increasing with the rising tide. The 68-ton schooner *Conquest*, of Padstow, Bellamy - Master, owner William Geake of St. Columb, Cornwall, was bound from Plymouth to Exmouth with a cargo of 80-ton on bones, valued at about £500 when she surprisingly ran aground on the Sands, the cause of the stranding apparently being a navigational error. The lifeboat was launched at 20.30 hours and reached the casualty within 20 minutes. At the request of Captain Bellamy the lifeboat crew assisted in laying a 'Bower' anchor astern of the schooner with a long warp and chain. Coxswain Knight then placed nine members of his crew onboard the *Conquest* who assisted the schooner's crew in heaving the vessel off the sands. A steam tug had been alerted and the lifeboat readied a towing hawser prior to its arrival. The *Joseph Somes* returned to her station at 23.59 hours.

The total cost of this service was £2.5s.0d, however a note to the Return of Service, made on 6 March 1894 records that:

'*£13.14.0 had been received from Mr Adams, Solicitor, as compensation accepted from the owners of* Conquest – *viz. £20 less £6.6.0 Law Expenses.*'

It was a dark, bleak winter day in Exmouth on Thursday 4 January 1894 when, at about 16.30 hours, a three-masted schooner was seen to be approaching the port, from the east. The wind was blowing a severe gale carrying snow squalls from the southeast. The heavy sea was breaking dangerously over the Exmouth Bar when the schooner was seen to take the bar but run beyond the passage onto the Pole Sands, at the top of the tide.

The *Joseph Somes* was immediately readied, and launched at 17.00 hours, to go to the assistance of the Danish registered vessel, the *John Grónsünd* of Svendborg. The schooner, which carried a crew of six, was on passage from London to Exeter with a cargo of beans and oats, valued at £2,100, under the command of her owner and master, C. Mikkelorn. The *Joseph Somes* pulled through the heavy seas and snow squalls and was within 150 yards of the vessel, amid heavy breakers, when she was struck by a sea on the Port beam, which filler her and knocked her to leeward. Three of the lifeboat's oars were carried away; spare oars were quickly in place but no effort by the crew could force the lifeboat against the heavy broken sea that continually washed over her from all sides. The force of the sea was such that Coxswain Knight was compelled to return inside the Pole Sand and pull into calmer water before a further attempt to reach the Schooner was made. Bitterly cold, some nearing a state of hypothermia, wet and exhausted, the crew of the *Joseph Somes* set out on a second attempt to reach the stricken schooner but their efforts were once again thwarted by the extraordinary force of the sea. The lifeboat returned to her station at about 19.00 hours.

Captain Greaves R.N., Inspecting Officer of Coast Guard, Chief Officer Cobden, the Lifeboat's Hon. Secretary and Coxswain, plus a Pilot, reviewed the situation facing the crew of the *John Grónsünd* and determined to once again launch the *Joseph Somes* as

soon as the tide had fallen a little. It was also agreed that the Coast Guard should send a Rocket Apparatus Team to throw a line to the vessel, from Pole Sands. The lifeboat was launched at 21.00 hours but in attempting to pull away grounded and remained fast until the tide made, at midnight, when she returned to her station.

Whilst this catalogue of unfortunate events took place, three local men John Bradford, Uriah Bradford and George Prowse took it upon themselves to launch a 15-foot open boat, from a point near the Pole Sands, and make for the Danish schooner. Throughout their hazardous journey, with each wave that they encountered, the heavy, breaking seas threatened to swamp their small boat. Miraculously, these three brave men reached the *John Grónsünd* and succeeded in taking off the crew of six. With the small craft now drastically overloaded they retraced their course and all landed safely.

In recognition of their bravery in saving the lives of the crew of the *John Grónsünd*, the Royal National Lifeboat Institution awarded Silver Gallantry Medals to John Bradford, Uriah Bradford and George Prowse.

The unrelenting seas continued to pound the Danish Schooner, the *John Grónsünd* until she became a total wreck.

The last occasion on which the *Joseph Somes* was launched under the command of Coxswain Edward Knight, took place on Friday 4 December

Recovering the Joseph Somes *ON41*.

1896, in most tragic circumstances. It was at about 06.45 hours that the Coast Guard Watchman saw a schooner take the ground outside the Pole Sands, slightly to the westward of the swash-way. It was nearing high-water, in a full south-easterly gale accompanied by driving rain, when the 69-ton schooner, the *Fowey*, owned by John Stephens, Master - John Miller, made a distress flare to summons the assistance of the lifeboat. At the same time as the lifeboat crew assembled and prepared their boat for launching, four local men readied a Pilot Cutter for launching, also intent on rendering service to the casualty.

The lifeboat crew watched as the schooner, with foresail, topsail and standing-jib set, gradually beat over the sands into the channel. Coxswain Knight launched the *Joseph Somes* at 07.35 hours, as was making for the swash-way when he was hailed by the crew of the Pilot Cutter who informed him that a punt, with three Pilots onboard, had capsized whilst endeavouring to put a Pilot aboard the schooner.

The Exmouth Lifeboats Station's Hon. Secretary recorded:

'*I immediately launched directing the Coxswain to endeavour to find the boat. The life boat remained out about an hour and a half but in the wild sea and very heavy rain were unable to see anything, they returned at 10 o'clock, and I am afraid three of our best Pilots must be counted lost. I watched the Life Boat the whole time and am well satisfied they did all that was possible. The schooner anchored safely in the bight.*'

The Exmouth Branch Committee met on Tuesday 22 December 1896 in consequence of a letter received, from a Mr Grenfell, calling the attention of the parent Institution to reflections on the lifeboat, given in evidence at an Inquest into the this tragedy. A second letter had been received from a Mr Thomas of Exmouth, in which he made several allegations in respect of delays in firing of the assembly signal, the launching of the lifeboat and other matters.

Evidence was taken from the Coast Guard Watchman, who was examined at considerable length, Mr P Lawe, Chief Boatman and Mr Driscoll, Chief Officer of Coast Guard; following which the Committee felt it unnecessary to examine further witnesses. Mr Thomas was called to explain his allegations following which, he was told by the Chairman, Admiral R Moorman that:

'*Not wilfully, but from his utter ignorance of his subject, his letter was full of erroneous statements and should never have been written. He had brought the Inspector (Inspector Kepple Foote) from London uselessly and caused great inconvenience to the influential gentlemen now assembled.*'

The Committee resolved;

'*That after full examination they are satisfied that even if the signal for launching the lifeboat had been fired by the Coast Guard at the moment that the schooner's signal of distress was seen it would have been impossible, considering the distance at which the crew live, to have launched the lifeboat before the schooner was again afloat and out of danger.*

Further that on hearing from the Pilot of the capsizing of their punt, no time was lost in launching the lifeboat and searching for the men.'

On Thursday 18 November 1897, after 17 years of loyal service, Edward Knight resigned his position as Coxswain of the Exmouth Lifeboat. On that same date Henry Squire was appointed Coxswain in his place.

Not all seafarers who find themselves in trouble are willing to accept the assistance of the RNLI; such was the case when the *Joseph Somes* was launched for the first time under the command of Coxswain Henry Squire on Wednesday 20 January 1897. The vessel in question was the schooner *Isabella Helen*, in cargo and in-bound to Teignmouth. It was a cold winter day with patches of thick mist being carried on an east-south-easterly gale force wind. It was at 08.30 hours that the Honorary Secretary received reports of a schooner anchored perilously close to the Clerk Rock, to the west of Dawlish, in a heavy, confused sea. The vessel was reported to be flying a 'Pilot' flag and French colours. The Hon. Secretary, Mr. Moresby, telegraphed the lookout at Dawlish who reported the schooner to be '*in a most dangerous position.*' With the sea rising and the wind freshening considerably, the lifeboat was launched, as a precaution, at 15.00 hours and proceeded to

Henry Christopher Squire, Coxswain 1897–1907.

Coxswain Squire and crew at new boathouse 1903.
Postcard Currie & Cliffe

being required, the lifeboat set course for her station returning ashore at 17.20 hours. Coxswain Henry Squire and Signalman Job Edwards kept watch all night but the services of the lifeboat were not called upon.

What proved to be the final service to be provided by the *Joseph Somes* took place on Friday 9 January 1903. The morning dawned to thick misty rain that was being carried on a moderate southerly wind. The sea was breaking heavily on the sands and bar. The weatherglass continued to fall. At about 06.00 hours, a schooner was sighted approximately 100 yards outside the Pole Sands, an estimated three-quarter of a mile from the entrance to the River Exe. Although the vessel was at anchor, with two anchors down, it being low water, she appeared to be striking bottom as she pitched heavily in the breaking seas. The schooners fore and aft mainsails and foresail were set. As the Hon. Secretary, Mr Moresby observed the vessel it became evident that her anchors were incorrectly set and had started to drag.

The lifeboat was launched at 07.45 hours, Mr Moresby instructing Coxswain Squire that if possible, in an effort to save time, he was to take the *Joseph Somes* out through the swash-way, a tricky business given the state of the tide and the prevailing sea conditions. At 08.30 hours the lifeboat reached the casualty, the 92-ton *Cardigan*, of Cardiff – J. W. Redd, Master and Owner. The vessel was light, seeking a cargo. As Coxswain Squire manoeuvred the lifeboat alongside the schooner, her crew of four, including the Captain, jumped into the lifeboat obviously intending to abandon their vessel. Henry Squire convinced Captain Redd and his crew to return to the *Cardigan* as he believed the vessel could be saved. In the meantime, a steam tug had set out, from Exmouth, to render additional assistance. Coxswain Squire placed two of his crewmen aboard the schooner and, upon the arrival of the tug, managed to pass a hawser between the vessels. By this time one of the anchor cables had parted, the second being slipped to establish the tow. Unfortunately whilst under weigh the hawser parted but in extremely difficult circumstances, the lifeboat crew took the tugs own hawser to the *Cardigan* and the schooner was towed safely into harbour. Having assisted to save four lives and vessel, the *Joseph Somes* regained the boathouse at 10.45 hours.

the schooner to offer assistance. For one hour, under sail and oars, the crew of the *Joseph Somes* battled through the confused seas before reaching the *Isabella Helen*. Coxswain Squire pointed out the imminent danger of the anchorage to the Captain of the schooner and the almost certainty of his anchors parting, should the strength of the wind increase further. The French Captain declined all offer of help saying that he could depend upon his cables to hold his vessel fast. Their services not

5
The Joseph Somes

(Second of Name)
17 November 1903 – 16 September 1933

Type: Self Righting   *Official Number: 519*
Propulsion: Pulling - Sailing   *Oars: 10*   *Crew: 13*   *Length: 35' 0"*
Beam: 8' 6"   *Displacement: 3T 16Cwt*   *Built: 1903*
Builder: Thames Iron Works, Blackwall.   *Launches: 10*   *Lives Saved: 4*
Coxswain: Henry Christopher Squire (1903-07), Edwin William Bridle (1907-18),
William Henry Mitchell (1918-28), Thomas Moore Horn (1928-33).

On 17 November 1903 the Exmouth station took delivery of a new 35-feet, self-righting lifeboat. The cost of this new boat, £683, like that of her predecessor, was defrayed by the generosity of Mrs Somes of Bideford. Likewise, this boat took the name the *Joseph Somes*. The new boat was 35-feet in length, self-righting with a revolutionary 10-foot sliding steel keel. She rowed 10 oars and was equipped with a mast and sails and No.1 rig.

With the arrival on station of the *Joseph Somes*, she became the 289th lifeboat to enter service with the Royal National Lifeboat Institution and the 14th to be stationed in Devon. Like her predecessors, the *Joseph Somes* relied upon horses and carriage for launch and recovery. The horses were obtained from Rowlands Farm which stood on the site that was to become the Madeira Bowles Club and Cricket Field. When the farm closed, the horses were transferred to sheds in Tower Street.

Due to the increased size of the new boat, it was necessary to demolish the existing boathouse and construct a larger one, albeit on the same site, at a cost of £800. The 'new' boathouse remains in use today, housing Exmouth's RNLI Life guards.

Although the Exmouth lifeboat was not called upon, for nearly five years, to provide an active service, in accordance with Royal National Lifeboat Institution Regulations, Coxswain Squire

and his crew regularly launched the Joseph Somes on training exercises.

Personal tragedy struck the Exmouth lifeboat crew on two such occasions. The first tragic loss occurred on Wednesday 9 August 1905 following the call-out for a training launch. The Station Signalman, F. H. Horne, duly reported to the boathouse and carried out his duty of firing the signals in order to summon the crew. He waited until the *Joseph Somes* was safely away and then headed for home; his body was later found amongst trees, near the lifeboat station, where he had died from a heart- attack. The Management Committee later voted the sum of £15 to a local fund. The second tragedy occurred, again whilst undertaking a training launch, on Thursday 14 March 1907 when Henry Squire, who had been the Coxswain of the Exmouth lifeboat for over nine years, collapsed and died.

A meeting of the Exmouth Life Boat Institution was held that same day; an extract from the Minute, records:

'*Present:*
Revd. C. R. Carr, Colonel Harvey, Capt. Grenfell, Capt. Plenderleath, Capt. Foote, Inspector, M. F. Moresby, Hon. Sec.
H. C. Squire having suddenly died at the moment of launching the Boat by Capt. Foote,

Crew of the second *Joseph Somes* ON519

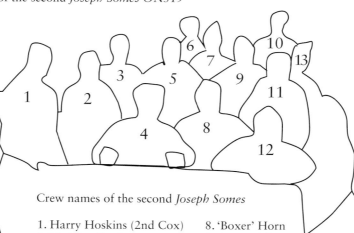

Crew names of the second *Joseph Somes*

1. Harry Hoskins (2nd Cox)
2. Ned Bradford
3. William Holman
4. William Mitchell (Cox)
5. George Carder
6. Ned Richards
7. Reg Searle
8. 'Boxer' Horn
9. Harry Tolby
10. Jack West
11. Lionel Bradford
12. Peter Shapter (Signalman)
13. Will Teschner

Inspector, it was unanimously resolved that a letter of sympathy and condolence be addressed to his widow, stating the high esteem in which the Committee held him and the value they placed in his long service. Also a letter in same sense to the Parent Institution, trusting some assistance could be bestowed on his widow.

That a meeting of the Committee be called on the 21st inst to select a Coxswain.'

The Committee of Management voted the sum of £150 to Coxswain Squire's dependents.

The minutes of a meeting held on Thursday 21 March 1907, record:

'*Present:*

Revd. C. R. Carr, Capt. Grenfell, Capt. Plenderleath, M.F. Moresby.

Committee selected 4 names for Coxswain and by unanimous wish of crew Edwin Bridle was appointed Coxswain.

4 names were then selected for 2nd Coxswain and Frank Squire was unanimously appointed.

In the event of Alfred Ferris, Bowman, resigning Edward Haupson to be appointed.'

An outstanding rescue took place on Thursday 10 October 1907 that called for the launch of both the Exmouth and Teignmouth lifeboats. Throughout the previous night a strong gale had been blowing from the south-southeast causing a high sea in the channel; towards morning the wind moderated and backed to south-southwest, but continued to carry constant heavy showers. In these horrendous conditions, a Russian three-masted schooner had been standing off Exmouth, waiting for a Pilot, but her position was such as to give the Coast Guard, and others who watched her, extreme cause for concern. At about 12.40 hours, under reefed fore and aft sail, the schooner turned her head off shore and those who watched her reportedly '*went to dinner.*' At about 12.50 hours the schooner attempted to 'wear' (hoist) sail but within minutes she stranded on the Pole Sand and heavy, violent, relentless seas started to wash over her from stem to stern.

The casualty was the 302-ton Russian schooner *Tehwija, (Tehvya)* of Riga, under the command of Captain Una Baarman; also on board were Alfons Bjorktof, first mate, Bruno Stromsten, second mate together with six crewmen. The schooner had left

Lappvik, Finland on 29 August experiencing bad weather throughout her voyage. She was now inbound to Exmouth with a cargo of timber for Messrs. R.W. & F.C. Sharp of Exeter.

In order to enter the River Exe, the Captain of the schooner had signalled for a Pilot and the Exmouth tug, *Queen of the Exe*, had set out with the Pilot but found it impossible to reach the schooner. As the *Tehwija* continued to drift towards the treacherous waters at the mouth of the River Exe the Captain dropped his anchors, but they failed to hold ground and, at 13.00 hours the vessel was seen to strand. The plight of the schooner had been observed from Exmouth by Mr Vernon; the Chief Officer of Coast Guard, who immediately fired the alarm signals. With the aid of the Coast Guard team, assisted by their wives and children, the *Joseph Somes* was launched in six minutes, by which time Coxswain 'Ned' Bridle and his crew had assembled. The lifeboat launched at 13.06 hours and, under oars, battled against wind and sea.

As the *Tehwija* was driven onto the Pole Sands, the crew of the *Joseph Somes* made several valiant attempts to reach the stricken vessel. Rowing directly into the teeth of the gale, the Exmouth crew were thwarted in their efforts to cross the Exmouth Bar. Unable to reach the schooner the lifeboat returned ashore at 16.30 hours where they remained in readiness to make further rescue attempts, should the opportunity have arisen. During the battle to reach the casualty, many of the crew of the *Joseph Somes* sustained lacerations and bruising. The lifeboat sustained one broken oar, whilst two that were washed overboard were recovered. Fortunately the lifeboat did not make water.

The pilot tug, *Queen of the Exe* and a pilot sloop also attempted to cross the Exmouth Bar, but it was impracticable to round the Fairway to attempt a rescue. The stranded vessel rested about at the end of the Swash Way, off Orcombe Point.

The Honorary Secretary of the Teignmouth lifeboat, Mr. W. J. Burden, was kept fully aware of the circumstances unfolding at Pole Sands and, upon Chief Officer Bennett, of the Coastguards, receiving a request for assistance, from the coastguard of Langstone Head, ordered the launch of the Teignmouth lifeboat, the *Alfred Staniforth*. The order to launch was given just before 14.00 hours and the boat was underway within ten minutes. The boat was launched under the command of Coxswain George Rice, with Mr Burden taking his place amongst the crew. It was now low water and the sea breaking over the Teignmouth Bar, was furious and dangerously shallow. In appalling weather conditions it took the crew nearly half-an-hour to cross the Bar and, in order to maintain headway, Coxswain Rice, together with the Second Coxswain and the Bowman found it necessary to double-bank the oars whilst the Branch Hon. Secretary, Mr Burden, took the coxswains position successfully steering the lifeboat over the Bar. The crossing was very hazardous indeed, the boat being subjected to a constant barrage of waves that repeatedly swamped the vessel; one particularly large wave knocked Coxswain Rice off his feet and swept the crew from their seats. Oars were washed overboard but fortunately were secured to the lifeboat by lanyards.

Once clear of the Bar, the *Alfred Staniforth* plunged into the breakers, being repeatedly devoured by the wave troughs and disappearing from the sight of onlookers ashore. In clear water Coxswain Rice hoisted canvas and with favourable wind, made good progress towards the stricken schooner. With first class boating skills and pure determination, the crew of the *Alfred Staniforth* reached the stricken schooner. The waters around the *Tehwija*, now firmly stuck on Pole Sands, were littered with timber from her deck cargo and it was evident that the vessel was fast taking in water. Coxswain Rice realised the danger to which his boat and crew would be exposed should he attempt to go alongside the schooner, the lifeboat therefore lowered her canvas and dropped anchor to seaward of the *Tehwija*. Coxswain Rice allowed the boat to veer down as close to the schooner as was possible when it was observed she had a hole in her stern and that her rudder was missing. The *Tehwija*'s mainmast had also been carried away.

Ropes were thrown to the crew of the schooner who were seen clinging to the lee rail. One man reportedly jumped, from the rail of the schooner, into the lifeboat, a drop of some 16 feet, whilst others were dragged from the wreck, to the lifeboat by ropes. The first man to leave the wreck had a lucky escape when he fell between the lifeboat and the hull of the schooner. At the moment both vessels were lifted by a wave, the lifeboat crew

The wreck of the *Tehwija* 1907
Courtesy of the Bill Sleeman Collection

fended off their boat from closing on the hull of the *Tehwija*, at the same time heaving the man into the lifeboat. The whole crew were rescued in a period of only three minutes.

At 16.00 hours the lifeboat landed the Russian crewmen safely at Exmouth Pier; the *Alfred Staniforth* was moored at Starcross and her crew returned to Teignmouth by train, '*where they received a well deserved ovation.*' The Pilot-tug, the *Teign*, towed the lifeboat back to Teignmouth the following day.

The *Tehwija* became a total wreck having split in half from stem to stern and eventually came ashore under the Battery, at Exmouth. When the deckhouse was subsequently washed ashore it was found to contain the ship's pet dog, apparently none the worse for his ordeal.

For this epic rescue, the Committee of Management of the Royal National Lifeboat Institution awarded the Silver Gallantry Medal to Coxswain George Rice and to the Honorary Secretary W. J. Burden. The Committee also gave additional monetary awards to the lifeboat crew.

Mr Moresby, the Honorary Secretary of the Exmouth Lifeboat wrote, in respect of this rescue:

'*The sea at the Bar was specially heavy and being low water the stretch of shallow dangerous surf considerable. For near three hours the Boat gallantly attempted to get through but in vain. The men never faltered, driven back, again and again reoccurred the attempt and though within 50 yards of the vessel she veered – no line or made any effort. Our crew returned exhausted, drenched having done their duty to the utmost.*'

The minutes of the Exmouth Life Boat Committee of 17 October 1907 resolved:

'*The Committee of the Exmouth Lifeboat having met this day and heard from the Hon. Secretary in full the account of the attempt to reach the wreck of the Russian schooner on the 10th inst, as watched by himself and by them and as given him that same evening by the Coxswain of the boat, desire to place on record in their minutes their high approval of the conduct of the coxswain and of the correctness of his judgement in adopting the course which he took in approaching the wreck; and their admiration of the gallant endeavours of the crew to save life on a most difficult and dangerous service.*

They find further that the Western Passage was absolutely impracticable at this time for want of water, and that very grave risk indeed would have been run both to crew and boat by any attempt to cross the Bar under the existing circumstances.'

The next occasion on which the Joseph Somes was launched was on Friday 17 November 1911, when she went to the assistance of the 38-ton Brixham trawler, the Ketch BM328 *Endeavour*. It was at 19.40 hours on a very dark night that continuous distress signals, in the form of lights, could clearly be seen emanating from a vessel on the Pole Sands. Mr Pett, the Chief Officer of the Coast Guard and a member of the Lifeboat Committee, ordered a signal to be made to summon the lifeboat crew. As Coxswain Bridle and his crew mustered, seeing that the distressed vessel continued to make signals, Mr Pett ordered the launch of the Coast Guard's own lifeboat. The Coast Guard boat made her way towards the stranded vessel and at 20.20 hours, on an ebbing tide, the *Joseph Somes* was launched, and in a strong force 5-6 south-westerly wind and heavy frequent showers, made her way, under oars, to the stricken vessel. The Coast Guard boat was the first to reach the *Endeavour*, which was aground on the 'western horn' of the Pole Sands. She was rolling heavily with the now heavy seas breaking over her. With great difficulty Mr Pett, and his crew of 5 hands, manoeuvred their boat up to the leeward side of the *Endeavour*, the boat barely floating in the shallow water. In approaching the trawler the rescue boat received considerable damage and became fouled in the *Endeavours* trawl. At one point the trawler rolled alarmingly and threatened to crush the Coast Guard boat. However, with great skill and determination, the Coast Guard crew rescued the four hands from the *Endeavour* and landed them safely at Exmouth.

Having launched the Joseph Somes, it had taken Coxswain Bridle and his crew 25 minutes to reach the casualty by which time, having completed the rescue, Mr Pett and his crew were returning to shore. Logic dictates that the two vessels must have passed each other but surprisingly Coxswain Bridle reported that he had not sighted the Coast Guard

Above left: Edwin William Bridle, Coxswain 1907~1918

Above centre: William Henry Mitchell, Coxswain 1918~28

Above right: Thomas Moore Horn, Coxswain 1928-33

Right: Launching the second *Joseph Somes ON519*

Below: The second Joseph Somes *ON519* under sail

boat. Having approached the *Endeavour*, Coxswain Bridle's hails went unanswered but as the lifeboat closed the trawler it became apparent that she was at anchor, her trawls had been stored and that the crew had been taken off. Unfortunately the tide having fallen, the lifeboat could not manoeuvre in the shallow water and had to wait until the tide made before she could return ashore at 23.45 hours, having failed to render service.

Monday 4 December 1911 had been a fine and calm day until about 21.00 hours when the wind rapidly strengthened from the south-southwest. By 23.15 hours it was raining heavily and, on the River Exe the wind had increased to Force 7 to gale Force 8, whilst outside the river, the south-southwesterly wind had reached Force 10 resulting in a heavy, confused sea. At this time the Coxswain of the Exmouth lifeboat, Edwin Bridle and the Coast Guard watchman were on the beach when they saw 3 or 4 flares fired from the direction of the eastern end of the Pole Sands. The alarm was raised and ten minutes later, at 23.35 hours, low water, the *Joseph Somes* was launched into a full gale. Under oars, the lifeboat headed for the main entrance that allowed access to the open sea, crossing the Exmouth Bar at 00.10 hours on Tuesday 5 December. Coxswain Bridle having ordered his crew to make sail, then took the lifeboat along the whole length of the Sands, from the Fairway Buoy to Langstone Point, the heavy seas, which were breaking on the Sands, constantly buffeting the lifeboat. Finding no sign of a wreck or a vessel in distress, Coxswain Bridle turned for home, the *Joseph Somes* being housed at 03.35 hours.

It subsequently established that five boats from Topsham, had been out fishing, four having returned by 18.00 hours on the Monday. It was further established that it was the fifth vessel, the *Chicken*, which had found herself in difficulty and fired the flares. Although the lifeboat did not locate the *Chicken* she returned safely to port.

An Annual Inspection of the lifeboat took place on 23 January 1912 and was itself not without incident, as reported in the contemporary press:

EXMOUTH LIFEBOAT
THE ANNUAL INSPECTION

The Exmouth lifeboat "Joseph Somes" was a day or two since launched for the annual inspection, when the crew were accompanied in the boat by the Inspector for the Southern District (Lieut. Keppel H. Foote, late R.N.) The members of the committee present at the launch included Col. G.L. Harvey, the Rev. C.R. Carr, Capt. Taylor, Mr. R. Tucker-Pain, Coastguard Chief Officer Pitts and Capt. M.F. Moresby (Hon. Sec of the local branch). There was an interested crowd of spectators. The lifeboat was smartly run down to the water's edge and launched after the firing of the signal rocket. The sea was calm, and there was no wind. The crew rowed to a position just off Warren Point, where the anchor was dropped and the gear overhauled and inspected. Subsequently various rockets were fired, and the sails hoisted. The boat remained out for about an hour. On its return the keel got embedded in the sand, and some difficulty was experienced in getting the boat to move. The hawser snapped, but was again attached and on being subjected to further strain the rope once more parted, each time precipitating the long line of men flat on the sand. One of the small posts used fore pulling up the boat was also snapped. When the boat was brought up on the road, it was placed on the carriage and taken around the town, with the object of testing the carriage.

The next recorded launch of the *Joseph Somes* took place in Wartime conditions on Sunday 5 November 1916. In common with many lifeboat stations, the Exmouth crew had been depleted of its younger members who had been called-up for active service, their places being taken by former crewmembers, together with members of the Coastguard and local volunteers often drawn from the fishing communities. Such were the circumstances in this instance.

It was at 07.00 hours that Mr Taylor, the Secretary of the Exmouth Lifeboat Station, received a report that distress rockets had been fired by a vessel that was outside the bar. Mr Taylor immediately made his way to the Coastguard Station only to find that the location of the distressed vessel was completely obliterated from view by heavy rain and a thick haze, which was being carried on a southeasterly gale force wind. Mr Taylor recorded:

'It would have been almost impossible to launch the Boat on account of the heavy gale blowing on the beach and inadvisable with the heavy sea on the Bar, nearly low water.'

The Return of Service records that *'the Teignmouth Lifeboat, the* Alfred Staniforth, *was launched and made her way to Exmouth but, finding that her services were not required, returned to her station.'* The Lyme Regis station was not alerted as there was *'no telephone or telegraph communication. '*

A message was subsequently received at the Lifeboat station, from the Coast Watchers, reporting a steamer to be aground under the 'highlands' between Orcombe Point and Straight Point. A Rocket Apparatus Team was immediately dispatched to the location only to find that the steamer lay outside the operational range of their equipment. By 0900 hours the wind had moderated and shifted to the southwest and at 10.00 hours the tug, *Queen of the Exe*, attempted to cross the Bar but was forced to return to port. The tug put out for a second time, at 10.40 hours, with the *Joseph Somes* in tow; the lifeboat being under the command of Coxswain Bridle. The vessels successfully crossed the Bar and reached the stranded steamer at 11.30 hours. The casualty was found to be the French registered 2-masted steamer, the *St. Paul*.

In truly atrocious sea and weather condition, Coxswain Bridle and his 'scratch' crew took a hawser from the tug to the grounded vessel. On the now rising tide the tug attempted to refloat the steamer but in so doing the hawser parted. With extreme difficulty, Coxswain bridle and his crew repeated the operation and were successful in attaching a second hawser to the Frenchman. This hawser held and at 12.30 hours the *St. Paul* was refloated and taken undertow, by the *Queen of the Exe*, to Torbay.

The Honorary Secretary wrote, in the Return of Service:

'The Life Boat sailed home, arriving at 4P.M. under oars and sail against a strong wind and tide, the wind having shifted to N.W. The sea was very heavy and taking into consideration the crew was principally composed of elderly men the younger members having left on Service, I consider it was an excellent

performance in face of one of the worst gales that have been known for 20 years.'

At the time of the original sighting of the *St. Paul*, a second steamer was seen lying outside the Bar, with both anchors down and was flying signals of distress. With the shift in the wind this vessel was able to weigh anchor and proceeded westward.

For their service that day the thirteen-man crew each received payment of fifteen shillings (15/). In further recognition of their dedication and commitment, on 9 December 1916, each crewman received an additional gratuity of ten shillings (10/), in addition to a 'Letter of Thanks', from the management Committee of the Royal National Lifeboat Institution.

The crew of the *Joseph Somes*, so honoured, comprised:

E. W. Bridle (Coxswain), W. Ferris,
W. Mitchell, H. Brackler, J. Bradford, W. Holmes,
E. Bradford, G. Curtis,
G. Holmes, W. Hocking, A. Hocking,
J. Back and T. Bradford.

Following eleven years in post, in 1918 Edwin William Bridle retired as the Coxswain of the Exmouth Lifeboat. Former crewmember William Henry Mitchell succeeded him.

The *Joseph Somes* was first launched under the command of Coxswain William Mitchell on Monday 5 January 1920, when she set out to assist the yawl the 49-ton *Zanita* of Guernsey, laden with a cargo of phosphate.

It was a typical January day with a rough sea being whipped up by a cold Force 4 wind that was blowing from the east-northeast, with heavy clouds gathering. A little after 14.30 hours the Coast Guard spotted a vessel that had stranded on the eastern end of the Pole Sands. Although the vessel was bumping heavily, with seas breaking over her, she was not showing signals of distress. In the absence of the Lifeboat Station's Honorary Secretary, the Chief Officer of Coast Guard, considering the vessel to be in a dangerous position, ordered the launch of the Exmouth lifeboat. The *Joseph Somes* was launched, on two hours of flood tide, at 14.45 hours, and proceeded under oars reaching the *Zanita* at 15.15 hours. Upon the lifeboat reaching the yawl, her Master requested assistance. Coxswain Mitchell place four of his crewmen onboard the *Zanita*, the men established a hawser tow and, on a rising, tide, the lifeboat refloated the yawl and towed her into harbour where the lifeboat crew docked her.

On this occasion the crew of the *Joseph Somes* were credited with the saving of four lives, these being the only lives credited to *Joseph Somes* lifeboat during her 30 years service at Exmouth.

It was the norm that when the *Joseph Somes* was launched she carried a crew of thirteen, the launch being assisted by twenty-nine persons. When launch to assist the *Zanita*, the *Joseph Somes* put to sea with a crew of fourteen; thirty-nine persons were engaged in assisting with the launch. At a meeting of the Exmouth Lifeboat Committee, held on 6 January 1920, the Committee ratified the justification for the engagement of the additional personnel, concluding the *'the launch was carried out with great promptitude.'*

The Return of Service in respect of the *Zanita* is the only recorded service launch to show William Henry Mitchell as Coxswain. In 1928 Thomas Horn succeeded William Mitchell as Coxswain of the Lifeboat.

At a ceremony held on Thursday 31 July 1930, the Master of Sempill, a member of the Royal National Lifeboat Institution's Committee of Management, presented to the Exmouth Station a Commemorative Centenary Vellum. The Vellum was delivered into the hands of the Chairman of the Exmouth Council for safe keeping. At the time of the ceremony, the Exmouth lifeboats have saved the lives of 26 persons.

What proved to be the final service launch of the Joseph Somes took place on Thursday 2 October 1930. The launch was one in series of four launches made to the same vessel, the motor vessel *Ben Johnson* of London, bound from Southampton to Exeter with a cargo of Benzyl oil, over a period of three days. It was cold and showery on that morning, the moderate easterly wind producing a moderate sea with a heavy easterly swell breaking on the Pole Sands. The Coastguard raised the alarm, by telephone, at 07.00 hours when the *Ben Johnson* was first sighted stranded on the Pole Sands, ¾ mile south-southeast, ½ mile east of the Lifeboat Station. The Hon. Secretary, .P. Shrubb alerted both the Teignmouth and Lyme Regis Lifeboat Stations of the incident.

With the tide ebbing for 3½ hours, the *Joseph Somes* was launched at 0815 hours and proceeded under both oars and sail to the casualty, reaching her at 08.30 hours. In spite of his ship's predicament, the Master of the *Ben Johnson* refused Coxswain Horn's offer of assistance, his crew refusing to leave the ship. Given the prevailing conditions, the lifeboat stood by the *Ben Johnson* until 17.00 hours when she returned to her moorings. The crew returned to the boathouse at 17.30 hours. As a heavy swell continued to run on the Sands, with waves breaking over the ship, the lifeboat went out for a second time at 00.01 hours on Friday 3rd October and stood by until 06.00 hours in the hope that the vessel would refloat on the rising tide. The tanker remained grounded, and with her crew remaining onboard, the lifeboat returned to her mooring. Coxswain Horn and his crew again put to sea at 13.05 hours and stood by the tanker until 18.00 hours when, in deteriorating weather conditions and with a falling glass she once more return to the mooring. The *Joseph Somes* was launched for s fourth time at 23.00 hours. By 23.59 hours the wind was blowing from the north and the lifeboat was yet again returned to her mooring at 01.00 hours having failed to provide a service. The lifeboat crew returned to the lifeboat to house her at 09.00 hours.

With a final shift in the wind, the sea moderated and the *Ben Johnson* was refloated by tugs.

The Station Hon. Secretary, C. P. Shrubb, wrote the following letter:

'The Secretary   Oct 4 1930
RNLI

Dear Sir
I enclose the return of service for as requested.

The helpers were not present at night as the Coxswain put the boat on the moorings each time. They stood bye all day on Oct 2nd they were present at 8am on Friday morning & again at 5pm & they housed the boat at 9am on Saturday.

I, personally, advanced the helper's 5/- each as some of them had left their jobs & they were mostly boatmen.

As the pilots went out to the ship before I launched the boat I waited to see what they did & as they couldn't get near her they advised me to stand by her. I should also like to report that the Coastguards did all they possibly could to help us.

I hope this will help our subscriptions this

year as people seemed to be very pleased with the quick was the boat was launched and handled.'

Yours faithfully

In 1932 the RNLI carried out a review and reorganisation of their operations in Lyme Bay. As a result of this reorganisation, the lifeboat station at Lyme Regis was closed, with greater responsibility falling upon the coxswain and crew of the Exmouth Station. In order to carry out these increased responsibilities, the Royal National Lifeboat Institution announced that the Exmouth Station was to receive a new motor-lifeboat.

Being condemned as 'unfit for service', after having serving as the Exmouth station lifeboat for nearly 30 years, the *Joseph Somes* was sold to Dr. R. Lee Michell, of Clifton Lodge, Taunton, Somerset, for the sum of £65.

In 1983, bearing the name *Panatelle*, the former lifeboat was in service, as a yacht, at the Marchwood Yacht Club, Southampton.

6
The Catherine Harriet Eaton
18 August 1933 – 9 October 1953

Class: Liverpool   *Official Number:* 767   *Crew:* 7
Propulsion: 35hp 'Weyburn' petrol engine   *Speed:* 7 knots
Length: 35' 6"   *Beam:* 9' 3"   *Displacement:* 6 tons
Builder: J. S. White, Cowes   *Services:* 34   *Lives Saved:* 31
Coxswains: Thomas Moore Horn (1933-38), Henry Turner 'Rent' Hockings (1939-43),
Reginald Mark Searle (1943-51), Harold John 'Dido' Bradford (1951-53).
Mechanics: William A. Mann (1933-53)

It was in August 1933 that the Royal National Lifeboat Institution's Exmouth Station took delivery of it first motor lifeboat. The lifeboat had been funded by a Legacy from the late Reverend Charles Pemberton Eaton of Milford Haven. The new boat, which cost £3,000, was 35ft 6ins in length with a beam of 9ft 3ins. She was a self-righting vessel and if capsized could, it was claimed, right herself in 4 seconds. The lifeboat was fitted with a 35 h.p. petrol engine, which could provide a maximum top speed of 7¼ knots. In addition to carrying her crew of 7, the new boat could carry up to 30 survivors.

The Inauguration Ceremony of Exmouth's new motor-lifeboat took place on The Front, Exmouth (opposite the Swimming Bath) at 14.30 hours on Tuesday 29 August 1933; it attended by some 8,000 people. The ceremony was conducted under the Presidency of The Rev. The Earl of Devon, Vice-President to the Institution.

The proceedings having been opened by The Rev. The Earl of Devon, the Chairman of the Exmouth Urban District Council, Mr J. Carter, J.P, welcomed those present. On behalf of the donor, Mr J. Kelly White presented the lifeboat to the Institution. The boat was accepted by Admiral Sir A. A. M. Duff, K.C.B. who was a member of the Committee of Management of the Institution who in turn presented it to Admiral F. C. Fisher,

Chairman of the Exmouth Branch of the Royal National Lifeboat Institution.

Lieutenant-Commander H. L. Wheeler, R.N., District Inspector of the RNLI gave a description of the lifeboat, and its capabilities of the vessel.

A short service of dedication was conducted by the Bishop of Crediton which closed with the traditional singing of the "Lifeboat-man's Hymn", *'Eternal Father, Strong to Save.'* A special choir led the singing with musical accompaniment being provided by the Exmouth British Legion Band.

Following the Service of Dedication, Miss

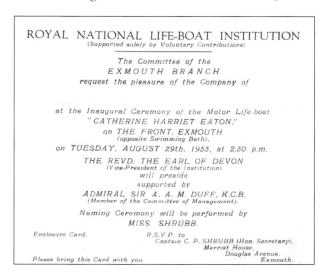

Invitation to the Inaugural Ceremony for Catherine Harriet Eaton 29 August 1933.

Shrubb, the daughter of the station's Honorary Secretary, Captain C. P. Shrubb, named the lifeboat the *Catherine Harriet Eaton*.

On behalf of the Institution, Rev. The Earl of Devon, presented binoculars to Lieut. Col. B. M. Hayes, O.B.E., in recognition of his services as Honorary Secretary of the Lyme Regis Branch.

The proceedings concluded with a vote of thanks to Rev. The Earl of Devon, Admiral Sir A. A. M. Duff, K.C.B. and the Bishop of Crediton, being proposed by Mr S. Couper, J.P. (Chairman of the Budleigh Salterton Urban District Council), seconded by Mr G. E. Saunders, J.P. (Chairman of the Sidmouth Urban District Council), followed by the singing of the National Anthem.

The official programme for the Inauguration provided the following information:

'The Record of the Life-boat Service'
63,363 Lives rescued from Shipwreck round the coasts of Great Britain and Ireland.
11 Lives rescued every week for 109 years!

The first 'shout' for the crew of the new motor lifeboat was something of an anticlimax. Captain C. P. Shrubb, Honorary Secretary of the Exmouth Station, received a telephone call, from the Hon. Secretary of the Brixham Station, on the evening of Tuesday 10 April 1934, reporting the loss of a small fishing vessel, the *Florence May*, the last reported position of the vessel being off Beer Head. The Brixham station requested that the Exmouth lifeboat crew be placed on stand-by. The maroons were not fired but at 21.00 hours Capt. Shrubb summoned Coxswain Tom Horn, together with four crewmen and the winch-man, to the boathouse in anticipation the first service launch for the *Catherine Harriet Eaton*. The lifeboat was not launched as a subsequent call from the Brixham Station reported that the *Florence May* had been sighted safe, in calm waters East of Lyme Regis. Tom Horn and his crew were stood down at 23.00 hours.

The crew of the *Catherine Harriet Eaton* were placed on standby at 15.54 hours on Friday 8 February 1935, following the receipt of a signal from the Seaton Coastguard Station that the *Record Reign of Haldon* was aground 2 miles West of Branscombe. Following the receipt of a further signal, the lifeboat was launched at 19.06 hours

The crew of the *Catherine Harriet Eaton*, (L-R) (?), Reg Searle (bowman) Rent Hockings (2nd Cox), Tom Horn (Coxswain), Billy Man (engineer), Cecil Hockings (asst. engineer) Capt. Shrubb,(Hon. Sec) Leaning against door Doggy Toby.
Courtesy of the Bill Sleeman Collection

A launch of the Catherine Harriet Eaton Sue Crellen

and proceeded towards the reported position of the casualty. The weather was fine, but cold, as Coxswain Horn fought an easterly wind and strong easterly swell until the lifeboat passed Sidmouth and entered the lee of Beer Head. The *Catherine Harriet Eaton* reached the casualty at 20.45 hours, only to find that the *Record Reign* had been abandoned. A signal from the shore, instructed the lifeboat to return to her station, which she did, arriving at Exmouth at 23.40 hours. On her first recorded launch the *Catherine Harriet Eaton* was not required to provide a service.

The first effective service launch of the *Catherine Harriet Eaton* took place on Wednesday 11 September 1935 when she went to the assistance of the sailing dinghy *Ripple*. An alarm was raised at 19.20 hours, by Mr Morgan Giles, a well-known local boat-builder of Teignmouth, via the Exmouth Coastguard, stating that a lady had left Teignmouth, for Exmouth, in a small sailing dinghy. Concerned was expressed for her welfare due to a deterioration in sea and weather conditions. The lifeboat was launched at 19.30 hours, one and a half hours into an ebbing tide. It was drizzling with a Force 3 southeasterly wind providing a moderate rising sea. The *Catherine Harriet Eaton* set out on an intercept course and found the *Ripple* at 19.50 hours, 1 mile from the Parson and Clerk Rock at Dawlish. The female occupant of the dinghy, Miss Whitton was taken onboard the lifeboat, her dinghy being taken in tow to Exmouth. Coxswain Horn recorded his opinion that, in the prevailing sea conditions, the state of the tide and failing light, the casualty would not have reached her destination.

To launch the *Catherine Harriet Eaton* for this

service required a total crew of 7 men plus 31 helpers.

Coxswain Tom Horn and the crew of the *Catherine Harriet Eaton* were themselves 'rescued' following a service launch that took place on Sunday 15 November 1936. The lifeboat was launched at 16.52 hours following the receipt of a signal from the Chief Coastguard at Wyke, to the effect that a trawler, the 40-ton *Crystal* of Dieppe, owner Andrew Tayot, was in distress approximately 1 mile off West Bay. The *Catherine Harriet Eaton* launched into a full southwesterly gale and very heavy seas; it was dark and raining with a flood tide. For three and a half hours Coxswain Horn battled against these conditions, finally reaching the distressed vessel at 20.30 hours. At the scene conditions were such that huge seas were sweeping over the disabled trawler but the crew refused to leave the Crystal. Tom Horn ascertained that the *Crystal* was at anchor, her trawl having fouled her propeller. A request had been made for tugs from Portland to assist the casualty but, as they were reportedly unable to round Portland Bill, the lifeboat stood by the trawler for the duration of the night. By about 07.00 hours the following morning, the storm had abated sufficiently to allow the *Catherine Harriet Eaton* to establish a line to the trawler, the *Crystal* weighed anchor and the lifeboat took her in tow to Lyme Regis, making her fast at 10.30 hours.

After a well-earned rest, and a meal, the crew refuelled the lifeboat (12 gallons of petrol) and at 12.15 hours Tom Horn set course for his home station. The passage was uneventful until the lifeboat suffered engine failure at a point approximately 4 miles off Sidmouth. A passing trawler, from Beer, took the lifeboat in tow recovering her from Ladrum Bay to a point off Straight Point, the Exmouth Pilot Boat then taking over the tow. The *Catherine Harriet Eaton* finally returned to station at 17.45 hours, credited with saving five lives, nearly 25 hours after her initial launch.

The *Exmouth Journal* reported:

'The men were cramped and tired by their 24 hours' trip, during which they had very little sleep, though they had managed to secure a meal while in Lyme Regis.'

A bizarre set of circumstances surrounded the launch of the *Catherine Harriet Eaton* on Saturday

15 January 1938. During Friday night, and into Saturday morning, strong south to southwesterly gale force winds, which in places reached a velocity in excess of 70 miles per hours, had swept the whole of Britain. The strongest gusts, of 76 miles per hour, were recorded at Pembroke. An area that particularly suffered the full ferocity of the gale was the English Channel.

At 04.45 hours that Saturday morning, a Dorset Constabulary Policeman, on his beat in Lyme Regis, reported seeing:

'a signal of distress shoot into the darkness in the direction of Seaton. A glow appeared in the sky as though a Verey light had been discharged.'

Acting on this information, the Coastguard at West Bay, Bridport, launched a full-scale search. Royal Air Force aircraft were scrambled from Dorchester and at 05.30 hours a request was received for the Exmouth lifeboat to be launched. The Beer Rocket Apparatus crew were also alerted and travelled the 20 miles by road to Lyme Regis, where they stood-by for several hours, before returning home on Saturday afternoon.

This distress signal was thought to have originated from the 320-ton vessel *Teasel*, of London, which had been due at Lyme Regis, with a cargo of cement, on Friday afternoon. A Coastguard, from the West Bay lookout, commented:

'We do not know for certain, but we believe it must be the Teasel. *We saw her late yesterday evening standing out off Lyme Regis unable to make the harbour owing to the heavy sea. It is possible that during the night her anchor cable parted. She has not been seen since, and we do not know whether she has gone ashore or drifted. Her motor would be quite useless in such a gale, and she may have drifted miles.'*

It was known that the *Teasel* was carrying a crew of five and that her skipper was Captain Capel. Anxiety steadily grew for their safety for it was in a storm such as this that, two years earlier, the vessel *Kentbrook*, a vessel similar to the *Teasel*, had disappeared in West Bay, known locally as Dead Man's Bay, without trace.

Having received a request for assistance, Coxswain Tom Horn and his crew of six men,

together with thirty-two helpers, set about launching the *Catherine Harriet Eaton* directly into the south-westerly gale. The wind and tide had driven the beach into what was described as '*a miniature sand bar*' and, when making the first attempt to launch, the boat failed to reach the water and had to be pulled back onto its carriage. At the second attempt, the heavy seas drove the *Catherine Harriet Eaton* broadside on to the beach. A local newspaper reported that:

'Fortunately, despite the early hour, there were plenty of willing helpers to render assistance, and after Herculean efforts the boat was again pulled up the beach. Another try was also unsuccessful, but at the fourth attempt at 7.15 the boat was got into deep water, with the foremost men who were launching her almost up to their necks in water. Despite this, they raised a hearty cheer as the lifeboat began forcing her way through the broken water towards the mouth of the River Exe, and then in the direction of Lyme Regis.'

Under motor and sail, after battling against heavy, confused seas, Tom Horn and his crew reached the search area at about 10.15 hours. In horrendous weather and sea conditions, an air/sea search was made of the 30-mile bay, with the Police searching miles of coastline. The *Teasel* was not found. At 10.35 hours a message was received *'NOTHING WHATSOEVER SEEN'* and the search was officially abandoned. The *Catherine Harriet Eaton* headed for Exmouth, passing Beer Head at 11.11 hours, her crew returning to the boathouse at 14.00 hours.

Speculation mounted that the yacht *Liberty*, which was on her way to a ship-breaking yard, might have made the distress signals but this theory was later discounted. The Berry Head Coastguard, at Brixham, had sighted the *Liberty's* lights shortly after 06.00 hours and it was thought highly unlikely that the vessel could have steamed into the teeth of the gale to reach Torbay in such a short period of time.

The mystery of the *Teasel* was however solved. Captain Capel and his crew heard a wireless broadcast reporting their vessel as being lost off Lyme Regis. Captain Capel immediately flashed a message to the Coastguard reporting that the *Teasel* was safely at anchor in Torbay.

The newspaper that reported '*the foremost men*

who were launching her (the lifeboat) *were almost up to their necks in water*' was no doubt referring to the Station's Honorary Secretary, Capt. C. P. Shrubb and the Exmouth Branch Honorary Treasurer, Mr J. G Moore, both of whom suffer exposure and hypothermia having waded into the sea.

The RNLI's magazine, *The Life-Boat*, of April 1938 recorded that:

It was a launch carried out with courage and great determination, and the Institution has made the following awards:

To Coxswain Thomas M. Horn, the thanks of the Institution inscribed on vellum and framed;

To the coxswain and each of the six members of the crew a reward of £1 in addition to the ordinary scale reward of £1 8s. 6., making a reward of £2. 8s. 6d. to each man;

To each of the thirty-two launchers a reward of 5s. in addition to the ordinary scale reward of 6s. 9d, making a reward of 11s 9d. to each launcher. Standard rewards to crew and helpers, £20. 15s. 6d.; additional rewards to crew and helpers, £15. Total rewards, £35.18s 6d;

T Captain C. P. Shrubb, the honorary secretary, and Mr J. G. Moore, the honorary treasurer, both of who were ill as a result of their exertions and exposure, letters of appreciation.

On 11 February 1938 a letter was sent to the Exmouth lifeboat Station in the following terms:

The Coxswain, Crew and helpers
Exmouth Life-boat.

Gentlemen.

At a meeting of the Committee of Management held here yesterday they had before them the report relative to the service launch of the Exmouth motor life-boat on 15th January.

During the whole S.W. gale with a heavy sea and rain squalls, rockets were reported to have been seen off Lyme Regis at about 5.30a.m. Owing to the formation of a bank of sand the launch of the life-boat was only accomplished with extreme difficulty at the fourth attempt, many men going into the sea in order to get the boat off. The life-boat then carried out a search

for over six hours but no casualty could be found.

The Committee were much impressed by the courage and determination shown by all and directed that this letter should be written to convey an expression of their warm appreciation of the splendid work of the crew and helpers of the Exmouth life-boat on this occasion.

Yours faithfully
Signed
Deputy Secretary R.N.L.I.

The origin of the distress signal, witnessed by the Policeman, was never established.

The shoreline at Exmouth was crowded with exited holidaymakers, eager to catch a glimpse of the motor lifeboat, as the *Catherine Harriet Eaton* was launched at 11.30 hours on Wednesday 27 July 1938 to assist a 10-ton auxiliary cutter, the *Florence II* of Southampton. The Hon. Secretary of the Exmouth Lifeboat Station, Captain Shrubb, received an initial alert at 08.40 hours when Mr Charles Pearcey, of the Budleigh Salterton Coastguard Station, made him aware of a motor vessel anchored, in a very dangerous position, in Ladrum Bay. At 09.30 it was reported that the vessel was unsuccessfully attempting to weigh anchor. Being concerned for the safety of the crew of the vessel, Capt. Shrubb, accompanied by Coastguard Station Officer Bates made his way to a point along the coast from where he could observe the distressed vessel. At 10.50 the vessel appeared to get under way but Capt. Shrubb reported '*she was steering a very irregular course.*' Realising that the vessel's sail was flapping and dragging overboard, Capt. Shrubb immediately order the maroons to be fired to launch of the lifeboat. The lifeboat was launched at 11.30 hours, and when addressing a subsequent meeting of the Exmouth Lifeboat Committee, Capt. Shrubb was able to report that the *Catherine Harriet Eaton* had been launched '*in a splendid time of 1 minute and 10 seconds, which was just two seconds above the record launch time.*'

Coxswain Horn located the casualty, the *Florence II*, in Ladrum Bay, with a crew of two on board. It would appear that the two yachtsmen, the owner Mr E.H. Johnson of London, and Mr S. Mynard, had anchored the vessel the previous evening, having set out from the Hamble, and had decided to move the vessel due to deteriorating weather conditions; however when they attempted to raise the anchor, they found that it had fouled in rocks. The men made an attempt to file through one of the links in the anchor chain but this initial attempt had failed. On reaching the vessel, a line was passed to the *Florence II*, from the lifeboat, and the vessel was taken in tow to Exmouth Harbour, arriving at 14.45 hours. The two yachtsmen made light of their experience, commenting that their greatest need was for a good meal!

Wednesday 28 December 1938 marked the retirement, from the R.N.L.I, of Coxswain Thomas Moore Horn. *The Exmouth Journal*, of Saturday 31 December 1938, carried the following headlines:

FORTY YEARS OF
LIFEBOAT SERVICE

Retirement OF Coxswain
Tom Horn

HONOURED BY ROYALTY.

Son of a fine old family of Exmouth fishermen and seafarers, Coxswain Thomas Moore Horn, for the past ten years coxswain of the Exmouth lifeboat, bade farewell to the lifeboat service on Wednesday morning, when the Exmouth motor lifeboat, Catherine Harriet Eaton was launched for a practice cruise.

Prior to the launching, the lifeboat was held up for a few moments in the roadway while Commander H. L. Wheeler, R.N., district inspector for the Royal National Lifeboat Institution, on behalf of the crew, presented Coxswain Horn with a parting gift of a case of pipes.

INSPECTOR'S TRIBUTE

A large crowd had assembled to give Coxswain Horn a cheery send-off, and to wish him "bon voyage" on his last official trip, and "Lifeboat-man Sam" (Mr. Sampson Bennett) made his usual collection for the lifeboat.

Commander Wheeler, who was accompanied by Capt. C. P. Shrubb (Hon. Secretary of the local branch), in making the presentation, commented that Coxswain Horn had been a member of the lifeboat crew for practically

forty years, a period broken only by his war service.

"He has a fine record," Commander Wheeler continued, "and we are all very sorry to know that, on account of his age, he is going. The crew, to mark their appreciation, have asked me to make this small presentation on their behalf, and I have much pleasure in presenting him, from the Exmouth lifeboat crew, these two pipes. I am sure you will join me in wishing him many happy years of retirement."

GOOD-LUCK WISHES.

Coxswain Horn, thanking the crew and the committee for their gift and for the kindness he had received, wished his successor and all the members of the crew the best of good luck.

Mr. Sampson Bennett called for three cheers for Coxswain Horn, and these were heartily given. The boat was then launched, and proceeded on a cruise along the coast.

Members of the crew present, in addition to Coxswain Horn, were Messrs. H. Hockings (second coxswain), R. Searle (bowman), H. Bradford, W. Mann (first mechanic), C. Hockings (second mechanic) and P. Gifford (signaller). Capt. Shrubb accompanied the crew on their trip.

Thomas Moore Horn had joined the Royal National Lifeboat Institution as a member of the 'first' *Joseph Somes* in 1899; he was the Shore Signalman from 1908 to 1919, and served as Second Coxswain from 1920 to 1928. In 1928 he became Coxswain of the second boat to carry the name *Joseph Somes*. At the time of his retirement, Thomas Horn was reported as '*being well into his sixty-seventh year.*' At this time it was a requirement of the RNLI that crew members retired at the age of 60 years. It was seen as being a tribute to the high regard in which he was held within the lifeboat service, that Tom Horn was permitted to remain in service after attaining retirement age.

With the imminent retirement of Tom Horn, the Local Committee convened and approved the following appointments to the crew:

R. Searle (Second Coxswain), H. Bradford (Bowman), with W. Horn being appointed to fill the vacancy in the crew. Henry Turner Hockings was appointed Coxswain of the Exmouth lifeboat.

Reginald Mark Searle, Coxswain 1943–1951.

Harold John 'Dido' Bradford, Coxswain 1951–1953.

Henry Turner 'Rent' Hockings, Coxswain 1939–1943.

William A 'Billy' Mann (Senior), Mechanic 1933–1953.

The last call-out of the *Catherine Harriet Eaton ON767* – a false alarm – 26 July 1953.

The first Wartime service to be undertaken by the Exmouth lifeboat took place on Wednesday 18 October 1939 when Coxswain Henry Hockings launched the *Catherine Harriet Eaton* following a request for assistance from the Royal Air Force. The request was received at 19.25 hours when the RAF station at Lyme Regis, reported that two of their speedboats were in trouble having broken-down approximately 12 miles southwest of Beer Head. The Honorary Secretary, Capt. Shrubb, immediately summoned the lifeboat crew and informed the Coastguard. The lifeboat was launched at 20.00 hours; the Return of Service records '*A very good launch helped by a company of the 8th Division stationed at Sidmouth.*'

Coxswain Hockings and his crew headed out into a moderate easterly swell, with a strong breeze blowing from the east-north-east. The *Catherine Harriet Eaton*, powered by motor and sail, made a search of the area and returned to shore at 01.15 hours, it having been established that the speedboats in question had been located by a passing vessel and towed to Lyme Regis.

With the outbreak, of the Second World War, the R.N.L.I. in common with numerous other services and occupations lost volunteers to War Service. In times such as these the lifeboat crews often supplemented crew numbers with the addition of members of the Coastguard, Royal Naval ratings who were on leave, and indeed local fishermen who by the very nature of their trade had a wealth of experience and knowledge of local waters.

Throughout the war years, the English Channel and the waters along the South Devon Coast were awash with warships and smaller craft. In many instances it was these craft that rendered assistance to distressed seafarers. The number of vessels in the surrounding waters, not surprisingly, gave rise to many 'false alarms'; such were the circumstances in numerous launches undertaken by the Exmouth lifeboat. With reporting restrictions in place many incidents were not commented upon in the press; the following details however are amongst those recorded in the Exmouth stations Returns of Service:

Monday 28 March 1940 – red flares sighted 1½ mile E.S.E. of Orcombe Point. Area searched for 2½ hours with a negative result.

Monday 6 June 1940 – the Budleigh Salterton watch reported red flares or flames an estimated 6 miles out to sea. The launch was curtailed when it was established that the flares were in fact off Portland Bill.

Sunday 3 July 1940 – the *Catherine Harriet Eaton* was launched at 02.05 hours following the receipt of a report from the Coastguard of a ship being on fire about 15 miles off Exmouth. The lifeboat was stood-down, having reached Orcombe Point, the Naval Authorities having signalled that they had the matter under control.

Friday 22 July 1940 – red flares reported 2 miles E.S.E. of Orcombe Point. The lifeboat was launched at 01.15 hours but was ordered back to station, having reached Orcombe Point. Upon returning to station, Coxswain Hockings and his crew were held on stand-by, until 02.45 hours, as further sightings of flares were reported.

Thursday 11 August 1940 - Coxswain Hockings launched the *Catherine Harriet Eaton*, at 11.38 hours, following a report from the Coastguard that an aircraft had entered the water some 4½ mile offshore at a point between Exmouth and Teignmouth. For reasons not recorded, the lifeboat was ordered back to her station, arriving at 12.50 hours. The Return of Service, signed by H. Hockings, however informs us that

'*When the boat was being hauled-up, one of the helpers, Sapper T. E. Mitchell, 573 R.E., Devon & Cornwall Regt. had his arm caught by the hawser and one of the shafts of the carriage. There were no bones broken but I expect he will have a nasty bruise. I do not expect you will hear more of this.*'

The bravery of the lifeboat-man is usually exemplified in acts of courage carried out at sea, but this is not always the case. Members of the Exmouth crew showed outstanding courage on Thursday 12 February 1942, brief details of the act being recorded in the Return of Service log.

The night of Wednesday 11, into Thursday 12 February, the city of Exeter, and surrounding areas, ha been subjected to another night of intense bombing. It was at 09.00 hours on the Thursday morning that the Station Mechanic, W Mann, reported that two unexploded bombs were lying very close to the Exmouth boathouse. The crew were immediately summoned with a view to getting the *Catherine Harriet Eaton* afloat. To launch the lifeboat required the boat to be pulled across the road, a manoeuvre which on this occasion was initially blocked by the Chief Constable as the boat had to pass within feet of the unexploded bombs. The Chief Constable was of the opinion that the passage of the lifeboat could well cause the bombs to explode.

It would appear that the lifeboat gained the safety of the River Exe as records show that '*The Military turned out to help launch the boat.*' It was also recorded that: '*As the bombs were so close to the boathouse the crew showed great courage in staying in the boat whilst about to be launched.*'

The crew referred to comprised H. Hockings (Coxswain), R. Searle (2nd Coxswain), W. Mann (Mechanic), C. Hockings (2nd Mechanic) and H. Bradford (Bowman).

A full twenty-two months passed before the *Catherine Harriet Eaton* was again launch for Service. By this time Henry Turner Hockings had retired as Coxswain of the Exmouth lifeboat and had been succeeded by Reginald Mark Searle.

A rough sea was being whipped up by a Force 6 to Gale Force 8 wind blowing from the South-south-west on Tuesday 21 December 1943 when, the lifeboat was launched at the request of the Resident Naval Officer (R.N.O). The circumstances leading up to this launch however commenced eight days earlier, on Monday 13 December 1942, when, at 08.45 hours, the Cardiff registered cargo vessel the *South Coaster*, ran aground at the eastern end of the Pole Sands, '*West by South ¾ from Orcombe Point.*' The 750-ton vessel, laden with 450-ton of coal, was out of Marsden, bound for Exeter. She carried a crew of thirteen. The lifeboat crew were mustered and stood-by from 09.00 hours until 12.00 hours, and again from 17.30 hours to 21.30 hours the same day but their services were not required, the R.N.O. having sent a tug and Landing Craft to assist the stricken vessel. Over the following week several attempts were made to re-float the *South Coaster*, the lifeboat crew 'standing by' on each occasion in case the assistance of the lifeboat was needed. The 'Head Launcher' stood-by from 17.00

hours until 20.00 hours on Saturday 18 December and J. Shepherd, the Assistant Launcher, stood-by from 11.00 hours until 13.00 hours on Tuesday 21 December. The launch of the lifeboat was not requested.

Shepherd had just been stood-down when at 13.15 hours the Resident Naval Officer requested the launch of the *Catherine Harriet Eaton* as the *South Coaster* was being battered and buffeted by a heavy sea and broken water. Coxswain Reg Searle put into the heavy confused sea with his crew of five, plus two Royal Naval Ratings, who were taken onboard at the request of the R.N.O. With expert seamanship Coxswain Searle took the lifeboat in to the broken waters surrounding the *South Coaster* and skilfully manoeuvred the lifeboat up to the casualty. Whilst experiencing some difficulty, in a textbook operation the lifeboat took off the full crew of thirteen from the cargo vessel and landed them safely at Exmouth at 14.10 hours, there receiving the congratulations of the Resident Naval Officer.

It is worthy of note that the launch and recovery of the *Catherine Harriet Eaton* was, on this occasion, carried out by 10 'helpers' with the assistance of 61 Royal Naval Ratings.

The final wartime launch of the *Catherine Harriet Eaton*, prior to V.E. Day, took place just under a year later when on Sunday 17 December 1944 notification was received of a vessel in distress off Beer Head. The lifeboat was launched at 16.40 hours and on this occasion a Coastguard Signalman and a Royal Navel Petty Officer volunteer accompanied the crew. The boat launched into a South-south-westerly wind of Force 5 – 6 and a rough sea, both the wind and sea conditions were deteriorating. The lifeboat came up to the stricken vessel, 1 mile off Beer Head, at 18.45 hours and found her to be the 500-ton Dutch motor vessel *Ooster Haven*. The steamer was at anchor having suffered a disabled propeller. In addition to her own crew, she carried eleven survivors, some of whom were injured, that she had earlier picked up following a pervious engagement in the English Channel. At the request of the Naval Authorities, Coxswain Searle stood-by the *Ooster Haven* to await the arrival of a tug. With deterioration in weather conditions, a Royal Navy destroyer and escort vessel were dispatched to the scene, arriving at 19.30 hours. The lifeboat transferred a Doctor from the destroyer to the

Dutchman, to tend the injured. A trawler was the next vessel to arrive on the scene and attempted to take the motor vessel in tow. The hawser parted and it fell to the lifeboat to re-establish the tow. The tug finally arrived on scene at 22.30 hours and took the *Ooster Haven* in tow. When it was clear that the vessel was no longer in danger, Coxswain Searle set course for home, returning to shore at 03.20 hours. With a distinct lack of helpers at that time of the night, the *Catherine Harriet Eaton* was moored in dock until morning.

The Exmouth lifeboat station certainly seems to have responded to its fair share of reported sighting of aircraft ditching in the sea. Coxswain Reg Searle and the crew of the *Catherine Harriet Eaton* responded to one such launch on Monday 27 August 1945. It was at 21.51 hours that The Honorary Secretary received a signal, from the Coastguard, reporting '*Aircraft crashed at sea 4 miles S.W. of Orcombe Point.*' The assembly signal was sounded at 21.59 hours. It later transpired that the 8-minute delay in sounding the assembly signal was due to the fact that a Coastguard was not available to make the signal. However the lifeboat crew assembled and with the help of 26 helpers, comprising local people and visitors, '*fully 70% of who were women*' an exceedingly creditable launch was achieved, the boat being actually in the water by 22.10 hours.

On a ¾ flood tide, calm sea and with a slight northwesterly wind, Coxswain Searle headed the *Catherine Harriet Eaton* directly across the Pole Sands directly to the scene of the disaster, which proved to be about 6 miles from her station, arriving at the scene of disaster at 23.00 hours. Two R.A.F. Search and Rescue vessels were already searching the scene and Coxswain Searle established that the aircraft had in fact exploded in mid-air. All that was to be found of the aircraft was an area of sparsely scattered wreckage and burning petrol on the surface of the sea. The R.A.F. vessels withdrew from the search at 22.30 hours but the Exmouth lifeboat continued to search, in a large circular sweep, until 02.00 hours when, realising that there were no survivors, she return to Exmouth.

The lifeboat was once more launched to assist an aircrew following a report being received by the Coastguard, from the Budleigh Salterton Police, that an aircraft had '*fallen in sea two miles from Budleigh Salterton.*' It was a fine but cloudy night with a southerly Force 3 breeze and moderate sea, when the Deputy Honorary Secretary ordered the launch of the lifeboat at 17.45 hours on Tuesday 21 May 1946. Coxswain Searle launched with a full crew of seven and on this occasion was accompanied by Surgeon Lieutenant R. Moore of the Royal Naval Voluntary Reserve.

On reaching the search area, the *Catherine Harriet Eaton* found no trace of either aircraft wreckage or oil spill. After communicating with Exeter Airport, at 19.45 hours, who confirmed that all of their aircraft were accounted for, the lifeboat returned to shore at 20.20 hours.

The Exmouth lifeboat literally supplied a Pilot to the collier, *Martha* of Amsterdam on Friday 9 January 1948. At 18.16 hours the Exmouth Honorary Secretary received a message to the effect that a vessel was seen to be firing distress flares approximately 3 miles off Sidmouth. The message had originated from the Police at Sidmouth. Having verified the authenticity of the call, the maroons were fired at 18.18 hours and the lifeboat was launched at 18.25 hours. As often was the case, the launch crew experienced difficulty in launching the *Catherine Harriet Eaton* as a bank had formed off the slip. The Return of Service records that *'this difficulty would not have been so with a tractor.'* The lifeboat set out into a rough sea, with a wind of Force 6-7 blowing heavy, squally showers from the west-north-west, reaching the casualty at 19.30 hours. Coxswain Searle found the 'casualty' to be the Dutch registered collier the *Martha*, inbound to Exmouth, from Amsterdam, laden with 300-ton of coal. The *Martha* had strayed from her intended course and, when approximately 5 miles off Sidmouth, had fired flares in an attempt to attract the attention of a Pilot. In the rough sea Coxswain Searle succeeded in placing his 2nd Coxswain Harold Bradford, a qualified Pilot, onboard the collier. Harold Bradford was able to manoeuvre the Dutchman, under her own power, to a safe anchorage, off the fairway buoy, to await a suitable tide for entering Exmouth. The lifeboat regained the boathouse at 21.50 hours.

The difficulties encountered in launching a lifeboat across the road and Exmouth foreshore were lessened, on Thursday 5 August 1948, with the arrival at the station of the 'Clayton' Tractor, T12. With a tractor unit, it was anticipated that fewer persons were required to launch and recover the lifeboat and the launch time was greatly

The *Catherine Harriet Eaton* towed by 'Clayton' tractor (T12) 1948. The tractor was built in 1924.

reduced. Only time would tell!

At 20.29 hours on Friday 8 October 1948, the Hon. Secretary received the following message from Exmouth Coastguard:

'*Yacht off Budleigh Salterton Beach, approx 100 yards. Heavy swell, request lifeboat from Exmouth. From Police B. Salterton, to CG Exmouth 20.25 hours.*'

The maroons were fired and with the help of 30 helpers, the lifeboat was under way in 11 minutes. Upon reaching the distressed vessel, at a position 3-miles south of Budleigh Salterton, Coxswain Searle established that she was the 35-ton auxiliary ketch, the *Cresta*, on passage from Poole to Salcombe. She carried the owner's boat-hand plus a temporary crew of three. The vessel had run into difficulty approximately 3-miles off Budleigh Salterton, having sustained damage to her rigging. Now, finding themselves in a heavy swell and south-easterly on shore wind, as well as and running low on fuel, her crew requested that their vessel be taken in tow by the lifeboat. The *Cresta* was taken in to Exmouth Bight where she was moored on a ring buoy. Two lifeboat-men were left onboard the ketch whilst the boat-hand, who had sustained a crushed thumb, was conveyed to Hospital. Following refuelling, the lifeboat remained in Exmouth Dock, returning to the boathouse at 11.30 hours on 9 October.

The Exmouth Return of Service records that, on this occasion, '*The crew wish to claim salvage.*'

In his report on this service, the Honorary Secretary states:

'*Owing to the quick launch several of the regular crew failed to get down to the boathouse in time and so missed the passage.*

It is found that the maroons are very rarely heard by the crew, when fired in the evening, they are in their houses and most likely got the wireless going, and if not on the phone have to rely on neighbours running in and telling them.'

The launch of the *Catherine Harriet Eaton*, on Friday 10 December 1948, was in fact the first to record the services of a Tractor Driver, albeit assisted by an Assistant Tractor Driver, a winchman and 27 other helpers. Once again the launch was to assist a ditched aircraft.

At 11.37 hours the following message was received from the Exmouth Police: '*Royal Marine Officer at Start Point Marine Camp reported Spitfire crashing in sea ½-mile south Budleigh Salterton.*'

At 11.46 hours the Coastguard fired the maroons and the lifeboat took to the water at 12.00 hours. Once again the boat was under the command of Coxswain Reg Searle, a crew of six accompanied him.

Due to the fact the tides had formed a sandbank, the carriage was brought to an abrupt halt in water that was too shallow to facilitate the launch. Fortunately the tractor had followed the launch party down the beach and immediately entered the water and pushed the carriage into a depth of water that allowed the lifeboat to slip from its carriage.

At 12.30 hours the Hon. Secretary received conflicting reports as to whether the aircraft had actually crashed. Enquiries were made with Exeter Airport, Devonport (Plymouth), and Lyme Regis Air Sea Rescue in an attempt to establish if indeed a Spitfire was missing. Confusion still prevailed.

By 12.45 hours the *Catherine Harriet Eaton* had battled her way through a south by east gale and reached the position where the aircraft had reportedly crashed. In a very rough sea, heavy rain and poor visibility Reg Searle commenced a search pattern. Information was subsequently forthcoming that a Spitfire, believed to be the one in question, had dived steeply, levelled off just above sea-level and was shortly afterwards seen proceeding towards Sidmouth. At 13.04 hours Coxswain Searle received a message, via Wyke and Niton R/T, to return to Exmouth. The Return of Service for this launch is the first to record the use of R/T communication by the Exmouth lifeboat.

In his remarks on this service, the Honorary Secretary wrote:

Self-righting lifeboat *Catherine Harriet Eaton* ON 767 Exmouth lifeboat 1933–1953.

'*On the return of the boat, the Coxswain reported having found no trace of the wreckage. He said they met the heaviest seas this boat had been out in. They had used the drogue while searching the reported position of crash, also when coming in over the bar on returning to station, in a very heavy broken following sea. I should like to very highly commend the Coxswain and his crew on the way they handled their boat and the spirit they showed in going out and on their return.*'

The full crew of the *Catherine Harriet Eaton*, on that day were, R Searle (Coxswain), W. Mann (1st Mechanic), H. Bradford (2nd Coxswain), C. Hoskings (2nd Mechanic), P. Gifford (Signalman), J Phillips (Bowman) and W. Horn (Crew).

The lifeboat and her crew were placed on stand-by at 23.25 hours on Wednesday 10 August 1949 following a report of a Firefly Class racing dinghy, the *Windfly*, No F352, being overdue whist on passage from Sidmouth to Beer. The two-man dinghy, which was being sailed by Mr Pym of Sidmouth, plus a crew member, had not been seen since leaving Sidmouth at 20.30 hours. Fishing boats had put to sea, from Beer, to commence a search, whilst the Coastguard checked that the dinghy had not returned to shore. Being unable to locate that dinghy, the Beer fishing vessels requested the launch of the Exmouth lifeboat. The *Catherine Harriet Eaton* was launched at 00.20 hours on Thursday 11 August onto a choppy sea and a fresh westerly wind. The night was overcast with misty rain. The search continued throughout the night and culminated at 08.02 hours when the dinghy and her crew were located by the lifeboat. It transpired that the dinghy had capsized in a squall, at 21.25 hours the previous evening, the two man crew had cut away her sail and mast, righted the boat, and spent some ten and three-quarter hours in the waterlogged hull. The two survivors were landed safely back at Sidmouth, before the lifeboat returned to her station. The Honorary Secretary subsequently received the following letter from the wife of Mr Pym:

My Dear Mr Butler.

Would you please convey to all the crew of the Exmouth Lifeboat, my deepest thanks for all they did for my husband on the night of August 10th.

No words of mine can ever express what is in my heart, or what by the Grace of God they have restored to me.

Any works of this kind are very close indeed to my heart, and both my father. I have been associated for a great number of years with the St John Ambulance & Red Cross Association, which in a way are kindred organisation; their one aim "To save life."

May God bless and speed all your efforts, with deepest gratitude,

Yours sincerely
Doreen Pym.

By 5 April 1951, Harold John Bradford had succeeded Reginald Searle as Coxswain of the Exmouth lifeboat.

The night of Sunday 6 July 1952 was very dark and reverberated to isolated thunderstorms, however sea conditions adjacent to the Maer Rocks, Exmouth, were calm. It was in these conditions that a 25-foot Royal Naval motor launch set out from Exmouth Docks to return to her mother ship, the destroyer *HMS Battleaxe*. The motor launch was carrying twenty-five ratings.'

Initial reports, received from the Coastguard at 02.00 hours stated that the launch appeared to be aground on the Maer Rocks, but distress signals were not being made. It was however understood that the Battleaxe had dispatched another launch to the area. On a rising tide, the stranded launch lifted free but it became abundantly clear that she was badly holed. The naval ratings clambered from the sinking launch and scrambled for the shore: it was only after a head-count that it was discovered that two of their number was missing. At 02.45 hours the Police informed the Coastguard that two men were believed missing, upon confirmation of the information, the lifeboat was launched at 03.24 hours. Coxswain Harold Bradford and his crew diligently continued the search until dawn. They located an area of oil in the vicinity of when the launch sank, but there was no sign of the two missing sailors. The *Catherine Harriet Eaton* was returned to the boathouse at 06.00 hours. A signal was subsequently received from the Commanding Officer, HMS Battleaxe, in which he tanked the lifeboat authorities for their assistance and the action taken.

The tragic events of this evening were further compounded in that Signalman P. Gifford fell from his pedal-cycle whilst responding to the 'shout.' He sustained multiple cuts, abrasions and bruising as a direct result of the fall. His injuries however did not deter him from reporting for service and going to sea as a member of the crew. Upon returning from the service, Samuel Gifford was taken to hospital; he was not detained but remained off work for a week. Sadly he later suffered a stroke and passed away on Christmas Day 1953. Mrs Gifford received an allowance, from the Institution, until her death in 1980.

Saturday 18 July 1953 was Lifeboat Flag Day in Budleigh Salterton and Sidmouth, with the *Catherine Harriet Eaton* making a goodwill visit to support the events. It was at 12.05 hours when, during a thunderstorm, two 12-foot racing dinghies capsized off Sidmouth. In a strong wind and choppy sea, Coxswain Bradford immediately took the lifeboat to their assistance, the crew of two were rescued from the dinghy *Moonstone* and their dinghy towed ashore. This service, which literally was a case of being in the right place at the right time, was the final service undertaken by the *Catherine Harriet Eaton*, at Exmouth. .

At the conclusion of her 20 years 2 months of service as the Royal Lifeboat Institution's Exmouth Station Lifeboat, the *Catherine Harriet Eaton* had undertaken 34 services and was credited with saving 31 lives.

The RNLI sold the *Catherine Harriet Eaton* in 1954, the vessel subsequently being renamed the *Sharon*. In August 1996 the *Sharon* was taken to Kingholm Quay, Dumfries, where she underwent conversion and refurbishment. She finally left Kingholm Quay in August 2002, her current whereabouts being unknown.

7
The Maria Noble
1 October 1953 – 1 January 1962

Class: Liverpool   *Official Number:* 916   *Crew:* 7
Propulsion: Twin 20hp 'Kadenacy' diesel engines   *Speed:* 7¼ knots
Length: 35' 6"   *Beam:* 10' 8"   *Displacement:* 8 ton 6 cwt.
Built: 1953   *Builder:* Groves and Gutteridge, Cowes   *Services:* 30   *Lives Saved:* 35
Coxswains: Harold John 'Dido' Bradford (1953-57), Thomas Henry Litton (1957-61)
Mechanics: William Frederick Mann

Thursday 1 October 1953 saw the arrival, 'on station', at Exmouth, of a new replacement lifeboat the ON 916, *Maria Noble*. She was a Liverpool Class lifeboat, 35ft 6ins in length and, although non-self-righting, she was much beamier, 10ft 8ins, and less likely to capsize than her predecessor. The cost of building the boat, which was nearly £14,594, was provided by the combined legacies of Mr Henry Noble of Hove, Sussex, Mr Arthur J. West, Mrs Louisa Andrew and Mr Ernest J. Williams.

Hundreds of holiday makers watched the Dedication and Naming Ceremony of the ON 916 when it took place 11 months after her arrival in Exmouth. The ceremony was held on the slipway opposite the, Exmouth Lifeboat Station, at 3pm on Wednesday 1 September 1954. The ceremony also, somewhat belatedly, commemorated the 150th Anniversary of the station.

Admiral Sir Arthur Peters, K.C.B., D.S.C, President of the Exmouth and Budleigh Salterton Branch of the RNLI, opened the proceedings recalling that the first Exmouth Lifeboat Station had been established in 1803. Captain G.R. Cousins, D.S.C., R.N., District Inspector of Lifeboats then described the new motor lifeboat. He said that the new boat was one of the first to be fitted with Diesel engines; they were each of 20h.p. Whilst on trial, the boat reached 7.6 knots, giving

a range of 125 miles. At its more normal speed of 7 knots it could travel 176 miles without refuelling, giving an operational radius of about 80 miles. In rough seas the lifeboat could carry 30 people, whilst in calm weather 48 persons could be carried.

Sir Arthur Reed, J.P., a member of the Committee of Management, formally handed over the lifeboat to the Exmouth Branch. The boat was accepted by Admiral Sir Arthur Peters. Prayers were said by Rev. R.F. King, Vicar of Littleham-Cum-Exmouth, and the Lesson was read by The Rev. W. Clark, Free Church Minister. The Dedication was conducted by The Right Rev. Bishop Willis, C.B.E., D.D., and Benediction was followed by the traditional singing of "Eternal Father, strong to save."

The Naming ceremony was performed by Air Vice-Marshal H.V. Satterly, C.B., C.B.E., D.F.C., a native of Exmouth and former Grammar School pupil. In christening the lifeboat with the traditional bottle of champagne, the Air Vice-Marshal officially name the lifeboat the *Maria Noble*. It was reported that as the bottle struck the starboard bow of the lifeboat, a group of spectators standing on the slipway received a liberal shower of champagne, blown on the wind.

Lady Peters presented a Certificate on Vellum to the Station in commemoration of the 150th Anniversary of the establishment of the Exmouth

The Maria Noble is brought from Cowes to replace the *Catherine Harriet Eaton ON767*, October 1953. In boat:- Joe Gorfin, Signalman; Bill Mann, 2nd Mechanic. Standing:- Brian Rowsell, Deckhand; Cecil Hockings, 2nd Mech.; Harold (Dido) Bradford, 1st Coxswain; Bernard Bradford, Bowman; and Jack Phillips, 2nd Coxswain.

THE
ROYAL NATIONAL LIFE-BOAT INSTITUTION
(Supported solely by Voluntary Contributions)
President: H.R.H. THE DUCHESS OF KENT

EXMOUTH BRANCH

Naming Ceremony of the Motor Life-boat
"MARIA NOBLE"

at the
LIFE-BOAT STATION, EXMOUTH
on
WEDNESDAY, 1st SEPTEMBER, 1954, at 3 p.m.

The Life-boat will be named by
Air Vice-Marshal H. V. SATTERLY,
C.B., C.B.E., D.F.C.

The cost of this life-boat was defrayed from the legacies of
Mr. Henry Noble, of Hove, Sussex, Mr. Arthur James West, of Solihull, Warwickshire,
Mrs. Louisa Andrew, of Rhos-on-Sea, Denbighshire,
and Mr. Ernest Jenkins Williams, of Salcombe, Devon.

Naming of the *Maria Noble*.

Programme for the Naming Ceremony of the *Maria Noble* 1st September 1954.

Lifeboat Station. Lady Peters also presented Certificates of Service to two former crew members, Bowman Frank Hockings and Motor Mechanic William A. Mann. The Vellum was received by the Coxswain, Harry Bradford who also received Mr Hockings Certificate in his absence.

William Frederick Mann succeeded his father, William A. Mann as Motor Mechanic of the new lifeboat.

At the time of this ceremony the Exmouth Station lifeboats had made 69 service launches saving 57 lives.

The Service Reports, of the Royal National Lifeboat Institution's Exmouth Station, record the first service launch of the *Maria Noble* as having taken place on the evening of Sunday 19 September 1954 following the receipt of a message from the Exmouth Coastguard, at 21.40 hours, that cries for help, accompanied by flashes of a torch, were emanating from the vicinity of Maer Rocks. The Station Honorary Secretary telephoned the lifeboat Coxswain, Harold Bradford and, by car, they made their way to Maer Rocks where, in the headlights of their vehicle, they saw a 20-foot cabin cruiser, the *Nicky*, riding at anchor, in heavy breaking seas. The occupants of the boat appeared to be bailing and pumping furiously. The two lifeboat men could clearly hear shouts and cries for help. As, having made an initial assessment of the scene, and given the state of the tide, it appeared utterly impossible to get any boat within 200 yards of the casualty, the Coastguard were requested to attempt a rescue by using Life Saving Apparatus. Attempts to fire a line to the casualty failed with the rocket falling 20 – 30 yards short. It appeared that any chance of rescue would depend upon the cabin cruiser remaining afloat until high water when, hopefully, a rescue attempt could be made by the lifeboat.

William F 'Billy' Mann, Mechanic.

The *Maria Noble* was launched at 23.57 hours, reaching the casualty ten minutes later. The casualty was being severely buffeted by the very heavy swell and heavy rain squalls. Coxswain Bradford realised that the only hope of saving the fiver person aboard the *Nicky* was to take the lifeboat in over Maer Rocks at dead, slack, high water. Realising that there would be a grave risk of damaging the lifeboat, the Coxswain and crew agreed that it was a risk worth taking. As the *Maria Noble* descended into the wave troughs, on three occasions the keel of the lifeboat grounded out on the rocks. Showing great skill and first-class seamanship, Coxswain Bradford closed the

Maria Noble Leaving Exmouth   Courtesy of Geoff Holman

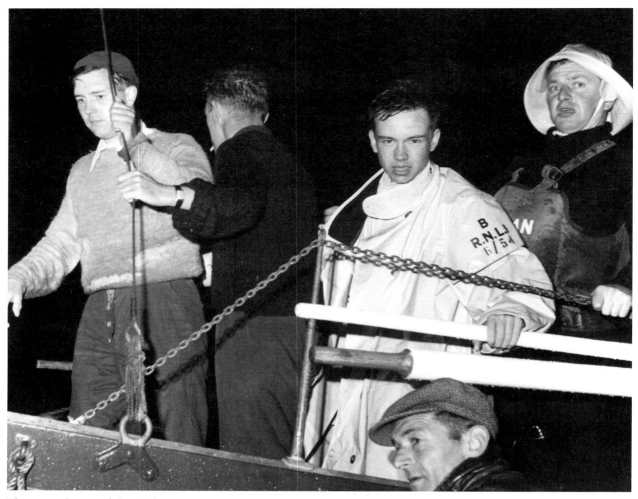

The rescued crew of the *Nicky*.

casualty on three occasions. On the first run two men successfully jumped from the *Nicky* onto the lifeboat. The second run was equally successful with a further two men being rescued. A third run was made to take off the casualty but as he made his bid for safety he mistimed his jump and fell into the sea. Luckily the remaining casualty was immediately grabbed by members of the lifeboat crew and hauled bodily onto the *Maria Noble*.

The owner of the *Nicky*, William Palmer, told the 'Express & Echo' that a dozen or so cars had switched on their headlights to illuminate the scene but switched them off immediately when they realised that they were dazzling and hindering the lifeboat crew. Mr Palmer continued:

'I was astonished that the lifeboat managed to get virtually alongside us in such a difficult situation. The lifeboat crew did a wonderful job of work.'

The cabin cruiser, *Nicky*, became a total loss,

almost at the same spot where two years prior, the liberty boat of *HMS Battleaxe* hit rocks and foundered, with the loss of two lives.

The Service Report for this launch records that the *Maria Noble* handled *'exceeding well under very difficult conditions.'* The report also records that the lifeboat was undamaged and that Coxswain Bradford completed the three rescue runs to the *Nicky* in an amazing time of 5 minutes. The *Maria Noble* returned to shore at 00.23 hours and was one again ready for service at 01.15 hours.

For his outstanding leadership and seamanship during this rescue, Coxswain Harold Bradford was awarded the Royal National Lifeboat Institution's Bronze Medal for bravery. In acknowledgement of the part that he played in the rescue, the Institution awarded a 'Letter of Thanks' to Lifeboat-man Brian Rowsell.

The Exmouth Coastguard received information at 04.18 hours on Wednesday 27 October 1954,

HRH The Princess Marina presenting a RNLI Bronze to Coxswain Harold 'Dido' Bradford for the rescue of the crew of the 'Nicky' on 19th September 1954.

don't think we should have stood a chance of getting in without a tow.' Although we were not far from shore she was leaking too fast for us to stop her sinking.'

The Service Records of the Exmouth lifeboat show that she was launched for service on five occasions in 1955. On the first occasion it was to assist a Liberty Boat, from *HMS Volage*; the liberty Boat having stranded on the Teignmouth Bar – lifeboat recalled, no service provided. The second launch was following receipt of a report of an aircraft crashing into the sea off Straight Point – lifeboat stood down by Fighter Command, no service provided.

On two occasions the crew responded to the alleged sighting of distress signals. On each occasion the area was searched, and the lifeboat recalled, without tracing the alleged casualty.

The only occasion on which service was provided was on Thursday 18 August 1955, the casualty being the 32-foot yacht *Saida*, of Lymington. The vessel, with a crew of 4, was on passage from Lymington to Torquay when she ran aground on the seaward side of Pole Sands. Coxswain Harold Bradford and his crew, launched the *Maria Noble* at 01.09 hours, reaching the casualty, the crew of which were flashing S.O.S. and burning red distress flares, at 01.35 hours. After two lifeboat men had been placed aboard the *Saida*, in a moderate sea, the yacht was towed into Exmouth Docks.

The *M.V. Arrowhead*, required the assistance and expertise of the Exmouth lifeboat crew when, on Thursday 2 February 1956 she found herself on the treacherous Maer Rocks, Exmouth, where many before her had foundered.

It was at 20.50 hours that the Hon. Secretary, Mr Butler, received a telephone call from Mr Bickford, Fairway, Mare Road, Exmouth, reporting that a vessel was perilously close inshore, near Maer Rocks. Mr Butler immediately telephone the Station Officer, Exmouth Coastguard, appraising him of the situation and confirming that the vessel in question was sending a 'MAYDAY'.

The assembly maroons were fired, by the Devon Fire Service, at 20.58 hours and the *Maria Noble* was launched, with her Coxswain and full crew of six, at 21.14 hours. The weather that evening was cloudy with a slight sea, but at the scene of the

that a white light had been observed approximately 3 miles southeast of Orcombe Point, Exmouth. At 04.21 the assembly maroon was fired, by the Fire Service, and by 04.39, just 18 minutes later, the *Maria Noble* was underway with a full crew. The lifeboat was launched into a force 4 south-south-westerly wind, which was accompanied by a moderate sea and heavy ground swell. At 05.10 hours, the lifeboat reached the casualty, the 32-foot cabin cruiser *Ruth*, of Poole, which was on passage from Poole to Dartmouth. The *Ruth* was 4 miles southeast of Straight Point and taking in water at an alarming rate; her two-man crew fighting a loosing battle as they attempted to bail her out.

Harold Bradford took the *Maria Noble* alongside the *Ruth* and transferred 2nd Mechanic C.W. Hockings onto the casualty. It was quickly established that the cabin cruiser's engine had failed due to the fact that the interior of the vessel was flooded to an estimated depth of 3½-feet.

It was agreed that the casualty should be taken in tow and a line was passed, from the *Ruth* to the lifeboat, but this soon parted in the heavy sea. A more substantial line was then passed from the *Maria Noble* to the *Ruth* and the lifeboat commenced to tow the cabin cruiser, at approximately 4 knots, to Exmouth Docks. The lifeboat returned to shore at 06.35 hours.

One of those rescued commented to Mr Butler, the Station Honorary Secretary:

'When the engine stopped all the lights went out and we were unable to see or charts. I

The wreck of the *Arrowhead* 2nd February 1956.

incident there was a very heavy swell breaking over the Maer Rocks.

The casualty the 198-ton *M.V. Arrowhead*, a wartime torpedo recovery craft with a single hull, owned by the Island Shipping Co. Guernsey, on passage from St. Malo, France, to Exmouth; was laden with 110 tons of grain and carried a crew of seven.

Upon arriving at the casualty, at 21.25 hours, Coxswain Bradford found the *Arrowhead* to be hard aground and leaking badly. The crew of the stricken vessel had lowered away one of the ships lifeboats and were preparing to abandon ship. By skilfully manoeuvring the *Maria Noble* up to the *Arrowhead* the lifeboat took off the Master and crew. The ships lifeboat was taken in tow but in the very heavy swell the securing rope parted and the boat was lost. The lifeboat landed the crew of the *Arrowhead* safely, at Exmouth Lifeboat station, at 22.05 hours.

When interviewed following the rescue, the skipper of the vessel, Mr Hocart, confirmed that the vessel was not under pilot as she attempted to enter the River Exe. He was unable to say why they went aground in calm weather and good visibility other than that the *Arrowhead* had adopted a course to starboard of the fairway before running onto the rocks.

It was to the aid of a '*person stranded*' that the Exmouth lifeboat was launched on Wednesday 8 August 1956, following an alarm being raised by two boys, that a man, who could not swim, was marooned on a cliff-face. The lifeboat was launched at 19.04 hours and proceeded to Otterton Head. Members of the public from a local holiday camp, organised themselves into a chain along the cliff-top and, using shirts and towels, signalled to

the lifeboat and directed Coxswain Harold Bradford towards the man, who was stranded on a ledge at Brandy Head. The ledge on which the man was marooned was only 1-foot wide but, with another 1 hour and forty minutes of flow tide and with the tide lapping at the very edge of the ledge, Harold Bradford was able to take the *Maria Noble* right in to the cliff face and rescue the casualty. The man was a Dr. Walker who had been attempting to walk along the rocks from Sidmouth to Budleigh Salterton. The lifeboat landed the man, at Exmouth, at 19.40 hours.

In respect of the holiday makers who lined the cliff-top throughout the rescue, an entry made in the Service Record, by P.H.C Butler, reads:

'*The Coxswain tells me they were a great help and that it would have been very difficult to locate the man without their help.*'

The call for assistance to which the *Maria Noble* responded on Wednesday 15 August 1956, involved not only the RNLI but also the Coastguard, Police and aircraft of the RAF Coastal Command. At 13.55 hours that day the Secretary of the Exmouth lifeboat station received a telephone message, from the police at Dawlish, informing him that two children had been missing from Dawlish since 11.00 hours the previous day, Tuesday 14 August. The Police sought advice, as during Wednesday morning, they had received information that an 11-foot dinghy was missing from the boat-cove. The dinghy could be accounted for, up until 17.00 hours the Tuesday and was discovered to be missing at 21.00 hours. There was no evidence to directly link the dinghy to the missing children. Mr Butler advised the

Police that a dinghy adrift in the prevailing wind, a westerly force 2-3, could be anywhere up to Portland. The Police were advised to immediately contact the RAF Coastal Command and that the lifeboat would be ready to launch, if required.

The expected request was forthcoming and the *Maria Noble* was launched at 17.30 hours to commence a search pattern in conjunction with the Torbay 'Barnett' Class lifeboat, the ON 734 *George Shee*, Coxswain Henry O. Thomas, and a Shackleton aircraft of the RAF Coastal Command.

The Shackleton was at the extremity of the first sweep when the crew sighted the dinghy, *Tina*, with the two children onboard, approximately 18 miles east-southeast of Straight Point. The lifeboats were alerted as to the position of the dinghy and both the *Maria Noble* and the *George Shee* started to close on to the casualty. The Exmouth lifeboat was only two miles from the given location when, at 20.30 hours, the Torbay boat reached the scene and successfully rescue the casualties.

It would appear, from the Station records, that although the two Krohn family children had been missing since 11.00 hours on Wednesday 14

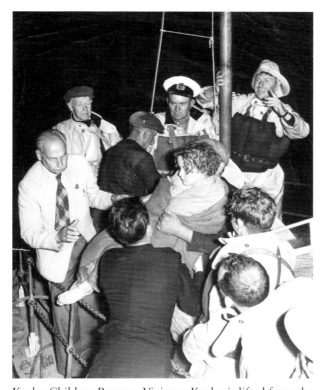

Krohn Children Rescue. Vivienne Krohn is lifted from the lifeboat. Background (l-r): Major Butler (Hon. Sec.) Henry Thomas (Torbay Cox), Dido Bradford (Exmouth Cox) and Joe Gorfin. 15 August 1956.

August, it was not until the following afternoon that their mother confirmed to the Police that the children had hired a boat. The Service Record records that it:

'*Would have been impossible for the Exmouth L/B and Torbay L/B to locate the dinghy without the help of the Coastal Command aircraft. They would not have seen the dinghy more than ½ to ¾ of a mile away in the choppy sea.*'

With a feeling of great relief the crew of the *Maria Noble* returned to shore at 23.05 hours.

Christmas Day is a time when, traditionally, families come together to relax and share in festive celebrations. But to the men and women of the Royal National Lifeboat Institution Christmas Day is like any other day; if a request for assistance is received, without fear or favour, the lifeboat crews will forsake their own enjoyment to readily go to the assistance of others. Such was the case on Christmas Day, Tuesday 25 December 1956, when tragedy struck the crew of the Exmouth lifeboat, the *Maria Noble*, as they responded to a distress call from the *Minerva*. On that fateful evening two members of the lifeboat crew were washed overboard, not in one incident as was first believed but by two separate waves; however both men were subsequently found in the same cove, beneath the 60 foot high cliffs, between Orcombe Point and Sandy Bay.

The *Maria Noble* was launched at 17.20 hours on that Christmas Day following a report that a vessel, which proved to be the 336-ton Dutch registered vessel, the *M.V. Minerva, of Amsterdam*, was burning red distress flare 4 miles southeast of Orkum (Orcombe) Point. Due to the location of the boathouse, Coxswain Bradford launched the lifeboat into a sheltered sea but very soon encountered a very rough, confused sea and poor visibility, in continuous squally, heavy rain which was being driven on a force 6-8 south-easterly wind. The lifeboat crew comprised:

H.J. Bradford (Coxswain), J. Phillips (2nd Coxswain), W.F. Mann (Mechanic), C. Hockings (Asst. Mechanic), B.J.B Bradford (Bowman) and lifeboat men C. Lane, B. Rowsell and Wm. Carder.

The launch appeared to go without a hitch; the first indication that the Station Honorary Secretary had of a potential disaster coming at 18.15 hours when, whist talking on the telephone to the

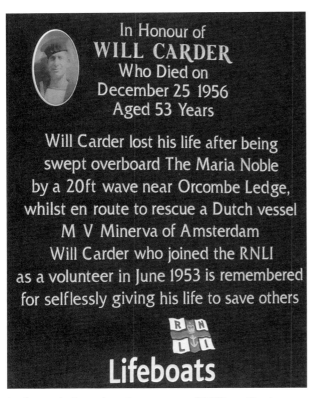

In Honour of
WILL CARDER
Who Died on
December 25 1956
Aged 53 Years

Will Carder lost his life after being
swept overboard The Maria Noble
by a 20ft wave near Orcombe Ledge,
whilst en route to rescue a Dutch vessel
M V Minerva of Amsterdam
Will Carder who joined the RNLI
as a volunteer in June 1953 is remembered
for selflessly giving his life to save others

Lifeboats

A plaque dedicated to the memory of William Carder.

The *Maria Noble* and crew return to station following the tragic loss of William Carder, 26 December 1956

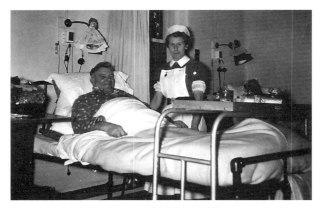

Sister Joyce Manning with Jack Phillips recovering at Exmouth Hospital Courtesy of the Bill Sleeman Collection

Coastguard, a Mr Putt broke in and reported to him that he had monitored a message from the lifeboat to the effect that lifeboat-man Carder and 2nd Coxswain Phillips had been washed overboard. Beach parties were immediately organised to search the coastline between 'Orkum' and Sandy Bay. The Torbay lifeboat was also requested to launch.

The first crewman to have been washed overboard, lifeboat-man Will Carder, was lost 10 minutes after the launch, at 17.40 hours, in the proximity of the No. 1 Buoy; ten minutes later the *Maria Noble* was struck by a succession of heavy seas and 2nd Coxswain Jack Phillips was lost in the vicinity of the Fairway Buoy. In the turmoil the lead to the lifeboat's radio mast had been damaged. Lifeboat-man Brian Rowsell attempted to carry out repairs but he was thrown against the mizzen mast sustaining head injuries.

At this point Coxswain Harold Bradford had to make what must have been one of the most heart-wrenching decisions of his Service, whether to turn the lifeboat and attempt to rescue his two friends and colleagues or to carry on, in the best tradition of the RNLI, and make his way on to the casualty. Repairs having been made to the aerial lead, and realising that any attempt to turn the lifeboat in the heavy seas would place his crew in extreme danger, the lifeboat made a distress call, which was monitored by Mr Putt; Coxswain Bradford then chose to continue on to the *Minerva*. Showing great determination, and trying to put personal thought behind them, the remaining six crewmembers of the *Maria Noble*, pushed onward on their errand of mercy, eventually reaching the M.V. *Minerva* at 18.45 hours. Upon drawing within hailing distance of the casualty, Harold Bradford established that the *Minerva* was lying to anchor, albeit the anchor was in imminent danger of dragging. The lifeboat stood-by in heavy seas that were relentlessly crashing onto the cliffs, the rebounding swell tossing the *Maria Noble* like a toy boat. Thankfully, at 20.00 hours Coxswain Bradford and his crew were relieved by Coxswain Thomas and the crew of the Torbay lifeboat, the *George Shee*.

As in the prevailing sea and wind conditions entry into the River Exe would be extremely difficult, the Exmouth lifeboat made her way to the Torbay Station, arriving at 22.00 hours. At Brixham Brian Rowsell received hospital treatment for his head injury and overnight accommodation was provided for the Exmouth crew.

Rested, but suffering from shock and bruised, the Exmouth crew returned the *Maria Noble* to her home station on Wednesday 26 December, re-housing the lifeboat at 14.00 hours.

The sea makes no distinction when dealing a fateful blow and on that day, while risking his life for the benefit of others, the cruel sea claimed the life of lifeboat-man, William "Will" J Carder.

Will Carder, aged 53, was the popular licensee of the Volunteer Inn, which stood in Chapel Street, Exmouth, and had served as a member of the lifeboat crew for more than 30 years. The sea spared the life of Jack Phillips, the second coxswain, who after receiving a terrible buffeting, was cast ashore, exhausted but alive.

First-hand accounts of the unfolding drama and consequent tragedy were reported, at length, in the *Exmouth Chronicle*, as set out below:

'*The sea drama which was to end in death began about 5pm on Christmas Day when Mr Thomas Tutton, a coastguard on bad weather watch at the Orcombe Point look-out, saw a distress flare from the 313-ton Dutch coaster* Minerva, *which had developed engine trouble about four miles offshore and dragged her anchor. The lifeboat was called out and was launched with a crew of eight into boiling seas, whipped up by a wind above gale force. Said Coxswain Mr H ("Dido") Bradford: "I have never seen such mountainous seas out there."*

At 5.20 the lifeboat was afloat and off on its severest test yet, watched by anxious eyes from the shore. Unknown to them, the boat's radio mast was soon carried away by a huge wave. Then came the first hint of tragedy.

At the Pierhead Stores, Exmouth, Mr Edwin Putt and his father, Mr Bert Putt, happened to be listening in on a trawler band radio and after hearing that the Exmouth lifeboat had gone out on a service call, Mr Edwin Putt went to the lifeboat station where he found that messages were not being received from the lifeboat. Then, at home, Mr Bert Putt picked up a weak signal from the lifeboat that the two men had gone overboard. He immediately telephoned the lifeboat station and volunteer search parties, including Special Constables,

were organised by Mr P.H.C. Butler (Hon. Secretary of the local R.N.L.I.).

Members of the Budleigh Salterton life-saving apparatus team had by this time reported for duty and coastguard Mr Tutton divided them into two parties to search the beach between Exmouth and Sandy Bay.

Mr Tutton lead the first party consisting of Mr C.R. Richards and his young son, Courtney, and Mr Harry Maers. They had not gone far when their torches picked out Mr Phillips trying to struggle to his feet at the water's edge. "It's a good job you've come. I couldn't have gone any further," he told them. They carried the 16st. Mr Phillips up the steps to the cliff tops where Mr Richards had left his car and he was driven to the lifeboat station for attention. Mrs Phillips and Mr Tom Phillips, brother, were there to go with him to hospital in the waiting ambulance.

Just after Mr Phillips had been found, the second party of searchers, consisting of Mr Michael Hayward and Mr Fred Veal, of the Budleigh Salterton rescue team, along with Mr Michael Heard, the Exmouth lifeboat winchman, discovered Mr Carder not far away.

"He was lying face down at the edge of the water," said Mr Tutton. "We started applying artificial respiration at the foot of the cliffs, having sent back a call for aid. Police and ambulance men joined us but after a time Dr R. Hardy told us that Mr Carder was dead."

Meanwhile the Exmouth lifeboat was ploughing its way through the gales and savage sea to the coaster, as was the Torbay lifeboat from the other direction. By then their services were not required and both lifeboats made for Brixham, where the Exmouth boat stayed overnight, and returned bruised and battered on Wednesday. Stanchions were bent, part of the guard rail had gone, and even the steel support for the searchlight had been twisted by the force of the ferocious waves.

Recovering in Exmouth hospital from shock and exhaustion after nearly an hour in the icy water, Mr Phillips told a "Chronicle" reporter the story of his adventure.

Mr Phillips, a harbour pilot and deputy coxswain of the lifeboat, said of his escape: "It was the luckiest break of my life. The boat was taking 20ft. high waves and I wondered that

Above left: Recovering the *Maria Noble*.

Above right: Launching the *Maria Noble*.

Right: Cox Harold 'Dido' Bradford opens the first National Boat Show at Olympia, London 1955.

she did not turn right over. I was standing aft with some of the others when I suddenly felt myself being swept away."

"There was nothing I could do but float with my cork life jacket. I knew I was being swept towards the shore and when I felt the sand under my feet I half crawled out of the water. I remembered that there was a beach hut café somewhere near and I found it. Then I thought of the tide coming up and not wanting to be trapped, walked along the beach looking for some steps. Then I saw the lights of the search party coming towards me and I certainly was glad. When I was in the water I never thought I would make it."

The missing links in this drama of Exmouth's Black Christmas were supplied when the lifeboat returned to base from Brixham about 1.30pm on Wednesday. Large crowds who had waited in the fine weather which was such a contrast to the wild winds of the previous day closed in as it hoved in sight and some members of the crew, spotting their relatives, leaped from the boat as soon as it was

beached and hugged them in a scene charged with emotion.

The crew looked grim and shaken after their ordeal, some had their clothes torn, and one, Mr Brian Rowsell, had a head injury. Then it was ascertained that it was not one giant wave, but separate waves which had knocked the men overboard.

"I have never seen such seas," said Coxswain Bradford. "I tried to keep the bows to the seas all the time, but it was impossible. Near the Bell Buoy the seas were massive and we were under water. We were being knocked for six and at times the masthead light was under water as we went over."

"We took one particularly big sea then we found that Will Carder had gone when we got the boat right again. Nobody saw him go. Even had we seen him we could not have turned the ship round. Then another terrific wave hit us in the same way and afterwards we found that Jack Phillips had gone. I was knocked flat myself with Billy Mann, the engineer, on top of me."

Expressing his grief at the loss of a colleague and his relief to know that Mr Phillips was alive, Mr Bradford added: "But you know, if the maroons went again tonight there would be a crew there."

Another member of the crew, Mr Brian Rowsell, came back with a black eye and a gashed forehead, sustained when he was thrown against the radio mast and knocked out. Mr Rowsell, well-known local yachtsman and a regular member of the lifeboat crew prior to joining the Royal Navy, was home on Christmas leave when he answered the call and went out. "Every time I come home on leave the maroons go," he said as he nursed his injuries.

The consensus of opinion among members of the crew was "We just don't know how the boat didn't capsize," and "We don't know how we came out of it alive."

One of the crew Mr "Ted" Lane, said that Mr Bernard Bradford, the bowman, and Mr Carder went forward in the boat with him. "Will Carder said he was going aft. We were getting thrown about and even the masthead light was under water. I was suddenly knocked flat. When I picked myself up Will Carder was nowhere to be seen. None of us saw him go."

Another member of the crew, Mr C. Hockings, confirmed that Mr Phillips went overboard after Mr Carder. He said that after Mr Carder had been missed he spoke to Mr

Recovering the *Maria Noble ON916* to station.

Phillips, and it must have been 10 or 15 minutes later that they missed Mr Phillips. "I think that Will Carder must have hit something and been knocked out when he went over" he said, "because where he went in he really had a better chance than Jack Phillips of getting ashore."

Lifeboat engineer, Billy Mann, described the sea as being "like a spongecake that came upon us layer upon layer." The skipper of the Brixham lifeboat told me he had seen nothing like it in 30 years.

This tragic incident was also detailed in the RNLI's own publication, 'The Life-Boat' of March 1957, under the headline:

Loss of member of Exmouth Crew
At 4.59 on the afternoon of Christmas day, 1956, the coastguard informed the Exmouth honorary secretary, Mr P.H.C. Butler, that a vessel was burning red flares four miles south-east of Orcombe Point. This is about three-and-a-half miles south-east of the fairway buoy in the River Exe. A south-easterly gale was blowing and there were high seas with continuous rain. It was less than an hour before low water. The river running into the sea had been swollen by heavy rain.

Maroons were fired at 5.4, and at 5.20 the Exmouth life-boat Maria Noble, *one of the 35-feet 6-inches Liverpool type, was launched into the sheltered waters of the river.*

The coxswain, Harold Bradford, took her down river at reduced speed, as none of the channel buoys is lit. As she approached Flatledge buoy she ran into heavy broken water caused by the bar, and the coxswain ordered full speed ahead in order that the life-boat could gain steerage way.

On Beam Ends
As she approached Orcombe Ledge buoy the life-boat shipped a very heavy sea over her starboard bow. This laid her on her beam ends and caused her to sheer violently to port. At

Launching the *Maria Noble* for service 01/09/1954 – Bernard Bradford leaning on the rail. RNLI/Richard Tarr

this time there were three men forward. One of them was the bowman, Bernard Bradford. The other two were E. C. Lane and William Carder.

When the boat had nearly cleared herself of the first sea but still had a list to port, William Carder shouted that he was going aft for shelter. As he did so the life-boat shipped a second heavy sea. It is believed that it was this sea which washed Carder overboard, although nobody saw him go.

After a few minutes the bowman, Bernard Bradford, went aft to see whether Carder was safe. By this time the life-boat was nearly clear of the bar, but she shipped three further heavy seas in quick succession over the starboard side. The first of these seas caused the aerial down-lead plug to come adrift. One of the members of the crew, Brian Rowsell, tried to plug in the lead when he was hit by the second sea. This knocked him against the mizzen mast and injured his head. Almost at the same time the second coxswain, Jack Phillips, was washed out of the life-boat over Rowsell, striking the mizzen mast and bending it as he went. At the same time it was learnt that Carder was missing. The time was now about 5.50.

Search Must Be Hopeless

With the sea that was running and in the general conditions prevailing, Coxswain Bradford reached the conclusion that a search must be hopeless and that to turn the boat at that moment would be to invite certain disaster. He therefore decided to inform the shore by radio-telephone that two men were missing, and to make for the casualty. Because of the damage to the aerial it was some fifteen minutes before the message could be passed. As soon as it was received on shore Mr. Butler and the coastguard organised search parties.

Coxswain Bradford by this time was badly shaken and bruised and the second coxswain had been washed overboard. The mechanic, William Mann, took the wheel, and the life-boat made for the casualty. She was a Dutch motor vessel, the Minerva, *of 336 tons, in ballast. She had anchored because of engine trouble and was in danger of dragging.*

At 6.35 the Torbay life-boat George Shee *was launched. She too went to the* Minerva *and relieved the Exmouth life-boat, which made for Brixham harbour, arriving at ten o'clock. The Torbay life-boat stood by the* Minerva *until she had repaired her engines and was under way. The life-boat then returned to her station, which she reached at 10.25.*

Half Swimming and Drifting

Jack Phillips meanwhile had managed, half swimming and half drifting, to reach the shore to the eastward of Orcombe Point, where he was found by search parties and taken to hospital. He subsequently recovered. Shortly afterwards William Carder was found lying head down in the surf, and all efforts to revive him were unsuccessful. Brian Rowsell was treated in hospital for head injuries.

William Carder was unmarried, but the Institution is paying a pension to a member of his family. The funeral took place at Littleham Parish Church on 28th December 1956. Sir Arthur Reed, J.P., represented the Committee of Management of the Institution. A letter of commendation was sent to Motor Mechanic William Mann.

Rewards: Exmouth, rewards to the crew, £23; additional monetary rewards to the crew, £40; rewards to the helpers on shore £15 14s; total rewards £78 14s.; Torbay, rewards to the crew, £12 5s.; rewards to the helpers on shore, £1 4s.

This tragedy was unprecedented in the history of the Exmouth Lifeboat Station and profound sorrow was felt by all the townsfolk of Exmouth. The *Exmouth Chronicle* carried the following Editorial on Saturday 29 December 1956:

THEY SERVE

'The tragic death of a member of the Exmouth Lifeboat crew, and the miraculous escape of another, as the lifeboat set out on a Christmas day rescue mission, brought a sense of shock and dismay that was universal.

Of this it must be said of Will Carder. He served the sea for many years, and the manner of his death was fitting for a man who, with all his comrades of the lifeboat crew, counts no hazard too great when their services are needed by those in peril on the sea.

But no tribute could pay the debt which is owed to him and his fellows for duties which they give as volunteers, freely and unmasking, in the service of their fellow men.

It demanded heroism beyond the limits of many to set out in the gale-swept seas on Christmas night, as the lifeboat did and has done on many other occasions. Yet there were volunteers enough and to spare for the task, and that is how it will always be.

When the Exmouth lifeboat came home the next day, Coxswain Bradford spoke for his crew when he said: "If there is a call now, there will be a crew ready to answer it." Not bravado – to him a statement of fact, for that is how these men regard their lifeboat service.

It is for that unassuming acceptance of what they regard as their duty that those who serve the lifeboats should stand highest in our regard. They will never fail those who need them.'

The year of 1957 saw the retirement of three of the most experienced and respected members of the Exmouth Lifeboat crew, Harold Bradford who had served as Coxswain of the lifeboat for 6 years, the 2nd Coxswain Jack Phillips and 2nd Mechanic C.W. Hockings.

It was widely reported that the resignations were at the wish of the Trinity House Commissioners as the three lifeboat-men were also local pilots. Speculation linked the resignations with the tragedy of Christmas Day last when Jack Phillips had been washed overboard from the *Maria Noble* and William Carder had tragically lost his life.

The Exmouth Lifeboat Station Secretary, Mr Butler, commented:

'It is a fact that had the entire crew been lost that day the port of Exeter would have been left without any pilots. It was the Commissioners wish, though not their direct order, that in view of the increasing traffic on the Exeter Canal, the three pilots should resign and they have now done so, much to their personal regret.'

At the Annual General Meeting of the Exmouth Branch of the Royal National Lifeboat Institution, held on Saturday 5 December 1959, the President, Admiral Sir Arthur Peters, presented a posthumous Certificate for Meritorious Service to Miss May Carder in memory of her brother, William J. Carder. The Certificate was signed by HRH The Duchess of Kent and Lord Howard, President of the RNLI.

At the same meeting, Long Service Certificates were presented to Harold J Bradford, Jack Phillips and Cecil Hockings who, between them, had contributed nearly 60 years' service to the RNLI.

In presenting the Certificates, Admiral Peters commented:

'We are grateful for their past service as we are grateful for those who come to take their place. These men must feel a glow of happiness in the knowledge of their many years service to the community.'

Harold Bradford and Jack Phillips were succeeded by Thomas Henry Litton and Brian Leonard Rowsell respectively.

The *Maria Noble* was launched for service on a total of eleven occasions during the period between 7 June 1957 and 13 May 1959, actually providing a service on seven of those occasions and being credited with the rescuing of a further fourteen lives.

Rather bizarre circumstances surrounded the launch of the *Maria Noble* on Tuesday 18 June 1957 when the lifeboat put to sea, at 23.40 hours, to investigate a report of red flares being sighted at a location given as '*90° from the Dawlish Railway Bridge and southwest of Orcombe Point.*' At the time of the launch, the sea was calm but visibility was impaired by spasmodic thunderstorms which were carried on a north-north-westerly wind.

When, at 00.05 hours, the lifeboat reached the search area the crew saw a number of red flares but could find no trace of a casualty, and when red parachute flares were seen to be dropped from an aircraft, Coxswain Bradford requested that immediate contact be made with 19 Group, Royal Air Force. Information provided by the RAF subsequently revealed that an exercise was in progress, off the South Devon coast, in conjunction with HM Submarines of the Royal Navy. 19 Group apologised for not informing the Emergency Services of the planned operation and both the *Maria Noble*, and the Torbay lifeboat, the *George Shee*, which had joined the initial search, were recalled to their respective stations. The *Maria Noble* was re-housed at 05.15 hours.

Thomas Litton, Coxswain 1957–61.

This service was the last service to be carried out with Coxswain Harold John Bradford at the helm of the Exmouth lifeboat.

The first service provided by the *Maria Noble*, under the command of Coxswain Thomas Litton, took place on Friday 26 July 1957, following red flares having been reported near Langstone Rock. The maroons were fired at 02.18 hours and the lifeboat was away, just 21 minutes later, at 02.39 hours. The lifeboat reached the casualty, the 9½-ton Bermudan Sloop *Lady Isabelle of Poole*, which was on fire and out of control, just as she was being blown onto the seaward side of the Pole Sands. The weather was overcast with heavy rain squalls; the wind was recorded as being west-south-westerly force 4, backing south-westerly force 6 and increasing. The sea was short and steep.

As Tom Litton closed the casualty a line was passed, from the *Lady Isabelle*, to the lifeboat which succeeded in towing the yacht clear of the sand bank before the line parted. Coxswain Litton then placed 2nd Coxswain Brian Rowsell onboard the yacht who made fast a line passed from the lifeboat. The fire was dealt with and, at 04.40

hours, the *Maria Noble* towed the yacht, and her crew of two, in to Exmouth Docks.

Notification was received at 19.20 hours on Saturday 28 September 1957 that three red flares, followed five minutes later by a single red flare, had been sighted by Lyme Regis Coastguard, at a position approximately 8-10 miles south of Lyme Regis. It was reported, at that time, that a RAF Range Launch was proceeding to the scene to commence a search. Having initially been requested to 'stand-by', the Exmouth lifeboat was subsequently launched at 21.48 hours and reached the search area at 01.10 hours on Sunday morning. Having assisted with a methodical search of the area, without locating a casualty, the lifeboat was recalled to station at 05.35 hours.

At 06.30 hours, as the *Maria Noble* was nearing the Exmouth Fair Way Buoy, the crew sighted red flares being fired from the direction of the Orcombe Ledge. Coxswain Litton altered course and on approaching the ledge found the 3½-ton sloop, *Westwind of Lyme Regis*, hard on Orcombe Ledge. Luckily the weather was clear with the force 2-3 wind providing only a slight swell.

The Master of the *Westwind* reported that upon entering the Fair Way, the vessel's engine had broken down, he had dropped his anchors but they had failed to hold and his vessel was driven onto the rocks. A towrope was established and the *Maria Noble* towed the *Westwind*, and her crew of four, in to Exmouth.

Whilst the *Maria Noble* was 'off station' in 1959, she was replaced by the Liverpool Class, single screw, Relief Fleet Lifeboat the *ON 795 Frank and William Oates*. The *Frank and William Oates* was the first lifeboat to be moored afloat on the River Exe. Whilst at Exmouth she was

Liverpool Class relief lifeboat *Frank and William Oates ON795* Courtesy of Geoff Holman

launched for service on only one occasion. The maroons were fired at 22.03 hours on Sunday 7 June 1959 and the lifeboat was launched in a record time of six minutes, at 22.09 hours. The launch was made following information being received from the Police at Dawlish that a boat some 2 miles off Dawlish, was making distress signals by flying clothing from the end of a spar. On reaching the position given the crew of the lifeboat saw a flare burning about 1½ miles to their southwest. On making their way to that location, which was approximately 2 miles south of the Parson and Clerk Rock, they found the 18-foot motorboat, *Donald of Teignmouth*. The motor boat had suffered engine failure and together with her crew of four, was taken under tow by the *Frank and William Oates* to Exmouth Docks.

What proved to be the last service launch of the *Maria Noble*, from the Exmouth Station, took place on Thursday 13 August 1959, when Coxswain Tom Litton and his crew set out to assist a canoeist reportedly in trouble near the Langstone Rock. On this occasion the lifeboat was recalled without providing a service.

Following service at Exmouth, as the official Station Lifeboat, the *Maria Noble* was transferred into the R.N.L.I's Relief Fleet. She subsequently served as the Blackpool lifeboat before returning to the Relief Fleet in 1970. Following her discharge from the R.N.L.I. she carried the names *Endurance*, *CA49*, *Valerie Marilyn* and *Jack Sam*. Having had a wheelhouse added, in December 2003 the former lifeboat was known to be in use as a fishing boat at Holyhead Marina. In September 2009, with a wheelhouse added, the former lifeboat was under restoration as youth training boat at Limerick, Ireland.

During the time that the *Maria Noble* was stationed at Exmouth, she was credited with 30 service launches and the saving of 35 lives.

8
The George and Sarah Strachan
29 February 1960 – 1 November 1963

Class: Watson   *Official Number:* 749
Crew: 8   *Propulsion:* 2 x 40hp petrol engines   *Speed:* 7½ knots
Length: 45' 6"   *Beam:* 12' 6"   *Displacement:* 19ton 12cwt.
Built: 1931   *Builder:* J. S. White, Cowes   *Launches:* 11   *Lives Saved:* 0
Coxswain: Thomas Henry Litton   *Mechanic:* W.F. Mann

The *Exmouth Journal* reported that '*Exmouth's "New" Lifeboat is 29 Years Old*', following the arrival of the *George and Mary Strachan*, O.N. 749, at Exmouth, early on the morning of Monday 29 February 1960. She arrived with a skeleton crew on board, having been brought up to her new station from Plymouth. Within three hours the boat was at sea again, this time with a full crew of eight. The reason for the quick turnaround, was given, by Coxswain Thomas Litton, as being '*To let the boy's get to know the boat.*'

The Watson Class, non self-righting, *George and Mary Strachan*, had been built in 1931, at a cost of £3,009, and was stationed at Exmouth initially for a 12 month trial period in order to evaluate the suitability of a larger craft being permanently placed on station.

The former Dunbar lifeboat (1931-1959) was altogether larger than the *Maria Noble* that she replaced. She was 10-feet longer and a much heavier vessel, being powered by twin 40 horse power petrol engines, turning twin screws, giving a speed of eight knots. One big advantage of the 'Watson' was that she provided far greater protection and shelter to her crew and was capable of carrying 75 persons. The *George and Sarah Strachan*, was named on Saturday 15 August 1931; she was fitted with wireless which enabled her to maintain communication within a 50-mile radius of Exmouth. Her all-round capabilities were

summed up by Coxswain Tom Litton who told a reporter for the *Exmouth Journal*: '*There's more power, more length, more draught, more room, in fact there's more boat.*' Mechanic, *Bill Mann*, expressed his delight with the boat's engines, stating: '*They are wonderful and good for another thirty years.*'

It is of note that in some images of this lifeboat, the name carried on the bow clearly reads '*George and Mary Strachan.*' Records of Service, made to RNLI Headquarters, have also been submitted

Watson Class lifeboat *George and Mary Strachan ON749*.

showing both variations in the name; all records however record the Official Number as *ON749*. Exhaustive checks made with the RNLI Headquarters, Poole, and at the vessel's original station, Dunbar, confirm that she was Named and Dedicated as the *George and Sarah Strachan*.

The *George and Sarah Strachan* was the first Exmouth lifeboat to be moored 'on station' at Shelly Beach. Up until the arrival of the Watson Class lifeboat, every launch of her predecessors involved manoeuvring the lifeboat and carriage from the boathouse, crossing the road and beach, and finally launching into River Exe. The launch typically involved, in addition to the crew, a Head Launcher, Shore Attendant or Signalman, Winchman, Tractor Driver, Tractor Driver Helper and Other Helpers; the latter group often numbering 13–18 persons. The fact that the new boat was to be kept afloat would greatly reduce personnel requirements.

Even with the new lifeboat on station, the *Maria Noble* remained in the boathouse and was maintained as a 'front-line' lifeboat, albeit it was the '*Strachan*' that would respond to service calls. Her first launch at Exmouth took place on Saturday 7 May 1960 when she was launched to search for a dinghy, containing two boys, missing from Lyme Regis. When the youths were located in Lyme Regis the *George and Sarah Strachan* was recalled without providing a service.

The Watson Class lifeboat was launched two months later, at the request of the Devon Constabulary, following their receipt of a report of a 'man overboard.'

The Honorary Station Secretary, Mr Butler, was contacted by Police Headquarters, at 23.05 hours on Saturday 16 July 1960, when he was informed that a crewman had been lost from a catamaran, off Starcross. The man, exhausted and suffering from exposure, had managed to reach the shore; he had been conveyed to hospital but had raised concern regarding a second member of the crew. It was believed that the second crewmember had remained onboard the catamaran which was being driven up the River Exe. In the knowledge that three police patrol cars had carried out an unsuccessful search of the river banks, the maroons were fired at 23.15 hours. The *George and Sarah Strachan,* under the command of Coxswain Litton, slipped her moorings into southerly gale force winds, heavy rain and a moderate sea, at 23.30

hours. She had been at sea for only fifteen minutes when, at 23.45 hours, a second message was received from the Police to the effect that the second crewmember had safely waded ashore.

The lifeboat was recalled to station by the Hon. Secretary who fired a flare from the Pier Head; the lifeboat acknowledging the recall by the combined use of her mast-head signalling lamp and searchlight. The lifeboat was moored in Exmouth Dock overnight and returned to her mooring at 09.00 hours the following day.

Whilst the launch had gone without hitch and the boat was reported to have performed '*very well*', the Coxswain and crew expressed concern that throughout the service contact could not be made with Niton Radio, the signal apparently being blanked by the topography of the land.

The Exmouth lifeboat crew were mustered for launch on a further five occasions without an effective service being provided, perhaps the strangest incident having occurred on Tuesday 21 March 1961. Coxswain Litton and the crew mustered following a report being received from the Coastguard that an Auster light aircraft had been seen flying exceptionally low and vanished over the cliffs at Seaton.

It was fortunate that, before the lifeboat could slip her mooring, a further signal was received from the Coastguard in which they confirmed that the location of the incident was not Seaton, East Devon but Seaton, near Looe, Cornwall!

The first effective service for the *George and Sarah Strachan* took place on Friday 31 March 1961, when a local Exmouth fisherman, Edward Lane, took a party of four on a deep-sea angling trip, in his 22-foot open motor boat, *Madam Moon*. By early evening the *Madam Moon* had not returned to port and, knowing the vessel to be overdue, Brian Rowsell, 2nd. Coxswain of the Exmouth lifeboat and Roy Knight, the winch-man, set off along the Exmouth seafront in search of the craft. Using a telescope, at 19.55 hours Brian Rowsell spotted an orange coloured flare, apparently south of Orcombe Point. The sighting was confirmed by the Coastguard and upon the instruction of the 2nd. Coxswain the assembly signal was made at 20.00 hours. At 20.20 hours the lifeboat slipped her mooring and proceeded in the direction of the flare. The flare had also been observed by the crew of the local Pilot Cutter which was on her way to a rendezvous with a tanker. The Pilot Cutter reached Orcombe Point some fifteen minutes before the arrival of the *George and Sarah Strachan* and found the casualty to be the overdue *Madam Moon*. The fishing boat had suffered engine failure.

As a tow had been established between the cutter and the fishing boat, the lifeboat escorted both vessels in to harbour.

On the afternoon of Friday 30 June 1961 Coxswain Tom Litton, accompanied by Mechanic Bill Mann and two crewmen, were on passage from Plymouth to Exmouth where the *George and Sarah Strachan* had undergone a refit. When approximately 2 miles south of Berry Head the lifeboat came alongside the 32-foot cabin cruiser, *Gladina* of Torquay; the cruiser having suffered engine failure. The vessel had a crew of three men and two women onboard. A towline was quickly established and the vessel taken in tow. When approximately half-a-mile from Torquay Harbour the owner successfully restarted the *Gladina's* engines, the tow was slipped and the lifeboat continued on to Exmouth.

Not all requests for the launch of a lifeboat are to assist crews or vessels that are in imminent danger. One such request was received by the Exmouth Station Honorary Secretary, Mr C. S. Chown, on Saturday 7 October 1961 when the lifeboat was requested to undertake a 'medevac.' The request for assistance was received from the Port Medical Officer who sought the services of the Royal National Lifeboat Institution to convey him to the 85,000-ton (gross) Liberian tanker, the *George Champion*, which was 6 miles south of Beer Head. The Port Medical Officer was responding to a report that a crewman on the tanker has suffered severe lacerations to his arm. The assembly signal was sounded at 19.30 hours and the crew of the *George and Sarah Strachan*, under the skilful eye of Coxswain Brian Rowsell, slipped the mooring at 19.50 hours. In fine weather, and with good visibility, the lifeboat made excellent progress towards the casualty; and in winds of force 4/5 and a moderate sea the Port Medical Officer was quickly transferred to the Liberian tanker.

The lifeboat stood-by for some thirty minutes whilst the injured seaman, Peter Stintz, of Bremen, received medical treatment. Following initial treatment, Stintz was lowered, by a sling, to the waiting lifeboat and conveyed to Exmouth Dock

before being taken by ambulance to the Royal Devon & Exeter Hospital.

The trials of the larger Watson Class lifeboat having proved satisfactory, on the 12 October 1961 *George and Sarah Strachan* was designated the Exmouth Station Lifeboat. It became abundantly clear that henceforth the larger Watson Class lifeboat would retain her deep-water mooring in the River Exe. With this decision having been made, a question-mark now hung over the future of the existing boathouse. Plans were subsequently put in place to convert the boathouse into a Lifeboat Display Centre and crew facilities were constructed on the quayside.

The Liverpool Class lifeboat, *Maria Noble* which had served at Exmouth for some 8 years, as both the station boat and relief boat, was reallocated to Blackpool to become the station lifeboat.

On Thursday 21 June 1962 the former boathouse was formally opened having been converted into Lifeboat Display Centre. The centre was later to house the Inshore Lifeboat (ILB).

In common with all RNLI lifeboats, the *George and Sarah Strachan* was taken 'off station' when she became due for a routine overhaul. In order to maintain lifeboat service at Exmouth, she was replaced, on Saturday 30 June 1962, by the reserve fleet Watson Class lifeboat, *Cecil and Lilian Philpott, O.N.730*. Within days of her arrival in Exmouth the relief boat, with Coxswain Tom Litton at the helm, answered her first call.

It was on Friday 20 July 1962 that the Coastguard notified the lifeboat station that a 12-foot boat with two persons onboard was overdue at Beer. The craft had left Beer, on an assumed pleasure trip, at approximately 15.00 hours and was last seen, at approximately 17.00 hours, south-east of Beer Head. As the craft had not returned to Beer by 21.00 hours, the Coastguard dispatched an Auxiliary team to act as a lookout at Beer Head. A local fishing boat from Beer was also utilised in the search.

It was an hour before high water with a strong tide running. The weather was deteriorating as the wind increased and visibility closed in. At 21.05 hours Mr. Chown, station Hon. Secretary, author-ised the launch of the lifeboat; the *Cecil and Lilian Philpott* slipping her moorings at 21.30 hours.

As is often the case in call-outs of this nature, the lifeboat was only about 1 mile out to sea when a message was received from the Coastguard, to the effect that the missing craft had been located. In this instance the boat was found safely beached at a small cove near Branscombe, some five miles to the west of Beer. The occupants had left the craft and were presumed safe. The lifeboat was recalled by the use of flare and regained her mooring at 22.30 hours.

On the evening of Thursday 16 August 1962, the Coastguard received information, from five persons, that they had witness a yacht 'disappear' approximately a half-mile off Ladram Bay, near Sidmouth. Whilst the Coastguard took steps to confirm the report, Mr Chown contacted as many of the lifeboat crew as possible, informing them of the impending call-out. Confirmation of the alleged disappearance of the yacht was forthcoming and at 21.40 hours the maroons sounded to summon the crew. Coxswain Tom Litton, and his crew of seven, launched the lifeboat at 22.00 hours. At the time of launch the wind was blowing from the south-west, force 4/5, and visibility was half-a-mile to one mile.

As Tom Litton steered the lifeboat towards the given position of the casualty, the weather deteriorated, the wind backed southerly and increased in strength to a force 6/7 as visibility dropped to less than half-a-mile in heavy rain. Hampered by the weather conditions and rough sea, the *Cecil and Lilian Philpott* carried out a search pattern finally locating the casualty at just after mid-night. Tom Litton established that the yacht, with the owners, Mr & Mrs H.J. Greene on board, was on passage from Weymouth to Torbay; the crew having become distressed due to the deteriorating weather conditions. Mrs Greene was transferred onto the lifeboat, from the 7-ton Bermudan-rigged yacht, *Caravel II*, which was taken in tow by the lifeboat, reaching Exmouth at 02.20 hours on Friday 17 August 1962.

Watson Class lifeboat *Cecil and Lilian Philpott ON730.*

At this time the Exmouth Station's Honorary Secretary, Mr Chown, was aware that the Torbay Barnett Class lifeboat, *ON945 Princess Alexandra of Kent*, (Coxswain – Harold Coyde), was on service searching for a 20-foot motorboat with two persons on board that had been reported 'overdue.' Mr Chown contacted the Torbay station and offered the assistance of the Exmouth lifeboat and crew. His offer was accepted but was not to be taken up until dawn when, it was anticipated, weather condition would improve. Very shortly after Mr Chown had received this reply the weather started to improve as recorded in the Exmouth Service Record:

'...the weather cleared in about 30 minutes & the sky was clear with a full moon. I therefore instructed the crew to proceed & assist Torbay at once, rather than wait for dawn. The Exmouth L.B. proceeded at 3.00am in rapidly improving weather with the wind veering to the N.W. & decreasing.'

The Torbay station had also sought the assistance of an air search and succeeded in locating the missing motorboat which the *Princess Alexandra of Kent* escorted in to Paignton harbour. Upon the motorboat being located, the *Cecil and Lilian Philpott* was 'stood down' and instructed to return to station. The lifeboat arrived at Exmouth Dock at 07.40 hours, having completed in excess of 10 hours continuous duty; the crew were dismissed to obtain breakfast following which they returned to refuel and re-provision the lifeboat which regained her mooring and was fully operational for service by 10.00 hours.

The local Coastguard could hardly believe their ears when they were contacted by the owner of a vessel late on the evening of Monday 25 March 1963. The Hon. Secretary of the lifeboat station that was informed that *someone speaking with a foreign accent had asked where he could go where there were no Preventative Officers!'* The vessel from which the call originated had apparently broken-down off Sidmouth. In contacting the Coastguard the owner had indicated his intention of sailing and paddling westward along the coast. At 01.45 hours on Tuesday 26 March Mr Chown received a further call in which he was alerted to a gale warning that had been issued for the area. The Duty Officer of Coastguard also expressed his

concern for the safety of the broken-down yacht which was lying on a lee shore. Mr Chown advised many of the crew of the impending launch by telephone, authorised the firing of the maroons at 02.10 hours and watched the lifeboat cast off her moorings at 02.25 hours. The lifeboat launched into continuous rain with poor visibility, the wind blew from the west at force 4/5 and a moderate sea was running, the tide being at low water on a Spring Tide.

As the *Cecil and Lilian Philpott* made her way to the casualty the wind backed to the south and increased to a force 5; visibility increased to 4 miles. Whilst the lifeboat was en-route, Coxswain Tom Litton received a signal from Niton Radio informing him that a force 9 gale was imminent. The lifeboat came up to the casualty, which was anchored some 500 yards off Sidmouth beach, at 03.30 hours and found the vessel to be the 5-ton motor yacht, *Sgumain*; Owner and Master Neil Gamble. The yacht had been bound for Teignmouth when it suffered engine failure. Initially the owner refused the offer of a tow but soon changed his mind when Coxswain Litton informed him of the impending gale.

When the *Cecil and Lilian Philpott* towed the *Sgumain* in to Exmouth they were met by a Customs Officer, 2 CID officers and a Police Constable. The whole incident however proved to be something of an anticlimax for although a thorough search was made of the *Sgumain* all that was found was half a bottle of rum, the property of the owner!

The Pole Sands claimed yet another victim on the afternoon of Sunday 14 April 1963, the casualty on this occasion being the 22-foot sailing cruiser, *Kalora*, on passage from Plymouth to Christchurch.

At 15.45 hours, when the alarm was raised, it was half-an-hour before low water; raining heavily and a rough sea was being whipped up by a south-westerly wind of force 5- 6. It was in these conditions that the *Kalora*, with five persons on board, was blown onto the south-west side of the Pole Sands and became stranded in the pounding breakers.

On this occasion the maroons were not fired, the crew being mustered by telephone. By 16.00 hours the yacht had been driven right on to the sands leaving her almost high and dry. In the light of the prevailing weather conditions, in order to carry out the rescue, Mr Chown, the Station's Honorary Secretary, in consultation with acting Coxswain Brian Rowsell, agreed that the rescue would be attempted by using the station's Boarding-Boat. The boarding boat was launched and upon reaching the sandbank, the crew alighted and walked across the sands to reach the stranded craft. The crew returned to the Exmouth station bringing with them three children, aged 5, 9 and 10 years, who were placed in the safe-keeping of the wife of the 2nd Coxswain. John Tomlinson, the owner of the *Kalora*, and one other person remained onboard. With the wind steadily increasing to a full gale force 8 and the tide beginning to make, the *Cecil and Lilian Philpott* slipped her mooring and proceeded towards the casualty. At 17.10 hours the crew of the lifeboat passed a line to the *Kalora* and by 17.30 hours, with the aid of two local skin-divers, the cruiser was re-floated and towed in to Exmouth Docks. The service was completed at 18.15hours.

The former Exmouth station lifeboat, *George and Sarah Strachan* carried out Relief Fleet duties from 1963 – 68 before being sold from the RNLI fleet. She underwent restoration at Inveraray and, with a cabin added, became a work-boat.

9
The Michael Stephens
1 November 1963 – 13 August 1968

Class: Watson *Propulsion:* Twin ferry diesel engines *Crew:* 8 *Official Number:* 838
Speed: 8 knots *Length:* 46' 0" *Beam:* 12' 9" *Displacement:* 20ton 2cwt.
Built: 1939 *Builder:* J. S. White, Cowes, Isle of Wight *Launches:* 25 *Lives Saved:* 11
Coxswains: Thomas Henry Litton (1963-64), Brian Leonard Rowsell (1964-1968)
Mechanics: William Mann

A 46-foot Watson Class lifeboat, the *Michael Stephens*, O.N. 838, arrived at Exmouth, on Friday 1 November 1963, to take up duties as the Temporary Station Lifeboat. Built in 1939 for the Lowestoft station, where she had served for 24 years, she was slightly larger than her predecessor in length, beam and displacement. Together with her sister boat, the Great Yarmouth and Gorleston lifeboat, the *Louise Stephens*, O.N. 820, she had been purchased from a legacy gifted to the Royal National Lifeboat Institution, by the Stephens family after whom they were named. The *Michael Stephens* was one of the famous armada of '*little ships*' that, on Saturday 1 June 1940, played such a crucial role in the evacuation of British troops from Dunkirk.

In the chaos that surrounded the operation, the lifeboat was twice rammed by motor-torpedo boats, whilst entering and leaving harbour.

The crew of the *Michael Stephens* successfully rescued fifty-two allied soldiers.

The first service launch undertaken by the *Michael Stevens*, at Exmouth, took place on Saturday 14 December 1963, when she went to the assistance of the 24-foot open motor fishing vessel, *Nil Desperandum*. The vessel, owned by the 2nd Coxswain Brian Rowsell, had left port at 14.00 hours and was reported over-due, by the Shore Attendant, at 21.15 hours. Initially checks were made to locate the vessel and crew, by telephone,

but when these attempts proved negative the lifeboat launched at 21.50 hours, with a volunteer crew of local fishermen. The *Nil Desperandum* was located at 22.15 hours, having suffered a broken gear box shaft, between the Fairway and

Brian Leonard Rowsell, Coxswain 1964–1982.

No.2 buoys. A tow line was quickly established and the casualty was towed in to Exmouth, by the *Michael Stevens* at 22.45 hours.

In common with entries previously made in Exmouth Station's Return of Service Book, in respect of the *Cecil and Lilian Philpott*, the Hon. Secretary, Mr Chown, once again complained of the bad interference experienced when the lifeboat attempted to establish radio communication with Niton Radio. The possible cause of the interference was recorded as being 'blanketing by the coastline.'

At 13.25 hours on Sunday 17 May 1964, William Mann, the Exmouth Lifeboat Station's Motor Mechanic, observed a yacht aground on the Pole Sands in what he knew, through local knowledge, to be a rather dangerous position. Mr Chown ordered the maroons to be fired at 13.30 hours and within 10 minutes the *Michael Stevens* slipped her mooring, with the Boarding Boat in tow. It was 2 hours after high-water, with a force 4–5 wind blowing from the east, as Coxswain Tom Litton carefully manoeuvred the lifeboat through the breakers towards the Pole Sand. The casualty was found to be the 28-foot yacht *Pippa* which has been on a pleasure cruise, with two persons on board. It had been Tom Litton's intention at take the lifeboat as far as possible in to the beakers and

then make a final approach to the casualty using the Boarding Boat. Having been assured by the owner of the *Pippa*, a Mr Harper, that his vessel was in no immediate danger, the *Michael Stephens* returned to her mooring.

At 15.30 hours, the 2nd Coxswain, Brian Rowsell, Assistant Motor Mechanic Bradford and crewman Peter Rowsell returned to the casualty in the Boarding Boat taking with them kedge anchors and ropes. At this time the *Pippa* was high and dry on the sands thus allowing the lifeboatmen to set the anchors to assist in re-floating the yacht on the rising tide. Coxswain Tom Litton and the crew of the *Michael Stephens* had been instructed to muster at 20.30 hours and the lifeboat, with the Boarding Boat in tow, once more slipped her mooring at 20.45 hours. Upon reaching the Pole Sands, Coxswain Litton stood off the casualty and allowed the Boarding Board to recover the kedge anchor line and pass them to the lifeboat which, with very little effort, successfully re-floated the *Pippa*, towing her to her mooring some 2 mile up river. The service was completed by 21.45 hours.

Second Coxswain Brian Rowsell was the Coxswain in charge of the lifeboat when the *Michael Stephens* was launched on Tuesday 29 September 1964. The Station's Assistant Secretary,

Watson Class lifeboat *Michael Stephens ON838*.

Mr R.L. Stevenson, authorised the firing of the maroons, by the Shore Attendant, at 22.05 hours, following the report of an open beach boat being overdue at Beer. The fishing boat was the E155, owned by a Mr Stewart which had a crew of four. The weather that night was fine with reduced visibility due to a sea mist. The sea was moderate and a force 2 – 3 wind blew from the east. With Coxswain Tom Litton on annual holiday, 2nd Coxswain Brian Rowsell slipped the *Michael Stephens'* moorings at 22.25 hours and was instructed to search an area south-southeast of Beer Head, known locally as Tenants Fishing Ground.

Throughout the search communication with the lifeboat was hampered, the Station Return of Service Book recording that '*atmospheric interference was very bad on all R/T.*' However at 00.45 hours on 30 September Coxswain Rowsell received a signal, from the Coast Guard, recalling the lifeboat to station; the signal read:

'*Fishing boat E155 towed in to Lyme Regis by Mr Roy Gollop. Boat found 4 miles offshore with engine trouble. Crew of 4 all safe.*'

The Station Return of Service Book also contains the following entry:

Note: '*Mr Roy Gollop of Lyme Regis is registered as an auxiliary to RNLI under inshore rescue scheme.*'

At 03.03 hours the Assistant Honorary Secretary informed the Coast Guard that the Exmouth lifeboat was '*safe home.*'

On 29 October 1964, Thomas H. Litton retired as Coxswain of the Exmouth lifeboat, a position which he had held for 17 years.

Tom Litton was succeeded, as Coxswain, by former 2nd Coxswain Brian Rowsell.

Brian Rowsell had to wait only six days before answering his first 'shout' as the acknowledged Coxswain of the Exmouth lifeboat, it came on the afternoon of Wednesday 4 November 1964. At this time the *Michael Stephens* was 'off station', her place being taken on 30 September, by the reserve lifeboat, O.N. 730 *Cecil and Lilian Philpott*.

At 13.30 hours, the Hon. Secretary, Mr. Chown received information from the Coast Guard that a yacht was dragging her anchor, off the coast of Seaton. A local fishing boat, from Beer, was reported to have gone to assistance of the vessel with a view to towing her in to Lyme Regis. At this time, at the lifeboat's launch position, the weather and tidal conditions were recorded as '*Overcast and hazy with visibility of 5 miles*', the wind was recorded as, '*North-easterly, force 4-5*' and the sea was '*rough*'. At 15.30 hours the R.N.L.I received a second signal reporting that the fishing boat had located the casualty and taken her in tow but was now unable to make headway in a strong East wind and heavy swell. The fishing boat had in fact slipped her tow and requested the launch of the Exmouth lifeboat. Coxswain Brian Rowsell summoned his crew by firing the maroons at 15.38 hours; the *Cecil and Lilian Philpott* slipped her mooring just 12 minutes later at 15.50 hours.

The lifeboat located the casualty some two and a half hours later, at 18.25 hours, in wind conditions that had deteriorated to an east-north-east force 6-7, gusting Gale Force 8. Brian Rowsell found distressed vessel to be the *Cap Lizard*, a converted Cornish Crabber, owned by R. S. Thomas, and carrying a crew of two. Her mizzen and punt had been carried away, her main-sail was extensively torn and she had suffered engine failure. The casualty was now about two-hundred yards from the shore and attempting to ride to a small anchor which was visibly dragging. The *Cecil and Lilian Philpott* was skilfully manoeuvred up to the casualty and the lifeboat crew quickly established a tow.

Due to the state of the tide, and knowing the *Cap Lizard* to have a draught of 8 – 9 feet, Coxswain Rowsell realised that he would be unable to manoeuvre the crabber over the Exmouth Bar and therefore decided to tow her to the safety of Brixham harbour. The tow took five hours and even then the casualty grounded when entering Brixham Inner Harbour. The vessel was freed and the *Cap Lizard*, with her crew of two, berthed safely before midnight.

The crew of the *Cecil and Lilian Philpott* refuelled the lifeboat and elected to sleep onboard, at Brixham, and return to Station at first light. The lifeboat was back 'on station' and fully operational, at 08.15 hours on Thursday 5 November, her crew having been on duty for a full 18 hours.

The reserve lifeboat, *Cecil and Lilian Philpott* was launched again, just three weeks later, following the loss of an aircraft belonging to the Royal Navy. The Station Hon. Secretary, Mr Chown, had been made aware of the missing aircraft at 20.30 hours the previous evening, but it was not until 10.01 hours on Thursday 26 November 1964 that a request was received, from the Coast Guard, for the Exmouth lifeboat to assist in the search for the two missing crew members of a Royal Navy De Havilland Sea Vixen. The lifeboat slipped at 10.20 hours, Coxswain Rowsell having been requested to search to the north of a line extending from 2 miles south of Straight Point, Exmouth towards Abbotsbury, Dorset.

R/T communication was very weak at times but the Exmouth lifeboat received instructions to carry out a search pattern by zigzagging along the line, predominately keeping to the north, until she met up with the Weymouth lifeboat, which was working from Portland Bill. The two lifeboats met off Golden Cap at 14.20 hours and were respectively instructed to return to station searching inshore of the line that they had previously taken.

As neither survivors nor aircraft wreckage was found, at 15.30 hours the search was abandoned; the crew of the Sea Vixen were presumed to have lost their lives.

The Temporary Station Lifeboat, O.N. 838 *Michael Stephens*, returned to duties at Exmouth on Monday 30 November 1964.

The first recorded service combining the skills of the crew of the Royal National Lifeboat Institution's Exmouth lifeboat with air support by a helicopter, took place on Saturday 17 April 1965. It was at 17.25 hours that the Exmouth Station Hon. Secretary was informed that two single-seat canoes were in trouble, in gale force winds and rough seas, off the Langstone Rock, near Dawlish. Due to his close proximity to the reported incident a local boatman, Mr Rackley, was reported to be launching and making his way to the distressed persons. Thirty minutes later, Mr Chown received notification that Mr Rackley had not launched as he would have been unable to make headway in the force 8 north-westerly winds that were blowing. In the meantime, Mr Chown had alerted Coxswain Brian Rowsell and Motor Mechanic Bill Mann who, in turn, had alerted crew members who lived nearby; consequently the maroons were fired at 18.05 hours and the lifeboat slipped her mooring at 18.10 hours. As the *Michael Stephens* made her way towards the reported position of the casualties, Coxswain Rowsell received an R/T call from a helicopter. Brian Rowsell requested the

helicopter to search an area approximately 1½ miles southeast of the lifeboat. Lady Luck was certainly with the rescue crews as this request placed the helicopter directly over one of the canoes. Within minutes a young girl, aged 14, was lifted into the helicopter and conveyed directly to hospital in Exeter, suffering from exposure and shock. The helicopter marked the position of the canoe with a smoke float thus allowing the lifeboat to recover the canoe.

At the Exmouth Lifeboat Station Mr Chown received a report of a body in the water. Details were immediately passed to Coxswain Rowsell with instructions to carry out a zigzag search pattern along a line between the position of the recovered canoe and Langstone Rock. The search failed to locate either the reported body or the second canoe. At about 20.05 hours information was received that the occupant of the second canoe had reached the beach and was safe and well. With all Canoe Club members accounted for the *Michael Stephens* was recalled and back on station by 21.00 hours.

Coxswain Brian Rowsell and the crew of the *Michael Stephens* undertook two services, totalling over nine hours at sea, on Sunday 25 July 1965. The first service took place following information being received from the Coast Guard, at 00.15 hours, that a 'Cruisette' - a 15-foot cruiser with two outboard engines, was overdue. The craft, owned by Mr Sidney Pearce of Kings Langley, Hertfordshire, had reportedly left the River Teign on a fishing trip at 10.30 hours the previous day. The party was believed to be bound for the area off Sandy Bay, Exmouth. The lifeboat was not required to launch at this time but should the necessity arise the lifeboat would be requested to launch at first light. The request to launch was received at 05.10 hours and the maroons fired at 05.25 hours. *The Michael Stephens* slipped her mooring at 05.40 hours. The previous day, the *Michael Stephens* had attended the Flag Day for the R.N.L.I's Lyme Regis Station and on the run up to Lyme Regis, once clear of land, had experienced a moderate to rough following sea, the waves being about 4-foot from trough to crest. The lifeboat now put to sea on a clear night with full visibility and a north-westerly wind of force 3-4, to commence the search. Coxswain Rowsell initially commenced his search to the east but being fully aware that since the casualty had left the River Teign there had been two flood tides and an ebb tide, he set the lifeboat on a westerly course, zigzagging towards the River Teign. On completing this search pattern the lifeboat turned eastward.

At 09.00 hours air support was requested and within 30 minutes a helicopter had arrived on the scene and commenced a search pattern. At 10.15 hours the crew of the *Michael Stephens* spotted the wreck of a small boat approximately 5 miles south of Beer Head. Directed by the lifeboat the helicopter circled the wreck and located a body floating in the sea.

Coxswain Rowsell took the lifeboat alongside the casualty and found the cruiser to be fitted with two outboard engines; a 40 h.p. Perkins and a Seagull. Due to the weight of these engines and the fact that the craft had been swamped by the sea, she was floating stern down with her bow just above the water. She was being kept afloat by air trapped in the bow and cabin. The crew of the lifeboat experienced great difficulty in raising the casualty to a level position in order that the interior of the vessel could be searched. During the time that this task was being undertaken, the helicopter recovered a second body from the sea. The helicopter transferred the two bodies, both of which had been located within a 100 yard radius of the casualty, to the lifeboat and returned to base to refuel before returning once more to the scene of the tragedy. The lifeboat continued her search for the third crew ember of the cruisette. Upon the return of the helicopter, the crew of the *Michael Stephens* attempted to take the stricken craft in tow but as the vessel was constructed from plywood everything seemed to carry away. The forward cleat, to which the tow was attached, was held by three one-inch screws and pulled out as soon as a strain was placed upon it. Members of the lifeboat crew, whom Coxswain Rowsell and placed on board the stricken craft, managed to disconnect the two outboard engines and pull them inboard; they also secured a rope around the cabin but, like the forward cleat, the cabin was carried away as the strain of the tow was exerted. A tow was eventually established and, believing the casualty to be a danger to other shipping, Brian Rowsell managed to make very slow progress towards Sidmouth. In view of the slowness of the tow, Coxswain Rowsell requested that the lifeboat be relieved of the tow and with the assistance of the Sidmouth Police the *Michael Stephens* was relieved of the tow some three miles out of Sidmouth.

The body of the third missing crew member, a 19 year old youth, was subsequently recovered, the lifeboat landing the bodies at Exmouth after 10½ hours at sea.

On Sunday 25 July 1965, Coxswain Brian Rowsell and the crew of the *Michael Stephens* undertook a rescue which was described by Mr Chown, the Honorary Secretary, as being *'undoubtedly one of the most aggravating services any Life-boat could go on.'* The initial call for assistance was received by Mr Chown, via a telephone call from the Coast Guard, at 19.35 hours, reporting the Niton Radio had picked up a message from the *MFV Bien* that she was experiencing engine trouble and steering difficulties. Apparently the skipper of the *Bien* could make out the lights of Torquay and had given his position as being 10 miles north-east of Torquay. Mr Chown recorded in the Return of Service, *'This position worried me at the time and has ever since, as if she was in the position she said she was, she could not see the Torquay lights.'* The maroons were fired at 19.45 hours; the *Michael Stephens* slipped by 19.55 hours. It had been established that the *Bien* was a 40-foot motor fishing vessel, owned by the 29th Newport Sea Scouts, on passage from Weymouth to Plymouth with a crew of 16 Sea Scouts and 3 adults.

Upon reaching the location given by the casualty, the crew of the lifeboat were unable to locate the vessel. Due to excessive atmospheric interference on 2183kcs, neither the lifeboat nor the radio station at Wyke Regis could communicate with the *Bien*. At 20.36 hours a radio relay was established whereby the lifeboat switched frequency, leaving Wyke Regis to monitor the *Bien's* transmissions on 2182kcs and relay messages on to the lifeboat on 1662kcs. At 20.59 hours Wyke informed the lifeboat that they were unable to read the *Bien* and at 21.02 hours Wyke asked Niton Radio for 'Mayday' working. At the same time a request was made for the casualty to fire a flare.

At 21.37 hours, a coaster, believed to have been the *Sincerity* signalled the *Michael Stephens* to inform the lifeboat that she was receiving the *Bien* 'loud and clear' but immediately lost the signal. At 21.40 hours the lifeboat reported sighting a red flare, Coxswain Rowsell immediately set course for the approximate position of the flare but on arrival could not locate the casualty. At 22.06 hours Wyke again requested the casualty to fire a distress flare; Beer Coast Guard immediately reported sighting a red flare approximately six miles south-east of Beer Head, to which position the lifeboat immediately proceeded. At 22.56 hours Wyke requested the launch of the Weymouth lifeboat and asked the crew of the *Bien* to fire two flares or Very lights in quick succession, in order to identify herself; simultaneously Coxswain Rowsell reported sighting a flare some 4 – 5 miles from his position, which put the position of the casualty approximately 6 miles southeast of Beer Head. By 23.54 hours the *Michael Stephens* was about 3 miles south of Lyme Regis, Dorset, and at 00.12 hours on Monday 26 July, Coxswain Rowsell reported the lifeboat had located the *Bien* two miles south of Lyme Regis and was now alongside the casualty and preparing to escort her back to Exmouth.

Thankfully, throughout the duration of the search, which had taken some four hours, the weather had been fine and clear with full visibility and a moderate sea. Whilst the *Bien* was under escort to Exmouth, her steering became very erratic and Coxswain Rowsell took the decision to take the vessel in tow and placed the Bowman, T Rowsell onboard the vessel to assist with the steering and to bring the casualty in to the River Exe and in to the dock. The casualty was finally berthed at 03.00 hours.

Returning to Mr Chown's remarks in the Returns of Service Book, he concluded:

'...the casualty every time she fired a flare, instead of stopping in the position where she had fired it, motored on! Each time the Coxswain and crew saw a flare and took a bearing on, steamed to that position, the next one was likely to go up three or four miles on the starboard beam. And so this went on for most of the night, with the Life-boat chasing her all the way up Lyme Bay, and with the casualty apparently zigzagging all over the place. The Coxswain is of the opinion that if she had not turned in towards Lyme Regis, and got herself almost land locked, he would have been chasing her, and the Weymouth boat, for another couple of hours.'

Coxswain Rowsell and the crew of the *Michael Stephens* carried out a medical evacuation from a beach between Otter Head and Brandy Head, near Budleigh Salterton, during the early hours of Thursday 19 May 1966. The Station Hon. Secretary had been informed, at 01.05 hours, that Colin Guy, aged 22 years, of Exmouth, had failed to return from a bird-nesting expedition. His car had been found at Sea View Farm, Otter Head, but his precise location was not known. At 02.40 hours information was received that the man had been located, lying on a beach, but could not be reached from the cliff top. The assembly maroons were fired at 02.45 hours and, suspecting that the man may have sustained serious injury, Mr Chown summoned the assistance of Dr Richard Hardy, the Exmouth Lifeboat Station's Honorary Medical Advisor. The *Michael Stephens* slipped her mooring at 03.00 hours, Dr. Hardy accompanying the crew. Having local knowledge of the rocky coastline, at the casualty's location, and in anticipation of difficulty in taking the lifeboat close to the shore, the station's Boarding Boat was taken in tow by the lifeboat to provide ease of landing. The lifeboat reached the location of the casualty at 04.00 hours, Coxswain Rowsell illuminating the scene by firing three parachute flares. With Dr. Hardy onboard, the Boarding Boat was skilfully steered between the rocks towards the beach but in carrying out this manoeuvre the boat struck a submerged rock and sustained damage to planking on her port side. Dr. Hardy was landed safely and found Mr Guy to be suffering from multiple injuries. After receiving emergency medical treatment, the injured man was transferred to the *Michael Stephens* and taken to a waiting ambulance at Budleigh Salterton for transportation on to the Royal Devon and Exeter Hospital.

Many dangers are faced by workmen who undertake construction work at sea. Such dangers were experienced on Wednesday 3 May 1967 by workmen engaged in laying a new sewer outfall off the coast of Dawlish Warren. Work had been carried out throughout the spring, by William Press Ltd. Civil Engineering Contractors, with materials being ferried out to the workmen who worked from a 'dumb pontoon.' On the morning of 3 May 1967 the Exmouth lifeboat crew had been exercising with the Inshore Lifeboat (ILB) No.89, under the watchful eye of the Divisional Inspector Lt. Cmdr. Cairns. With the wind backing and freshening, the crew formed the opinion that should conditions deteriorate further, the seven-man crew of the dumb pontoon would be in need of their services. The first intimation of distress came, via the Coast Guard, at 16.11 hours; the lifeboat slipped her mooring at 16.29 hours and reached the casualty at 17.20 hours. The pontoon, which was anchored 200 yards off Langstone Rocks, was held in place by six anchors, each of which was marked by buoy, but now in rough seas, whipped up by a gale force south-south-westerly wind, all securing wires tended to stretch away up-wind of the casualty. Coxswain Rowsell approached the pontoon on two occasions in an attempt to fully assess the situation and found it impossible to approach the casualty on her lee side. The situation was further complicated by the position of a large fixed metal gantry which stuck out from the pontoon, level with the cockpit of the lifeboat. The crew of the lifeboat were unable to obtain an accurate depth reading from the Echo-sounder due, in the opinion of Brian Rowsell, to the large amount of sand that was being stirred up by the turbulent sea. The Coxswain however estimated the depth of water below his keel to be approximately 8-feet. Brian Rowsell took the *Michael Stephens* upwind of the pontoon and dropped anchor with the intention of veering down onto the casualty. This operation was hindered greatly by the protruding gantry but by moving the lifeboat ahead and astern with skilful manipulation of the throttles, Brian Rowsell manoeuvred the stern of the Watson class lifeboat up to the dumb pontoon allowing six of the seven workmen to leap to safety. The seventh member of the crew insisted that he recover some personal belonging, thus causing the lifeboat to back off the pontoon and make yet another unnecessary and dangerous approach. Thankfully the man was taken off, the lifeboat's anchor recovered and the crew of the pontoon landed safely at Exmouth at 18.45 hours.

Shortly after the rescue operation had been completed, the anchors holding the dumb pontoon failed, the pontoon being driven on to the lee shore. Being flat-bottomed, the pontoon was subsequently reclaimed without having sustained serious damage.

Between Sunday 2 July and Sunday 1 October 1967, the *Michael Stephens* was absent from the Exmouth lifeboat station, her place being taken by the relief lifeboat O.N.713 *Elizabeth Elson*. This early Watson Class lifeboat was 45-foot 6inches in length and 12-foot 6inches in beam. Built in 1928 by the boatyard of J.S. White, at a cost of £8,235,

The relief Watson Class *Elizabeth Elson ON713*.

the lifeboat had been provided from the legacy of Mr Benjamin Elson of Hove, East Sussex. The lifeboat, which carried a crew of eight, was equipped with two 40 b.h.p. Weyburn engines, giving a top speed of 8 knots. Between 1929 and 1957 the *Elizabeth Elson* had served as the Station Lifeboat at Angle, Pembrokeshire, before being reassigned to the R.N.L.I's Relief Fleet.

The *Elizabeth Elson* was launched on Tuesday 22 August 1967 and again, one week later, on Tuesday 29 August; these launches proved to be 'false alarms' and the lifeboat was recalled on each occasion without providing a service. On Tuesday 19 September 1967 the *Elizabeth Elson* provided her first operational service at Exmouth when she went to the assistance of the cabin cruiser, *Sumatra*, owned by Mr Spicer of Exmouth. The vessel, apparently in distress, had been spotted at 22.55 hours by the Exmouth Lifeboat Station's Motor Mechanic Bill Mann, who was on annual leave. The maroons were fired and the *Elizabeth Elson* slipped her mooring at 23.10 hours, locating the casualty at 00.05 hours between Pole Sands and Dawlish. Upon reaching the *Sumatra* it was found to be crewed by three inexperienced 'trawlermen' who had managed to wrap their trawl around the propeller of the cabin cruiser. The *Sumatra* was taken in tow by the lifeboat and returned to her mooring off Shelly Beach, Exmouth at 00.45 hours.

The *Michael Stephens* returned to Exmouth and officially remained 'on station' from 20 September 1967 until 13 August 1968.

It was two-and-a half hours before low water, on a neap tide, when the *Michael Stephens* launched on Saturday 23 March 1968. In the River Exe a force 4-5 wind was blowing misty rain from the South-west. Outside the Exe, driving rain was being carried on a South-westerly gale force 8 wind, the sea was moderate to rough and visibility was one-and-a half to two miles. It was at 04.50 hours the Mr Chown received notification from the Coast Guard, that a motor coaster had gone aground approximately half-a-mile east of the Exmouth Coast Guard lookout. Mr Chown contacted as many crew-men as possible, by telephone, and then made his way to the lifeboat store where he fired the assembly maroons at 05.10 hours. Within 15 minutes, Coxswain Brian Rowsell, and his crew of seven, slipped the lifeboat's moorings and headed towards Straight Point. On reaching the casualty, at 06.30 hours, they found her to be the Dutch motor cargo vessel, the *Roelof Buisman*; Master, Conrad Smith. The 550-ton vessel which was on passage from St. Malo to Exmouth, in ballast, and carrying a crew of six, had driven ashore onto rocks on the West side of Straight Point.

The Master of the *Roelof Buisman* had broadcast a 'MAYDAY' requesting the assistance of a tug to assist in re-floating the cargo ship. The request had been monitored by the Coast Guard and tugs had been dispatched from both the Cornish Port of Falmouth and the French Port of Cherbourg.

The vessel was clearly well aground and having assessed that neither the vessel nor her crew were in imminent danger, Coxswain Rowsell returned to Exmouth to obtain a kedge anchor and ropes. The *Michael Stephens* returned to the casualty at 07.30 hours, with the Port's Chief Pilot onboard. At 08.27 hours, the lifeboat reported that she had laid the kedge anchor and that by veering down on his own anchor, Brian Rowsell had been successful in passing the anchor line (30 fathoms of 3" Nylon) to the casualty. A second 30 fathoms of nylon hawser had also been passed to the casualty, the latter to act as a tow-rope. The *Michael Stephens* then lay at he own anchor and waited for the tide to rise. At 08.50 hours the lifeboat reported that she had been successful in towing the casualty off the rocks, had put the Pilot on board and was escorting the casualty to Exmouth Docks.

Coxswain Rowsell commented:

'It was a bit of a gamble and I was frankly surprised that she came off so easily. The vessel put out the kedge anchor and got her engines working on it, and with the help of our tow line she came out of the shallow water and into the clear. It was a big relief because, with the wind freshening she would almost certainly become a total loss had she stayed there another hour.'

The Return of Service Book records that for this rescue the crew of the Exmouth Lifeboat received an Ex-Gratia payment of £500 from Lloyds Brokers.

On 13 August 1968, having served the Exmouth Station for nearly five years, in which time she had undertaken 25 Services Launches and saved 11 lives, the *Michael Stephens* was placed in the Royal National Lifeboat Institution's Relief Fleet, where she continued to serve until being sold by the R.N.L.I. in 1975. In June 2009, unaltered, the *Michael Stephens* was being used as a pleasure craft on the River Yealm at Newton Ferrers, Devon.

It is of note that throughout her time at Exmouth, the vast majority of entries made in the Returns of Service Book, relating to the *Michael Stephens*, record her name as *Michael Stevens*.

10
The Gertrude

13 August 1968 – 11 February 1970

Class: Watson   Propulsion: Crew: 8   Official Number: 847
Speed: knots   Length: 46' 0"   Beam: 12' 9"   Displacement: 20ton 10cwt.
Built: 1946   Builder: J. S. White, Cowes   Launches: 11   Lives Saved: 0
Coxswains: Brian Leonard Rowsell   Mechanics: W. Mann

On Tuesday 13 August 1968, another Watson Class lifeboat was placed 'on station' at Exmouth; she was the Temporary Station Lifeboat, ON847, *Gertrude*. Built in 1946, the *Gertrude* had been purchased from the legacy of Lady Struther of London, and had served as the Station Lifeboat at Holy Island from 1946 until the closure of the station in 1968.

Following her arrival at Exmouth, the *Gertrude* and her crew were put through a full training exercise on Saturday 31 August 1968, under the watchful eye of the RNLI's Divisional Inspector, Lt. Cmdr. Tears. Whilst the lifeboat was engaged on the exercise, Mr Chown became aware that Wyke Radio was attempting to contact the lifeboat but lifeboat did not respond. Wyke then called Niton Radio and requested that they attempt to contact the lifeboat but again the lifeboat failed to respond. The services of the lifeboat were required as a small motor boat, with two persons onboard, was

Watson Class lifeboat *Gertrude ON847*.

Cyril Chown Hon. Sec. Exmouth Lifeboat Station 1961~72.

drifting off Dawlish Warren having suffered engine failure.

Being aware that the *Gertrude* had suffered radio failure whilst on passage from Colchester to Exmouth, Mr Chown ordered the launch of the Inshore Rescue Boat to locate and stand-by the casualty until such time as the lifeboat could be informed of the situation. At Mr Chown's request

the Coast Guard fired a 'flash and sound' rocket and passed instructions to the lifeboat by Morse Code. Unbeknown to Mr Chown and the Coast Guard, Coxswain Rowsell had monitored the message passed by Wyke and was already on route to the casualty. The *Gertrude* came up to the casualty some 1000 yards off Dawlish Warren and took her in tow to Exmouth. It subsequently transpired that the reason for the lack of R/T communication with the lifeboat was that, as part of the exercise, the crew had lowered the mast and the aerial had been on the deck. Mr Chown commented, '*I suppose the odds of the aerial being down at a precise moment like that must be astronomical.*'

During the 18-month period in which she acted as the Exmouth Station's Temporary Lifeboat, the *Gertrude* was launched for service on a total of 11 occasions. Her last launch, on Sunday 23 November 1969, was to assist Police units in the search for the body of a girl, which had been reported floating off Langstone Point, Dawlish.

Following service to Exmouth, the Gertrude saw service at Sheerness, (1970–74) and in the Relief Fleet, (1974–80). Sold from the RNLI's fleet in 1982, unaltered and retaining her original name, the *Gertrude* plied as a pleasure craft in Mevagissey Harbour, Cornwall.

11
The City of Birmingham
11 February 1970 – 4 August 1983

Class: Solent   *Propulsion:* 2 x 110hp Gardner 6LX engines   *Crew:* 7
Official Number: 1012   *Operational Number:* 48-009   *Speed:* 9 knots
Length: 48' 6"   *Beam:* 14' 0"ft   *Displacement:* 28 tons   *Built:* 1969
Builder: Camper & Nicholson, Southampton   *Services:* 58   *Lives Saved:* 19
Coxswain: Brian Leonard Rowsell (1970-82), Geoff Mears (1982-83)
Mechanics: W. Mann (1970 -71), Bernard Bradford (1971- 83)

On 1 January 1969, the Lord Mayor of Birmingham, Alderman Charles Simpson, launched an appeal to raise £40,000 towards the purchase a new lifeboat; the boat was to be named *City of Birmingham*. By March the fund had risen to £6,000 and, as often is the way, increased considerably following a lifeboat disaster on 17 March 1969. On that fateful day the R.N.L.I's Longhope lifeboat, the *T.G.B.*, capsized whilst on service to the Liberian vessel the *Irene*; the lifeboat's entire crew of eight tragically lost their lives.

Due to the exceptional generosity of the people of Birmingham, and surrounding area, by early November of that same year, the Lifeboat Fund had risen to a staggering £28,000.

Although the Mayoral Fund continued to grow on Tuesday 18 November 1969, *The Birmingham Post* carried the following headline:

Lifeboat is ready, but Mayday call goes out for more funds

The City of Birmingham *is to be launched on Thursday and will go into service at one of the six oldest lifeboat stations in the country at Exmouth, Devon, early next year.*

Earlier this year it had been intended that one of the two 37ft self-righting boats being built at Littlehampton in Sussex would be named City of Birmingham. *These boats are of wooden construction.*

But last night the Royal National Lifeboat Institution announced that a much bigger boat, now nearly complete at a Southampton boatyard on the river Itchin, is to be named City of Birmingham.

The boat, 48ft 6in long, is a steel hulled design of the "Solent Class," and apart from an experimental life-boat, it will be the first all-steel hull boat to go into service for the R.N.L.I.

This new boat, the 1,012th built for the R.N.L.I., is going to cost £72,000 - £35,000 more than the boat originally planned to carry the city's name.

Last night a spokesman for the R.N.L.I. said: "The Committee of Management has decided to name the new lifeboat planned for Exmouth City of Birmingham. *At present we understand the Birmingham appeal stands at just over £28,000, but in appreciation of the efforts made in raising the money by Ald. Simpson, it has been decided to allocate this bigger boat to Birmingham, rather than the smaller one originally planned.*

Exmouth has many links with the Midlands through its holidaymakers, and as a new boat is needed there, we decided this would be most suitable."

The Secretary of the Exmouth Lifeboat Station, Mr Cyril Chown said, "The whole of the crew are West Countrymen, and they have never let anyone down - we have been trying to get a new boat for a long time now, especially one with radar." Mr Chown was pleased with the boat's number – 1012. "I am most thankful it is not the next boat that we are having. We are very superstitious when it comes to 13 and boats."

Work had started on the new boat at the shipbuilding yard of Camper & Nicholson, Southampton about 12 month earlier. The boat was launched into the adjoining river on Thursday 20 November 1969, prior to the completion of her fitting-out. The new lifeboat sailed on Tuesday 10 February 1970 in the skilful hands of Coxswain Brian Rowsell and his crew, on a 'night run' to Plymouth As they headed down-channel the crew had to contend with heavy seas whipped up by a full gale force wind. The lifeboat made an overnight stop at Plymouth, moving on to their home station the following day.

The arrival of the new Exmouth lifeboat was reported in *The Exmouth Journal*, of: Saturday 14 February 1970, in the follow terms:

Exmouth's new lifeboat, City of Birmingham *berthed at the local docks at 4.30 on Wednesday afternoon after two days of trials by the Exmouth crew at Cowes, and with an overnight stop at Plymouth.*

It was an informal arrival and she came into the docks with no fanfare – not so much as a cheer or the waving of a flag. But there was more than such outward signs – there was an atmosphere of pride and ownership amongst the hundreds of Exmothians who had waited hours in the cold for her.

The binoculars were out in force, but inferior in numbers to cameras. The boat looked good as she came in down the deep-water channel, and she put on a skittish performance at the entrance to the docks, circling fast in a heavy foamy wake and showing the waiting Exmothians that she could skip about freely and gaily.

The crowd liked it, but it was put on mainly for the Birmingham television crew aboard, who wanted shots of the piers and the waiting Exmothians.

Solent Class lifeboat *48-009 City of Birmingham* ON *1012.*

She then docked, and made the perfect picture for the many amateur camera users around. The television crew disembarked, and the girl reporter member of the crew spoke enthusiastically of the comfort. She told of a smooth trip, and reported that none of the landlubbers aboard had had the slightest suggestion of seasickness.

"It was comfort," she said, "and, oh boy, it had at toilet! Last lifeboat I went in hadn't anything like that. And the kitchen, begging your pardon, the galley, was real good."

The Exmouth crew have now to have more experience of handling her before she goes fully into service. She is equipped with radar and the latest in wireless telegraphy.

One has only to look at her to realise she has the best of everything. She looks good, and everybody who has had anything to do with her to date says she handles well. Exmouth is going to be proud of this boat, and of course, so will the people of Birmingham be.

Feeling on Thursday was that the City of Birmingham *will prove, however unwittingly, to be the best bit of publicity Exmouth has had for a long time.*

The formalities, the cheering and the flag waving are yet to come, most likely when the visitors are here in force, in the summer time.

The first Return of Service for the *City of Birmingham* records that she was launched on Sunday 1 March 1970 following a report being received at 23.30 hours, from the Coxswain of the Weymouth lifeboat, that the cruising sloop *Mayfly*, of Exmouth, was overdue. The sloop had left Weymouth at 06.00 hours on passage from Weymouth to Exmouth. The *Mayfly* was being run by a crew of two; both men being members of the Weymouth lifeboat crew.

Having made initial inquiries, Coxswain Rowsell contacted Wyke Coast Guard and was informed that the Weymouth lifeboat had launched to search for the missing sloop which was known to have passed the Bill of Portland at 08.30 hours. Brian Rowsell informed Wyke that Exmouth would also launch and search to the East until they met up with the Weymouth boat. The *City of Birmingham* slipped her mooring at 00.18 hours on Monday 2 March. At the same time Lifeboatman Handoll, of the IRB crew, took the station's

Boarding Boat and searched the Western side of the Exe estuary in case the missing boat had entered the river unobserved and picked up a vacant mooring.

The search was aided by good visibility, a force 3-4 North-westerly wind and moderate sea, and at 01.15 hours the *City of Birmingham* located the *Mayfly* three miles South of Sidmouth. The sloop was taken in tow and berthed at Exmouth at 03.00 hours.

Following this initial service the *City of Birmingham* revealed a few 'teething problems', as the result of which the Hon. Secretary, Mr Cyril Chown sent the following communication to Commander W.L.G. Dutton, R.D., R.N.R. Chief Inspector of Lifeboats:

Dear Commander Dutton,

With reference to the Service report herewith, several faults developed. Firstly, the compass is almost useless, and you may remember when you paid us an informal visit last Summer, that Brian Rowsell complained of the compass in the Loch Inver L-B, well this one is just as bad. When we made the night run from Weymouth to Plymouth when we were bringing her on station, had we not had a few stars to steer on, we might well have finished up in the Channel Islands. It is no uncommon thing to be almost 90 degrees off course, on this service, Brian relied mostly on the Radar. Secondly, after slipping, the engines were given full throttle, and very soon, the Starboard engine stopped, and took about ten minutes to re-start, due to air in the fuel line. Billy Mann has checked it over most closely, but can find no leak, and thinks that the air is getting into the line from the venting pipe. And lastly, after about twenty minutes, the VHF packed up, and the only thing obtainable was music from some station or other on all channels. I have contacted Harry Teare, and also Peter Young for the VHF, and Mike Wheeler regarding the engine, and they all are arriving at Exmouth on Wednesday.

I think you will agree that to have all these faults turn up in a brand new L-B is very disquieting, and since it was her first Service, I had several reporters on the phone, but in all cases told them that she went like a bomb, as adverse reports of this nature would be very

damaging to the public image of the Institution.

With regard to the engine, I think you will find that Billy Mann reported this fault when he was at Southampton for her trials.

With kind regards

Sincerely yours...

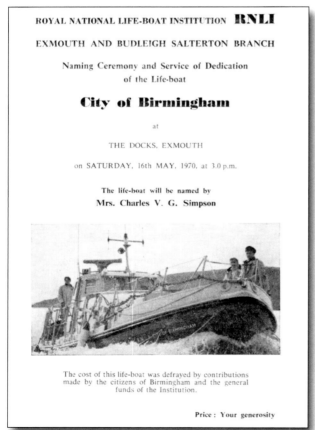

Top: Rail ticket issued for the Solent Class lifeboat, *City of Birmingham ON1012* naming ceremony.

Above: Programme for the Naming Ceremony of the City of Birmingham 16th May 1970.

Needless to say, this catalogue of complaints received immediate attention, and the faults were rectified swiftly.

The Official Naming Ceremony and Service of Dedication of the lifeboat took place at The Docks, Exmouth, at 15.00 hours on Saturday 16 May 1970. Lieut Colonel G.A. Haward, R.M. (Retired), Chairman of the Exmouth & Budleigh Salterton Branch, opened the proceedings. Lieut. Commander H. F. Teare, R.D., R.N.R., Inspector of Life-boats, gave a description of the boat. The specifications of the new lifeboat were truly impressive; the following details being taken from RNLI's official statistics on the Solent Class lifeboat:

This class of life-boat has a steel hull of all-welded construction,(a major change from the Mark I and Mark II versions, which had wood hulls), a cast iron ballast keel, and an aluminium super-structure. It is equally suitable for slipway launching stations and for those where the life-boat is permanently afloat.

The hull is sub-divided by watertight longitudinal bulkheads into centre and wing compartments, and further sub-divided by four main watertight bulkheads, by a watertight double bottom in way of the engine room, and a watertight flat in way of the aft cabin.

The double bottom compartments in way of the engine room, the fore peak compartment and the void compartments outboard of the longitudinal bulkheads are all completely filled with rigid polyurethane foam to provide reserve buoyancy in the event of hull damage.

Watertight scuttles are fitted to provide emergency access to clear a fouled propeller.

Watertight doors are fitted between the wheelhouse and after cabin, the wheelhouse and engine room, and the engine room and forward cabin. Warning lights are fitted in the wheelhouse to show whether any other door or hatch is open.

A watertight hatch is fitted at the aft end of the after cabin large enough to allow a stretcher to be passed through. A watertight hatch is fitted over the fore cabin for emergency access.

The Solent Class life-boat has excellent stability properties and also natural self-righting ability from any angle of capsize.

The machinery installation consists of two

Gardner 6LX engines with Gardner 2 UC reverse and 2:1 reduction gearboxes. Each engine develops 110 B.H.P. at 1,300 r.p.m. Propellers are 28-inch diameter aluminium bronze.

Engine cooling is by means of heat exchangers, mounted remote from the engines and arranged so that circulation of the sea water is obtained by means of inlet and outlet scoops mounted on the shell of the boat. The exhaust system is fitted with non-return valves of special design, to exclude water in the event of capsize. All ventilation inlets and outlets also have valves of special design for the same purpose.

There are two fuel tanks. One is an integral part of the double bottom structure forward of the engine room and has a gross capacity of 120 gallons. The other is a steel tank of 120 gallons capacity, separate from the hull structure, and fitted abaft the engine room.

All instruments, gauges, remote controls for the engines and steering wheel are mounted on a console in the wheelhouse.

The steering gear is of Mathway manual type and the boat has twin spade rudders. These give a useful improvement in manoeuvrability.

To aid navigation a Solent class life-boat is equipped with two compasses, radar – Decca 202, M.F. radio – Coastal Radio Curlew complete with D/F equipment,, V.H.F./U.H.F. radio – Redifon type 289/299, and echo-sounding equipment – Ferrograph combined inshore-offshore unit. An intercom is fitted between the after cabin and the wheelhouse for communication between radio operator and the helmsman.

The life-boat had a comprehensive outfit of equipment, including line-throwing apparatus, breeches buoy, stretcher, first aid equipment, emergency rations, blankets, scrambling net, etc.

The Deputy Mayor of Birmingham, Alderman Charles V. G. Simpson who, whilst Mayor of Birmingham in 1969 had launch the Lifeboat Appeal, handed over the lifeboat, on behalf of the City of Birmingham to the Royal National Lifeboat Institution. The boat was formally accepted by Admiral Sir Wilfred Woods, G.B.E., K.C.B., D.S.O., Chairman of the Committee of Management of the R.N.L.I. who, in turn, delivered the boat in to the care of the Exmouth Lifeboat Station. Mr C. E. Chown, Honorary Secretary of the Exmouth & Budleigh Salterton Branch, accepted the boat on behalf of the Branch.

The Lord Bishop of Exeter, the Right Reverend R. C. Mortimer, D.D., dedicated the lifeboat, assisted by the Rev, R. T. Urwin, Vicar of Littleham cum Exmouth, the Rev. A. Lester-Hetherington, Free Church, and Rev. Canon J. P. O'Malley, Roman Catholic Priest. The singing of the hymns "*O God our help in ages past*" and the traditional lifeboat-man's hymn "*Eternal Father, Strong to Save*" was followed by Benediction. A Vote of Thanks was proposed by Councillor H. C. Evett, Chairman of the Exmouth Urban District Council, following which Mrs Simpson, wife of Alderman Charles Simpson, officially named the lifeboat "*City of Birmingham.*"

It was reported in the *Express & Echo* that:

Several thousand people, including 500 from Birmingham who arrived by special train lined the flag-bedecked dockside at Exmouth to watch the official naming ceremony of the £72,000 City of Birmingham, which is stationed at the resort.

She is named after Birmingham in recognition of the city's contribution of £42,000 towards her cost.

Col. G. W. Haward, chairman of the Exmouth & Budleigh Salterton Branch of the R.N.L.I. said, "Exmouth had always been proud of their lifeboat and crew who were equal to any in the country." He also paid tribute to the crew's families who, he said "had their lives dominated by the service of their husbands to the lifeboat."

The station's Honorary Secretary, Mr Chown said that Exmouth lifeboat history went back 167 years, in which time 132 lives had been saved but, he added, "*not without loss to themselves.*"

Proud to be among the guests, and fellow lifeboat-men, at the ceremony was 93-year-old Bert Hockings, who had served in the Exmouth lifeboat under five coxswains.

The *City of Birmingham* was engaged in a full scale air and sea search which involved the lifeboat, a Royal Navy Minesweeper and three helicopters, on Friday 24 July 1970, albeit the service really began at 22.30 hours the previous evening when a

Top left: 48-009 City of Birmingham 'disguised' as the fictional 48-006 *St Teilo* for the BBC Television series Tim Mock.

Top right: The City of Birmingham undergoing self-righting tests.

Above left: HRH Duchess of Kent, escorted by Commander Dutton, meets the crew of *City of Birmingham*. (l-r): 'Spud' Rowsell, Geoff Holman, Ron Lavis, Jon Turner, Roy Richards, Martin Handoll. 14 May 1971.

Above right: 175th Anniversary Celebrations Local crew rowing the *Henrietta* with *D516* alongside. The *Henrietta* is the former Teignmouth self-righting lifeboat *Henry Finlay ON618*.

Left: HRH The Duchess of Kent, at the helm of the City of Birmingham with Coxswain Brian Rowsell.

boat was reported overdue at Exmouth. The boat in question was a 25-foot speedboat, the *Foam Prayer*, owned by Alan Richards of Payhembury, Nr. Honiton. The missing craft was on passage from the Hamble to the River Exe with two persons on board. Coxswain Rowsell contacted the Coast Guard who, from initial enquiries, established that the missing speedboat had rounded Portland Bill at 20.45 hours, travelling at an estimated speed of 12 knots. It was estimated that, if that speed were maintained, it would take the Foam Prayer a further 3 to 3½ hours to reach Exmouth. As by 01.30 hours on Friday, the vessel had not reached Exmouth Coxswain Rowsell sought authority to launch the lifeboat but, as the Coast Guard were making further enquiries at locations along the coast, the authority to launch was not given.

At 07.10 hours notification of an anticipated launch was received and Coxswain Rowsell and Mr Read, a boat builder who built the casualty, went out in a Pilot Cutter and searched the moorings on the West side of the River Exe where the casualty was normally moored. The search produced a negative result. Consequently, at 08.05 hours the assembly maroons were fired and the *City of Birmingham* slipped her moorings at 08.15 hours. At about 08.30 hours, Mr Chown was notified that the local ferry had carried two sailors from the West bank of the Exe to Exmouth. Acting on this information, Mr. Holman, the Lifeboat Station Launcher, took his own MFV out and once more searched the West bank moorings, extending his search further up-river than that of Coxswain Rowsell. Again the search met with a negative result.

Niton Radio broadcast a 'Pan-Pan'* alert message to all shipping subsequent to which, at 09.30 hours, the lifeboat received notification that the Royal Navy Minesweeper *HMS Highburton* had been diverted to search a line from Portland Bill to Straight Point, Exmouth. *The City of Birmingham* was requested to search in-shore of this line in the knowledge that three helicopters would take off to join the search at 10.30 hours; the Coastal Radar Station, Charmouth, would also assist in the search.

Whilst the Royal National Lifeboat Institution does not measure the cost of a service in monetary terms, in heavy rain showers, poor visibility and a moderate sea, whipped up by a Westerly wind, of

force 4 – 5, a very expensive search was under way.

At 1.00 hours, Mr Chown received a telephone call informing him that the missing craft, the *Foam Prayer* had been located moored on the River Exe, at Odam's Wharf, near Topsham, where that craft had in fact been built. Both occupants of the craft were safe and accounted for. The Coast Guard were informed and the search disbanded with the *City of Birmingham* returning to station. Subsequent enquiries revealed that whilst on passage the speedboat had developed engine trouble and sought the lee of Anvil Head to make temporary repairs, and then proceeded on to Exmouth, breaking down on several more occasions on route. The casualty reached Exmouth at 03.15 hours, the occupants deciding to limp up river to the boatyard at Odam's Wharf. Unfortunately the boat struck a mud bank and became stranded and did not re-float until after 10.00 hours, when finally she reached the boatyard.

The *City of Birmingham* regained her mooring, on the completion of service, at 14.15 hours.

*(A call of 'Pan-Pan' means that there is an emergency on board a ship or boat but that, for the time being at least, there is no immediate danger to anyone's life or to the vessel itself.)

Two consecutive services involving the *City of Birmingham* unfortunately culminated in the loss of life. The first of the two launches took place on Sunday 14 March 1971 when the lifeboat slipped at 20:40 hours to assist in the search for a young man who was missing from a dinghy which had capsized half-a-mile to the South of the Cobb Breakwater, Lyme Regis. One man had been found and taken to Lyme Regis Hospital. The lifeboat crew were joined in the search by motor fishing vessels, from Lyme Regis, and three Brixham trawlers. For six hours Coxswain Rowsell and his crew carried out their search in a moderate sea and heavy snow which was being carried on a Northerly. In the heaviest snow visibility was, at times, reduced from half-a-mile to less than 25 yards. Given the appalling weather conditions, and the fact that Coxswain Rowsell reported that he was running out of parachute flares, the *City of Birmingham* was instructed to make for Lyme Regis where she tied up at 04.15 hours. With her store of flares replenished and her crew rested, accompanied by two motor fishing vessels, the lifeboat put to sea again at 06.50 hours. At 08.45

hours a helicopter joined the search but by 10.35 hours, with all hope of finding the missing man alive, the search was abandoned. *The City of Birmingham* returned to station at 12.45 hours, her five man crew having completed at seventeen-and-a half hours service. Four days later, the body of the deceased was found near West Bay, Dorset.

The second fatality occurred on Sunday 16 May 1971. It was just after 17.00 hours that a 16-foot vessel, the *Rose* of Teignmouth had been towed into Dawlish with the body of a young girl on board. From items found in the boat, it was assumed that there had been a second person onboard. It was fortunate that, being a Sunday evening, most of the lifeboat crew was in the vicinity of the docks, thus enabling a crew to assemble and launch the Inshore Rescue Boat at 17.20 hours; the *City of Birmingham* slipping 10 minutes later at 17.30 hours. Having commenced a search pattern the lifeboats were assisted by a helicopter. The Police subsequently established that the deceased was in fact alone in the *Rose* and at 18.50 hours the lifeboats were recalled to station.

Saturday 28 August 1971 saw the start of the annual Cowes-Torquay-Cowes powerboat race. At Exmouth dock the weather was cloudy with poor visibility and a force 2 breeze blew from the Southwest. At 17.10 hours Cyril Chown received notification from the Coast Guard that one of the competitors had not been 'checked off' by the race control at one of their checkpoints. The craft in question was the *Fund Raiser*, an inflatable powerboat owned by the R.N.L.I., with three crew members onboard. The order was given to launch the lifeboat and at 17.40 the *City of Birmingham* slipped her mooring. Coxswain Brian Rowsell and his crew were instructed to search a line, five miles offshore, towards Portland Bill. Having been at sea for just fifteen minutes, the lifeboat received a signal confirming that the *Fund Raiser* had been

The relief Watson Class *Julia Park Barry of Glasgow ON819*.

located by the Coast Guard and was being escort in to Torquay.

This somewhat routine call closed a chapter for one crew member, W. (Bill) Mann, as it marked his last day of duty with the Royal National Lifeboat Institution. During his service Bill had been the Motor Mechanic of the Exmouth lifeboat for seventeen years.

The Exmouth lifeboat crew were required to muster on Tuesday 2 February 1972 but were stood-down without the boat slipping her moorings. The Station Lifeboat, *City of Birmingham* had been taken 'off station' for repair, on 13 January 1972, and was temporarily replaced, until 7 March 1972, by Relief Lifeboat *ON 819 Julia Park Barry of Glasgow*. Built in 1939, this 46-foot Watson Class lifeboat had been the Peterhead boat for 30 years before being allocated to the Relief Fleet (1969-78). Sold by the R.N.L.I. in 1979; in September 2002 the *Savell O Hicks*, as she had been re-named, was working as a pleasure boat out of Fahan Marina, Lough Swilly, Donegal.

A canoeing party, which turned in to tragedy, initiated the launch of the Exmouth lifeboat of Monday 8 March 1972. As the *City of Birmingham* remained 'off station', Coxswain Brian Rowsell and his crew responded to the 'shout' with the Reserve Fleet lifeboat, *The Royal British Legion Jubilee*. This Solent Class lifeboat carried the Official Number *O.N.1013* and Operational Number *48-010*, being the sister-ship of the *City of Birmingham*. *The Royal British Legion Jubilee* was built in 1971 and was immediately allocated to the Reserve Fleet (1972-78.) She subsequently served as the station boat at Fraserburgh (1979), in the Reserve Fleet (1979-87), and as the Peterhead Lifeboat (1987-88) before returning once again to the Reserve Fleet (1988-90.)

The alarm had been raised, by the Coast Guard, at 18.00 hours following the reported sighting of a man in the sea off Dawlish. The lifeboat slipped her mooring at 18.15 hours, Coxswain Rowsell on this occasion having mustered and additional two hands, making a total crew of eight. Having placed the crew on the lifeboat, the additional two hands were instructed to proceed, in the Boarding Boat to the reported position of the casualty, via the shallow waters of the Western Way as, due to the low state of the tide, there was insufficient water for the Solent class lifeboat to steer that course. It was therefore necessary for Brian Rowsell to navigate the channel out of the River Exe until such time as he found a

sufficient depth of water which allowed the *The Royal British Legion Jubilee* to cross the Pole Sands. Whilst negotiating the river estuary, Coxswain Brian Rowsell received a signal that a man was seen to be clinging to the Fairway Bell Buoy. Upon reaching the Bell Buoy, at 18.35 hours, the crew found two men, one clinging to the buoy, the other inside the buoy cage sounding S.O.S. on the buoy's bell. Both men were recovered safely by the lifeboat. At that same time, Coxswain Rowsell received notification that a vessel out of Teignmouth had rescued a third person and received the body of a forth. The Boarding Boat crewed by Bowman T. Rowsell and crewman P. Rowsell returned to station, as did the *The Royal British Legion Jubilee*, landing the canoeists 19.00 hours. The three casualties, David Oates (20), Harry Elliot (21), both of Kendel, Cumbria, and Graham Ramsey (20) of Witheridge, Devon, were taken directly to hospital. The deceased was Jonathan Page (20) of Aylesbury, Bucks. All were students at St. Lukes College, Exeter.

This service took place on the very first day that *The Royal British Legion Jubilee* was 'on station' at Exmouth and is the only service credited to her during this period of time on the Exmouth station. She remained at Exmouth until 4 July 1972 albeit two musters and a service that occurred between April and July 1972 are credited to the *City of Birmingham*. Sold by the R.N.L.I. in 1990, in November 2003 the re-named Ocean Jubilee was undergoing restoration, as a pleasure craft, at Pappleworth, Nottingham.

In the autumn of 1972, Cyril Chown who had been the Honorary Secretary of the RNLI's Exmouth Station for many years passed away. He was succeeded by Mr. W.L.C. Smith.

No matter how good a sailor or swimmer an individual may be, he or she must never fail to respect the moods and might of the sea. This lesson was learned by a local swimmer, from Exmouth, on Sunday 15 April 1973, when he entered the sea to recover a dinghy which was adrift.

It was at 20.44 hours that Station Hon. Secretary, Smith, received notification from the Coast Guard that a swimmer had entered the water, some 45 minutes earlier, in an attempt to salvage a rubber dinghy which was approximately a quarter of a mile off Exmouth Pier. His wife had observed his progress but in failing light had lost him from view at about 20.25 hours. The station's Boarding Boat, manned by Coxswain Brian

Rowsell and members of the lifeboat crew, was launched at 20.57 hours and a search initiated along the shallows of the Pole Sands. Coxswain Rowsell requested the assistance of additional crewmen to facilitate the launch of the *City of Birmingham* in order that a more extensive search of the area could be made. By 21.10 hours the Boarding Boat had transferred crew to the lifeboat and, having picked up additional crewmen, had rejoined the search. At 21.18 hours the *City of Birmingham* cast off her moorings and joined the search for the missing swimmer, concentrating on the area of the Exe Fairway as far as the Fairway Buoy, whilst the crew of the Boarding Boat, on an ebb-tide, continued to search the Pole Sands shallows.

At 21.50 hours a message was received at the Life Boat Station to the effect that a swimmer had reportedly come ashore on the main beach and was making his way to the boat house. At 21.54 hours the swimmer arrived at the boat house and was identified as the missing swimmer. Having failed in his attempt to recover the rubber dinghy, the swimmer had got ashore onto Pole Sands and eventually cross the Fairway at the narrowest point. No doubt his survival was in part due to the fact that he was wearing a wet suit.

Both the Boarding Boat and the *City of Birmingham* were recalled to station and by 22.36 hours were once again ready for service.

Between 7 September 1974 and 25 July 1975, four service launches were undertaken, at Exmouth, by the Reserve Fleet Lifeboat O.N. *828, The Princess Royal (Civil Service No.7.)* This 46-foot Watson Class lifeboat, built in 1939, had been the station boat at Hartlepool (1939-68) and the Humber No2 boat (1968-69), before being allocated to the reserve fleet in 1969. With the outbreak of the Second Word War, during the latter part of 1939, *The Princess Royal* was involved in rescuing the pilot of the first Spitfire to be shot down off the North-East coast, near Redcar. *The Princess Royal* was sold from the R.N.L.I. fleet in 1976, and was initially renamed *La Rochelle*. She was subsequently discovered decaying in a wrecking yard in Wales. A rescue party was formed and the boat was taken back to Hartlepool, at the cost of one penny. A team of volunteers spent nearly five years restoring the lifeboat to her former glory, to form part of a floating/working museum at the Hartlepool Marina.

It was at 18.47 hours on Monday 10 November 1975 that a report was received at the lifeboat house that red distress flares had been observed approximately 2 miles off Straight Point. Three minutes later, a confirmation signal was received from the Coast Guard who also reported that the casualty was believed to be on fire. The assembly maroon was sounded, the crew mustered and at 19.08 hours Coxswain Brian Rowsell, with his crew of six, slipped the *City of Birmingham* from her moorings.

In a slight sea, variable wind and moderate to poor visibility, in thick drizzle, the lifeboat made good headway towards the casualty, which had been identified as the 31-foot fishing boat, *E77 Winifred*. At 19.30 hours the Coast Guard signalled the lifeboat to inform the coxswain that the casualty was now approximately half-a-mile to the West of its original position and it was therefore possible that any survivors may be in the water to the East of the stricken vessel. As the *City of Birmingham* closed on the casualty, it was clear that the *Winifred* was on fire from stem to stern. With the use of the lifeboat's searchlight, Coxswain Rowsell commenced a methodical search for survivors; good fortune was certainly with the lifeboat crew that evening for, within two minutes, the two man crew of the *Winifred*, Gerald Stratham (23) and Charlie Smith (19) were spotted in the water just 20 yards of the bow of the lifeboat. At 19.36 hours the lifeboat reported that both men, who were suffering for hyperthermia and shock, were safely aboard the *City of Birmingham* which was returning, at full speed, to Exmouth Dock. On reaching the dock both men were transferred to a waiting ambulance and conveyed to hospital.

It subsequently transpired that the *Winifred* had caught fire as the crew were hauling the nets. The two men attempted to fight the fire with fire extinguishers before they were forced to don lifejackets and abandon ship. They had been in the water for some 45 minutes before being rescued by the lifeboat. The cause or the fire remains a mystery.

Sunday 3 October 1976 brought a report, from a member of the public in Dawlish, of red distress flares being sighted in the general direction of Orcombe Point, Exmouth. The original report, which was received at 05.55 hours, was confirmed at 05.57 hours by Berry Head Coast Guard,

Brixham, who had also observed the flare, at an estimate distance of 7 – 8 miles from Berry Head on a bearing of 021°. The Exmouth lifeboat crew mustered within 17 minutes, the *City of Birmingham* slipping at 06.12 hours into a force 7-8 Southerly wind with moderate to poor visibility. At 06.50 hours the lifeboat reported that she was alongside an inflatable dinghy from the 29-foot Elizabethan Class auxiliary sloop, *Mysterytu*. The dinghy contained the two man crew of the sloop, a Mr Goss and a Mr Stewart of Axminster; albeit there was no sign of the *Mysterytu*. The casualties were taken aboard the lifeboat and the dinghy recovered. The lifeboat then returned to Exmouth where she was met by a waiting ambulance; Coxswain Brian Rowsell and his crew, having had a hot drink, return to sea in a further attempt to locate the *Mysterytu*. At 08.00 hours the *Mysterytu* was reported to have been driven ashore at Shell Cove, between Dawlish and Teignmouth. The *City of Birmingham* was recalled to station.

Following his release from Hospital, Mr Goss, the skipper of the *Mysterytu* explained that he and Mr Stewart had left Exmouth at about 22.00 hours on Saturday 2 October in a Force 5-6 Southerly wind. It was their intention to sail throughout the night, reaching Brixham the following morning. They were not aware of a gale warning, albeit the

Hon. Secretary, Mr Smith records that the Coastal Water forecast, issued at 3.45 hours was given as '*Southerly 6-8 becoming Westerly 5.*' By 05.00 Goss and Stewart were cold and wet and in a Force 6-7, gusting 8, sought the shelter of Hopes Nose, Torquay, and 'hove too' while they prepared a hot drink. Mr Stewart went forward to reach a fire extinguisher and then apparently regained the deck via the forward hatch. Whilst making his way aft he was swept overboard. The fire having extinguished itself, Mr Goss got in to the inflatable dinghy, which was being towed behind the sloop, in an attempt to pick up Mr Stewart. Mr Goss explained that he had taken this action and not put the yacht about to pick up Mr Stewart as he did not wish to lose sight of his colleague. Mr Goss succeeded in recovering his crewmate nearly an hour later, but finding that they could not get back to the sloop, fired the distress flare from the dinghy. No oars were found in the dinghy when the *City of Birmingham* recovered the craft.

The *City of Birmingham* was temporarily off-station during the autumn of 1978, her place being taken by the relief fleet lifeboat, O.N. 912 *Euphrosyne Kendal*. The *Euphrosyne Kendal*, built in 1955, was a 52-foot Barnett class lifeboat and had served as the station boat at St. Peter Port (1954-72) and Dunmore East (1973-75) prior to being assigned to the Relief Fleet. During this

The relief Barnet Class lifeboat *Euphrosyne Kendal ON912*.

period of relief duty, 10 September to 20 November, the *Euphrosyne Kendal* was only launched on one occasion, that being on Tuesday 10 October 1978.

At about 22.10 hours, a member of the public reported to the Exmouth Coxswain, Brian Rowsell, that a yacht appeared to be attempting to enter the River Exe having failed to locate the Fairway. The yacht was crossing directly across the Pole Sands and was grounding heavily. At 22.13 hours the local Coast Guard received a signal from Brixham Coast Guard which also reported a craft in difficulty on the Pole Sands. The craft was kept under constant observation and, although no distress signal was made, at 22.30 hours it was decided to launch the lifeboat. The *Euphrosyne Kendal* slipped her mooring at 22.44 hours and in a rough sea with fair/good visibility reached the casualty within 15 minutes. The casualty proved to be the 5-ton Swedish yacht *Maria II*. Initially, due to the shallow waters on the sands, the lifeboat was unable to reach the casualty but established contact by firing a rocket line. By 23.10 hours a tow had been made fast and the yacht was manoeuvred clear of the Pole Sands and alongside the lifeboat. The sole crew member, and owner/skipper, of the *Maria II*, was taken aboard the lifeboat and two lifeboat-men place onboard the yacht. The yacht was moored at Exmouth at 00.10 hours.

It was subsequently established that the skipper of the *Maria II*, Djorknund Halward, was sailing the yacht, single-handed, from Sweden to the Canary Islands. Having put in to an East-coast port, he had been at sea for 72 hours and ill for the previous 24 hours, before arriving off Exmouth. Suffering from exhaustion and being unsure of his whereabouts, he had made for the nearest land, quite unaware of the potential danger that awaited him in crossing the treacherous Pole Sands.

Coxswain Rowsell and the crew of the Exmouth station lifeboat, the *City of Birmingham* slipped the moorings into a South-westerly wind of force 5-6 which accompanied a rough sea, with fair visibility, at 22.28 hours on Monday 13 August 1979, following the report of a vessel in trouble off Sidmouth Beach. The lifeboat battled a heavy sea as she made her way along the coast, sighting the casualty some 50 minutes later, at 23.20 hours. Due to a heavy swell, Brian Rowsell was unable to take the lifeboat alongside the casualty, which proved to be the 28-foot Mirage yacht, *Sharina*, of

Hamble. In addition to Mr Haughton, the owner/skipper of the yacht which was on passage from Alderney to Dartmouth, the crew comprised Mrs Haughton and two children. In a heavy swell the lifeboat crew fired three rocket lines across the casualty, but found difficulty in coaxing the crew of the *Sharina* out on to the deck in order to secure the lines. Eventually the line was taken and a tow rope secured and the homeward tow commenced; the casualty being moored at the entrance to Exmouth Dock at 03.19 hours. By 03.50 hours the *City of Birmingham* was re-fuelled and operationally ready for further service.

The crew members of RNLI lifeboats are ever vigilant in their respect for the sea and the safety of others. Such vigilance was rewarded on Saturday 19 September 1981 when Coxswain Brian Rowsell and Michael Clifton, a former Inshore Lifeboat crewmember and at that time ILB Training Officer, were relaxing in the local yacht club. A wind of Force 8-9 (gale gusting strong gale) was blowing from the South-southwest, accompanied by heavy rain and a very rough sea when, at 23.15 hours, they saw the 'S.O.S.' international distress signal being flashed from a vessel in the River Exe estuary. Brian Rowsell immediately contacted the station's Acting Honorary Secretary, Mr. Noakes, who at 23.17 hours sounded the assembly maroons. It was unanimously agreed that for the safety of the lifeboat and her crew, the rough, confused seas made the launching of the ILB totally out of the question. Likewise, due to shallow waters and semi-submerged moorings in that particular part of the estuary, it was impractical to launch the *City of Birmingham*. It was therefore decided that the service would be undertaken by launching the station's Boarding Boat. The boat was 17-feet in length with a beam of 6'10", wooden in construction, and kept on davits at the entrance to the docks. The craft was propelled by a Lister 8h.p. diesel-engine. On that evening the crew equipped the boat with an Aldis lamp, a focused lamp which can produce a pulse of light and primarily used for signaling Morse-code, and a portable radio.

At 23.28 hours Brian Rowsell and Michael Clifton launched the Boarding Boat into extreme weather conditions. Picking his course out through the rough, confused sea, whenever possible Brian Rowsell kept the sea on his bow thus reducing the possibility of catching a crashing wave on the beam and avoiding a possible capsize. Using all his skills of seamanship, in treacherous conditions, it took Brian Rowsell only ten minutes to reach the casualty, the sailing yacht *Michelle,* which had a crew of two onboard who having moored their yacht, due to the prevailing weather and sea state, had found themselves unable to reach the shore. The two men, one of whom was suffering for extreme sea-sickness, were wet, suffering from hypothermia and in a very nervous state when taken aboard the Boarding Boat. Having secured the safety of the crew of the *Michelle,* Brian Rowsell and Michael Clifton navigated their return journey and, with great difficulty, landed the two men at Ferry Steps.

The lifeboat crews of the Royal National Lifeboat Institution do not seek plaudits or rewards for their services but sometimes after a rescue a simple word of 'thanks' can mean an awful lot to them; such was the case following the service to the *Michelle* when the following letter, from Mr. H Green of Bristol, was received at the Exmouth Lifeboat Station:

Dear Sirs,
I'd like to take this opportunity to thank you for kindness and assistance given when on Saturday 20th September I was taken ashore from the boat Michelle, *in very rough weather conditions.*

Your understanding and kindness which was shown was a great comfort to myself and Mr Duck.

I have now fully recovered from my ordeal and would like to show my appreciation by donating the enclosed cheque.
Yours faithfully
H. Green.

In the 'Returns of Service' book, for this service, the Acting Honorary Secretary Mr J. Noakes, recorded:

'Although it transpired that the two men were in no immediate danger, this was not of course apparent at the time of the S.O.S. This was potentially a most dangerous service due to high confused seas off Exmouth Dock. I would recommend at very least a letter of thanks to both crewmen.'

The recommendation made by Mr. Noakes was acted upon by the Management Committee of the R.N.L.I. and on Wednesday 7 April 1982 the Royal National Lifeboat Institution, honoured members of the Exmouth lifeboat crew, and their supporters, in a ceremony that recognised both bravery and devoted long service. These Service Awards, which had only been instituted the previous January, were the first to be made in the country, in recognition of operational work. Of the 178 awards made throughout Great Britain, in the form of Long Service badges, Exmouth crewmen qualified for three.

On behalf of the Institution, Mr Les Vipond, Divisional Inspector for the South-West Area, made presentations to Coxswain Brian Rowsell and crewman Mike Clifton, who were honoured for rescuing the two crewmen from the yacht, *Michelle.* A framed 'Letter of Thanks', signed by His Grace The Duke of Atholl, Chairman of the Institution, was awarded to Coxswain Brian Rowsell with a 'Letter of Appreciation', signed by the Director of the R.N.L.I., being awarded to Lifeboat-man Michael Clifton for their respective roles in a service carried out in the true tradition of the R.N.L.I.

Geoff Holman was presented with a framed 'Letter of Thanks' in recognition of his 35-years service to the R.N.L.I.

Long Service badges, for 20 or more years of service, were presented to Coxswain Brian Rowsell (30 years), Bernard Bradford (35 years), and Peter Rowsell (20 years).

A milestone was reached in the career of Coxswain Brian Rowsell, on Sunday 14 February 1982, when assisted by four crewmembers, the *City of Birmingham* slipped her moorings to go to the assistance of a pleasure craft which had reportedly capsized at apposition between Warren Point and Langstone Rock, Dawlish. Initial information, received from the Brixham Coastguard, suggested that there were at least two persons in the water. The assembly signal was made at 16.36 hours and the lifeboat slipped her mooring at 16.48 hours into fine weather, good visibility and a relatively calm sea. As it was low water, the lifeboat had to take the long route seaward, following the channel, and only cutting across the Pole Sands where the depth of water allowed.

As the *City of Birmingham* approached within approximately 100 yards of the casualty, she ran aground on the sandbank, but by keeping his engines at 'full ahead' Brian Rowsell succeeded in

Bernard Bradford, Mechanic 1971–1983.

Bernard Bradford in engine-room of 48-009 City of Birmingham.

driving the lifeboat across the sandbank in order to regain deep water. As the lifeboat reached the casualty, one man was seen to slip below the surface of the sea; Lifeboat-man Simon Turl leapt into the water and successfully assisted the man onto the lifeboat. He then turned his attention to the second person who had been thrown into the sea and also succeeded in rescuing that person. The pleasure craft was left semi-submerged and was washed ashore the following day.

With three casualties on board, two of whom were suffering from extreme exposure and hypothermia, the *City of Birmingham* commenced her return journey to Exmouth. Whilst on route, at 17.30 hours, the lifeboat was joined by a helicopter from RNAS Chivenor, North Devon, which had been scrambled in response to the initial distress call. Following consultation between Coxswain Rowsell and the helicopter pilot, a winch-man was lowered and the two casualties were air-lifted to the Royal Devon & Exeter Hospital, Exeter, for treatment.

The *City of Birmingham* returned to station and was once again ready for service 18.01 hours.

Although the *City of Birmingham* was launched on Tuesday 9 March 1982 she was recalled to station without providing a service, thus the service of Sunday 14 February proved to be the last service launch undertaken with Brian Rowsell as Coxswain of the Exmouth lifeboat.

In a typically quiet and informal ceremony, held at the Royal National Lifeboat Institution's dockside hut on the evening of Wednesday 30 June 1982, Brian Rowsell who had served the Exmouth lifeboat for 30 years, and as Coxswain of the lifeboat for more than 18 years, retired.

Brian, who had served on Royal Navy motor torpedo boats and sailed racing dinghies to Olympic standard, was always considered an exceptional helmsman by his crew. He joined the Exmouth lifeboat crew in 1952 and became Coxswain in 1964. The *City of Birmingham* was the fourth Station Lifeboat that he had commanded. Brian holds the distinction of being Exmouth's longest serving Coxswain

In retiring Brian Rowsell knew that the boat and crew were being placed into good, experienced hands; his successor was Coxswain Geoffrey Mears. Geoff Mears had served on the lifeboat for 11 years, the last six in the post of 2nd Coxswain.

The Exmouth R.N.L.I Return of Service Book records the first service launch undertaken by Coxswain Geoff Mears, to have taken place on Sunday 12 September 1982. On this occasion Coxswain Mears, accompanied by his crew of three, B. Bradford, (M.M.), Tim Mock (A.M.M.), and R. Richards slipped the moorings of the Reserve Fleet lifeboat, O.N. 853 *Winston Churchill (Civil Service No 8.)* For this service 2nd

'Solent' crew '70's (l-r): Billy Mann (Engineer), Maurice Mellish (2nd Cox), Brian Rowsell (Cox), Bernatd Bradford (2nd Engineer), Terry Rowsell. Seated (l-r): Geoff Holman, Peter Rowsell and Doug Were.

'Solent' crew '83 (l-r): Reg Mogridge, Geoff Mears (Cox), Tim Mock, Bert Thomas, Front (l-r) Tom Chandler, Keith Graham (2nd Cox) and Bernard Bradford (Mechanic).

Coxswain Geoff Mears, Coxswain 1982–1984.

Coxswain, Keith Graham, and crewman R. Mogridge manned the Boarding Boat.

The *Winston Churchill*, a 46ft 9in Watson class lifeboat, had been built in 1947 serving as the Blyth, Northumberland, station boat from 1948–79 before being relocated into the Relief Fleet. She was on station at Exmouth from Saturday 8 May to Tuesday 2 November 1982.

The lifeboat was launched at 0338 hours following the receipt of information, from Brixham Coast Guard, that red distress flares had been sighted '*off Maer Rocks, Exmouth.*' The casualty proved to be the 18ft motor vessel '*DoDo*', out of Exmouth, with four persons onboard. The occupants of the small craft had been on a fishing trip, off Dawlish, but upon hearing a local radio warning of fog, decided to return to the River Exe. Unfortunately, on entering the Exe estuary, the rudder on the craft snapped and the *DoDo* broached on a strong ebb tide and was buffeted onto the Pole Sands.

Following the initial sighting of the distress flares, the Exmouth Mobile Coast Guard had made vocal contact with the casualty which, by this time was attempting to reach Exmouth beach. The propeller of the small craft had fouled a rope and Coast Guard Davies and former Exmouth I.L.B. crew member R. Griggs entered the sea, recovered a line and prevented the craft from being driven on to the Maer Rocks. When the *Winston Churchill* arrived on the scene, Keith Graham, in the Boarding Boat, took the fishing boat in tow to the lifeboat; the tow was transferred and the *DoDo* and her crew were returned to Exmouth at 04.15 hours. The Return of Service records:

'A very prompt, smooth, efficient service under our new Coxswain and 2nd Coxswain – their first in these Offices.'

The Exmouth Return of Service for Saturday 16 October 1982 carries the following endorsement,

The relief Watson Class lifeboat *Winston Churchill (Civil Service No8) ON853* Tim Mock

by the Acting Honorary Secretary Mr D.W.H. Sargeant:

'This service was carried out in atrocious weather condition and, while not resulting in a rescue, it must still be regarded as a successful and praiseworthy operation, worth of consideration for letters of thanks.'

It was at 06.55 hours that the duty Deputy Launch Authority received an *'immediate launch'* request from Brixham Coast Guard to assist a yacht that was on the rocks at the Western end of Sidmouth beach. An injured man had reportedly made his way ashore and had been removed to hospital but his female companion was missing. At 07.10 hours the *Winston Churchill* slipped her mooring, it was approaching high-water and the lifeboat immediately faced Force 8 - 9 southerly gale-force winds, which were accompanied by a rough sea.

In addition to the requested launch of the lifeboat, a 'Search and Rescue' helicopter had also been scrambled; arriving on the scene at 07.33 hours. At 07.35 hours the coast guard advised Geoff Mears that the casualty, that had now been identified as the catamaran, *'Hongi'*, was infact at the Eastern end of Sidmouth beach and not the Western end and initially reported. The skipper of the *Hongi* was a Mr G. Fielding, of no fixed abode; the missing female was his wife.

Having taken a heavy pounding as they battled atrocious weather conditions, which at the scene of the incident were recorded as being South-south-easterly, strong gale Force 9 winds, gusting storm Force 10, with a high sea; at 08.00 hours the lifeboat reported an estimated time of arrival at the casualty of 08.15 hours. At 08.10 hours the S.A.R.

helicopter pilot reported that he had located the missing female and intended winching her from the sea. At 08.14 hours the *Winston Churchill* was instructed to return to station. At 08.19 hours the helicopter reached a waiting ambulance but unfortunately Mrs Fielding was certified dead on arrival at Sidmouth Hospital. Mr. Fielding subsequently died in hospital from his injuries. The *Hongi* became a total loss, breaking up on the rocks.

The remarks of the Acting Honorary Secretary Mr D.W.H. Sargeant, as quoted above, were well received by the Committee of the Royal National Lifeboat Institution and acknowledged by the sending of a 'Letter of Appreciation' to Coxswain Geoffrey Mears and all members of the Exmouth lifeboat crew who took part in a very demanding launch and operation, the letter read:

'Gentlemen
A report has been received on the service carried out by you in the lifeboat "Winston Churchill" (Civil Service No.8) on temporary duty at your station on 16 October 1982, when the Catamaran "Hongi" was driven onto the rocks at Sidmouth, with a man and his wife onboard.

It is noted that you proceeded in a south south-easterly gale and very rough seas and, although your services were not required, I wish to send you the Institution's warm and appreciative thanks for your efforts in the appalling weather conditions.

I also send you an expression of my personal appreciation.'

A service carried out by the Exmouth Lifeboat crew, in which an unusually high number of persons were rescued, did not infact involve the launch of the Exmouth Lifeboat. The rescue took place in fine weather, light breeze and calm sea on Saturday 23 July 1983.

It was at 23.10 hours that D.L.A. Sleeman sighted red distress flares from the Exe Sailing Club; he immediately notified Brixham Coast Guard and crew-member Reg Mogridge and Exe Sailing Club member C. Jacobs to investigate the signal in the Sailing Club's fast rescue dory. Sleeman then made his way to the Exmouth Lifeboat Station accompanied by A/Mechanic Tim Mock and G. Ingram. At 23.17 hours he received a request, from the Coast Guard, for further investigation to be made. Mock and Ingram were dispatched in the Boarding Boat to back up the sailing club's dory. The Boarding Boat returned with news that a pleasure craft, the 17ft 'Seacrest', had run aground on a sandbank. On a falling tide, the Inshore Life Boat helmsman, Simon Turl, offered to take out the Exe Water Taxi, on which he was a part-time employee. The water Taxi slipped her mooring at 23.30 hours and located the Seacrest stuck fast between No.17 buoy and Spit buoy. The pleasure craft had 51passengers and 2 crewmembers on board. Many of the passengers were young children who quite understandably were in a distressed condition. All were safely transferred to the Boarding Boat, Water Taxi or the Exe Sailing Club's dory and safely landed at Exmouth.

Although not directly involved in this service the City of Birmingham had infact completed her last service as the Exmouth lifeboat with an announcement that the RNLI was to place a Brede Class lifeboat on the Exmouth Station.

On Sunday 17 July 1983, Tim MOCK succeeded Bernard Bradford as Motor Mechanic for the Exmouth Station

Upon completing over 13 years of service as the Exmouth lifeboat, the City of Birmingham was transferred to the RNLI's Walton and Frinton Station where she served from 1984–93. The lifeboat then served in the Relief Fleet during 1993–94, before being discharged from the R.N.L.I. fleet in 1995. Thereafter, renamed ADES 14 and ILC 95, the former City of Birmingham continued her distinguished career as a lifeboat at Puerto de Colonia, Uruguay.

Solent crew on dockside, (l-r): Maurice Mellish (2nd Cox), Brian Rowsell (Cox), Bernard Bradford (Mechanic), Doug Were (Ass Mech) and Geoff Holman (launcher/crew).

12
The Caroline Finch
4 August 1983 – 9 July 1994

Class: Brede   *Propulsion:* 2 x 230hp 'Caterpillar' 3208 diesel engines
Official Number: 1088   *Operational Number:* 33-06   *Crew:* 4
Speed: 20 knots   *Length:* 32' 9"   *Beam:* 12' 2"   *Displacement:* 8.5 tons
Built: 1983   *Builder:* Lochin Marine, Rye.   *Services:* 178   *Lives Saved:* 64
Coxswain: Geoff Mears (1983-84), Keith Graham (1984-1994).
Mechanic: Tim Mock

The eagerly awaited arrival of a new Exmouth lifeboat, in June 1983, was apparently delayed, as it was reported in the *Express and Echo* of Monday 13 June, that:

'*The expected arrival of Exmouth's new lifeboat that Caroline Finch is likely to be delayed for a couple of weeks as modifications are to be carried out to the boat before she is commissioned.*

The RNLI plan to have shaft brakes fitted to the 33ft Brede Class lifeboat as it will be moored in the entrance to the Exe estuary, off Exmouth Docks.'

Anticipation however grew and grew in Exmouth during July 1983 as the town awaited the arrival of a new lifeboat. It was known that the boat would be of the 33-foot Brede Class and carry the name *Caroline Finch*. It was reported in the *Express &*

The Brede Class lifeboat *33-06 Caroline Finch ON1088.*

Echo, of Tuesday 12 July, she had already earned herself a reputation, having two services to her credit before officially going into service. During the last few weeks, whilst undergoing her final sea trials off the Dorset coast, the *Caroline Finch* had assisted a yacht which had become disabled in a severe electrical storm and latterly a fishing trawler that was in danger of being swept on to rock off the Channel Isles. With an estimated top speed of over twice that of the Solent Class boat that she was to replace, the new Exmouth lifeboat would be one of the fastest lifeboats stationed along the Southern coast.

The *Caroline Finch* arrived at her station on Sunday 17 July 1983, her arrival being extensively reported in the local press:

'*Flags were out at Exmouth yesterday to welcome the resort's new lifeboat to its home port for the first time.*

Dozens of boats turned out to form a welcoming flotilla for the £150,000 Brede Class lifeboat the Caroline Finch – *and as it arrived off Exmouth a severe electrical storm sent thunder and lightning rumbling and flashing around the bay.*

Heading the flotilla was the town's retiring lifeboat, the City of Birmingham, *decorated with flags and bunting. Also there was the Exmouth inflatable inshore rescue lifeboat, nipping in and out of the flotilla, completing a unique spectacle for the hundreds who lined the seafront and dockside to witness the arrival.*

Overnight

From the first moment the new 33ft lifeboat appeared on the horizon it proved an impressive sight as it skimmed over the heavy swell with a top speed of over 20 knots.

Exmouth coxswain Geoff Mears, who had brought the lifeboat on from Weymouth, after a high-speed overnight crossing from Alderney, eased right back on the throttles of the twin 208 hp engines to allow the old City of Birmingham – *with a top speed of just eight knots – the courtesy of leading the way home.*

"Like a racehorse and a carthorse" was how one lifeboat-man compared the new with the old as the Caroline Finch *came to Exmouth – giving the port the fastest lifeboat along the coast, packed with the most up-to-date radar*

and electronic equipment, and self-righting in just over two seconds.

Although not yet formally in commission, the new lifeboat has already shown her colours – saving seven lives in two dramatic rescue operations during her final sea trials over the past month.

The flags flying from the Exe Sailing Club starting box on the dockside spelt out the message "Welcome," and dozens of people crowded the quayside to echo the sentiment. Providing a civic welcome were Exmouth Town Committee chairman Mr Derrick Dray, and deputy chairman Mr David Scott, who were among the first to take the opportunity to look over the new boat.

The arrival of the Caroline Finch *marks a new era for the lifeboat rescue service at Exmouth. The old* City of Birmingham *could take up to 20 minutes to pull clear of the entrance channel to Exmouth with its notoriously strong tides and currents – so it has often been overlooked in preference to faster boats further along the coast.*

Now, when the call goes out for emergency help over a wide area off the coast, all eyes will be cast towards Exmouth.

"She is a fine craft – very fast and responsive," said coxswain Mears who completed the long Alderney to Weymouth crossing in just under 2½ hours.

On board with him were emergency mechanic Tom Chandler, lifeboat-men Reg Mogridge and Steve Baker, and RNLI district inspector, Chris Price and staff engineer Bob Elliott.

Over the next few days, the volunteers who make up the remainder of the Exmouth crew will be putting the craft through its paces and familiarising themselves with the controls – to be ready to provide 24-hour, 365-days-a-year rescue service that is the RNLI.

Quality

Exmouth lifeboat Hon. Secretary Mr Derek Sargeant observed: "it seems incredible that it was just 50 years ago that the first powered lifeboat was stationed at Exmouth – before that they were just rowed out.

The boats themselves have come a long way since then, incorporating the most up-to-date technological developments – one thing that doesn't change though is the quality of the men that crew them. They are exactly the same type of men now as those who risked their lives to row out into a gale to save others half a century ago,"

The *O.N. 1088 Caroline Finch* officially entered service as the Exmouth Lifeboat on Thursday 4 August 1983. In addition to her 'Official Number' the *Caroline Finch* was the first Exmouth lifeboat to carry an Operational Number - *33.06*, denoting her length, in feet, and her number in the class. The allocation of Operational Numbers was introduced by the RNLI in 1958 with the construction of the Oakley Class lifeboat *O.N. 942 J.G. Graves of Sheffield, Operational Number 37-01.*

The Caroline Finch answered her first callout just three days later on Sunday 7 August. On this occasion the lifeboat was under the command of 2nd Coxswain Keith Graham. The *Caroline Finch* joined the *I.L.B.*, which was out on exercise, in the search for a member of the Wellington Diving Club who had been reported missing between the Fairway Buoy and Straight Point, Exmouth. The diver made his own way safely ashore and the

Keith Graham, Coxswain 1984–1998.

Caroline Finch returned to station without providing a service.

As the next three calls to which the Brede Class lifeboat responded were all classified as 'No Service', it was not until Thursday 10 November 1983 that the *Caroline Finch* responded to her first call as the Exmouth lifeboat.

It was a fine evening on the River Exe when the alarm was raised for the immediate launch of the lifeboat to assist a cabin cruiser that was reported as being 'on the rocks at Jacob's ladder, Sidmouth.' At the lifeboat's moorings a light breeze of Force 1-2 was blowing from the East, giving rise to a moderate/choppy sea and slight swell.

Coxswain Geoff Mears slipped the *Caroline Finch* from her mooring at 21.53 hours and initially proceeded towards the casualty at full speed. At 22.00 hours Brixham Coastguard reported the casualty being battered by heavy surf; at this time the *Caroline Finch* was passing the Exmouth fairway Buoy and the Lyme Regis lifeboat, *B546 Independent Forester Benevolence*, was 1 mile from Axmouth. Condition at sea were quite different from those experienced at the lifeboat's mooring; here the weather was overcast, the Force 5 'fresh breeze' was churning up a very rough sea with a 9 foot swell. Both lifeboats reached the casualty at the same time, finding her to be the sailing cruiser *Smiler* with two persons from London on board. The skipper of the *Smiler*, Mr Fitzsimmons, was totally lost and had got into difficulty having run short of fuel. The incident was as the same location where, on the 16 October 1982, the *Winston Churchill* had provided service to the *Hongi*; on that occasion two lives were lost. Thankfully, on this occasion Coxswain Mears established a line and the *Smiler*, with her crew of two on board, were taken under tow to Exmouth Dock.

The Return of Service records that *'The speed of our new lifeboat on this latest service was of paramount importance. Coxswain Mears and the crew were thrilled with their L/B's performance in tricky condition.'*

The next four assembly/launches of the *Caroline Finch* resulted in 'recalls' or 'no service given'; so it was five months before the Exmouth Station provided the next service. The service of Sunday 29 April 1984 was undertaken by Second Coxswain Keith Graham with the sister boat to the *Caroline Finch*, the Brede Class lifeboat, O.N. 1087, *Merchant Navy*, Operational Number 33.05 From the time that she was accepted into the R.N.L.I's fleet, *Merchant Navy* was allocated directly into the Relief Fleet (1983-87) but subsequently posted to Scotland where she acted as the Oban station boat (1987-89) before entering storage. The *Merchant Navy* performed relief duties at Exmouth from 28 April 1984 to 15 July 1984. She was sold by the RNLI in 1990 and, sailing under the name *Lyonesse,* became a pleasure boat at the Delfzijl Marina, Groningen, Holland.

On that fine Sunday morning a gentle to moderate Easterly breeze blew onto the mooring of the Exmouth lifeboat. Coxswain Geoff Mears, with a crew of two, were on passage to Poole, Dorset, with the *Caroline Finch.*

Listening to a scanner at the ILB station, the Station Honorary Secretary, Derek Sargeant, was monitoring the progress of the Inshore Lifeboat, *D278* which, whilst on 'relief duty' at Exmouth, was out on exercise. At 11.45 hours he monitored a broadcast to the effect that the *D278* had capsized. Motor Mechanic Tim Mock, who had also been at the ILB station, immediately made his way to the

lifeboat station leaving Derek Sargeant to page Second Coxswain Keith Graham and fire the hand-held maroons. To assist in the speed of launch, Keith Graham elected to take Mr T Wreford and Mr K Walkey, two volunteer crew members, on the service enabling the *Merchant Navy* to slip her moorings at 11.50 hours. The lifeboat reached the ILB at 12.00 hours, took the two crewmen onboard and took the *D278* in tow. At the scene of the capsize the wind was Easterly, Force 5-6, the sea state was rough with a 3ft-4ft swell.

Whilst returning to station, the *Merchant Navy* was diverted to assist a wind-surfer who had been spotted in trouble off Pole Sands. The wind-surfer was located, his board recovered and all three casualties were conveyed safely back to Exmouth Docks.

The Naming Ceremony and Service of Dedication of the *Caroline Finch* took place at Exmouth Docks at 14.00 hours on Tuesday 24 July 1984. The Guests of Honour were Their Royal Highnesses the Duke and Duchess of Kent. Costing £155,000, the lifeboat was provided by the combined legacies of

The relief Brede Class *33-05 Merchant Navy ON1087.*

Royal National **Lifeboat** Institution

NAMING CEREMONY
AND
SERVICE OF DEDICATION
of the
EXMOUTH LIFEBOAT
RNLB "CAROLINE FINCH"

Photo: Julie Hodge, Exmouth & East Devon Journal

The lifeboat will be named by
HRH THE DUKE OF KENT
President of the Royal National Lifeboat Institution
at Exmouth Docks
on Tuesday, 24th July 1984, at 2.00pm

The Exmouth Branch of the RNLI welcome you
to this Ceremony and Service

Programme   Price – Your Generosity

Above: Their Royal Highnesses The Duke and Duchess of Kent at the Naming and Dedication Ceremony of the Caroline Finch 24 July 1984.

Left: Programme for the Naming Ceremony of the Caroline Finch 24th July 1984.

Below: Presentation of Vellum to Geoff Ingram (1986). (l-r): Keith Graham (Cox'n), Jack Stapley (Treasurer), Geoff Ingram, Charles Tate (Chairman), Bernard Hughes (Exmouth Town Committee Chairman), Les Vipond (District Inspector of Lifeboats), Tim Mock (2nd Cox'n/Mechanic), Derek Sargeant (Hon Sec) and Bert Thomas. Melanie Tolman

Mr W.H. Finch, Mr W.J. Orley, Mrs M.G. Shaw and Mr H.E. Rohll. Albeit her Operational Number was 33-06, she was in fact the fifth Brede Class lifeboat to enter service with the RNLI.

Their Royal Highnesses were welcomed by Vice Admiral Sir Peter Compston KCB, and following the National Anthem proceedings were opened by Mr L W Aplin, Chairman of the Exmouth Station Branch. The lifeboat was handed over to the Royal National Lifeboat Institution by Mr N.G. Finch, on behalf of all the donors. The lifeboat was accepted by Vice Admiral Sir Peter Compston KCB in his capacity as Deputy Chairman of the Institution. The lifeboat was then handed into the keeping of Mr D W H Sargeant, Honorary Secretary of the Exmouth Station Branch.

The Service of Dedication was conducted by The Right Reverend E A J Mercer, The Lord Bishop of Exeter; following which His Royal Highness The Duke of Kent named the lifeboat *Caroline Finch*.

Music for the occasion was provided by the Band of Her Majesty's Royal Marines, Britannia Royal Naval College, Dartmouth, under the direction of WO1 (Bandmaster) P.J. Rutterford LRAM, ARCM, RM. Together with the choir of St Peter's School, Lympstone.

Albeit mid July, the weather on the day was atrocious but that did not stop hundred of guests, supporters and well-wishers attending the ceremony. The occasion was captured in the headline of the following day, carried by the *Express and Echo*:

'Barefoot royal's winning ways'
'The Barefoot Duchess walked the plank at Exmouth yesterday and won the hearts of the crowds.

For the Duchess of Kent refused to be daunted when faced by a steep, slippery gang-plank to take her from the dockside to board the new £155,000 Exmouth lifeboat she had just christened the Caroline Finch.

"Don't be silly I can manage that," she insisted as lifeboat-men and officials suggested the gangplank was too dangerous for her to tackle and the ferry steps should be used instead.

To the delight of the crowds, the smiling Duchess simply slipped off her high-heeled shoes and completed the journey in her stocking feet – gallantly assisted by two RNLI officials who she asked in mock seriousness

"Can you catch me if I fall?"

The crowds of residents and holiday makers who packed every vantage point on the dockside for the lifeboat's christening ceremony quickly warmed to the popular royal couple's friendly manner.

As soon as the formal welcome to the Duchess and the Duke, who is President of the RNLI, was complete, the Duchess went over to the waiting crowd for a chat with two young Exmouth girls – Elizabeth Beaton and Emma Payne – who had been waiting in the front of the crowd.

A bout of measles meant the opportunity of a lifetime for two other Exmouth girls. Lifeboat men's daughters Amy Smith, nine, and Debbie Graham, 12, stepped in to make welcoming presentations of bouquets and souvenir programmes when illness prevented the great grand-daughter of the lifeboat donor from attending.

It was Debbie's father, Second Coxswain Keith Graham, who also quietly saved the day when the Duchess formally christened the lifeboat. She had pressed the button that should have sent the traditional bottle of champagne crashing against the bows, but for a second nothing happened.

The quick thinking lifeboat man moved swiftly – and pulled out the retaining pin to send the bottle smashing against the bows.

The formal naming of the craft was met with three rousing cheers – and a sudden torrential downpour.

After conquering the gangplank, and completing a trip around the bay in the high speed lifeboat, the Royal party returned for tea at the Exmouth Pavilion with over 350 guests.

As a foot note, it is recorded that the Duke and Duchess were presented with afresh 10lb Exe salmon, specially dressed for the occasion by Mrs Annette Quilter of Exmouth Fisheries.

On Monday 20 August 1984, following the retirement of Coxswain Geoff Mears, Second Coxswain Keith Graham was appointed Coxswain of the Exmouth Lifeboat. Motor Mechanic Tim Mock was appointed Second Coxswain/Mechanic.

Throughout the remainder of 1984, and in to 1985, the *Caroline Finch* undertook several 'routine' service launches which necessitated

Tim Mock, Mechanic 1983–1998.

assistance being rendered to wind-surfers who got in to trouble off Exmouth and the Pole Sands.

Coxswain Keith Graham, Second Coxswain/ Mechanic Tim Mock and crewmembers Geoff Ingram and Bert Thomas launched the Exmouth Lifeboat, *Caroline Finch*, to undertake an outstanding service on Sunday 7 April 1985. The Hon. Secretary, Derek Sargeant fired the assembly maroons at 11.06 hours having received a report from Brixham Coastguard that they were receiving calls of a speedboat having sunk 'somewhere between Teignmouth and Exmouth.' The *Caroline Finch* slipped from her mooring at 11.20 hours. Encountering heavy seas on the notorious Exmouth Bar, Coxswain Graham had to reduce speed and on crossing the Bar encountered a Southerly Force 6 wind and a rough sea with a 2-3 foot swell. Initially, on searching the area the casualty could not be

located but as the search area was extended, the 17-foot craft, which was being pounded by 8-foot waves and a heavy swell, was located one and a half miles east by south of Exmouth. As the lifeboat closed on the casualty, the three occupants, having been thrown into the sea, were sighted in the heavy surf. A male person appeared to be supporting two females but his task was hampered as no-one appeared to be wearing a lifejacket. Calling upon all his skills of seamanship, Keith Graham attempted to close in on the casualties but he was prevented from doing so by the height of the waves. Geoffrey Ingram leapt into the sea and located the male casualty, Mr M. Kearns of Birmingham, allowing the man to swim to, and gain the safety of, the *Caroline Finch* by climbing the scramble net. With his lifejacket fully inflated, Geoff Ingram and was able to support the two female members of the crew,

Michelle Greenham (14) and Amanda Thompson (12) until he was joined by lifeboat-man Bert Thomas who had also entered the water.

Geoff Ingram and Bert Thomas each assisted a girl to the side of the *Caroline Finch* where they were assisted aboard by Coxswain Keith Graham and Mechanic Tim Mock. Throughout the rescue Michelle Greenham had been rendered unconscious but was thankfully revived upon reaching the lifeboat. Michelle Greenham was air-lifted by Search and Rescue helicopter, '*Rescue 69*', which had been joined the lifeboat at the scene of the rescue, and was conveyed direct to Torbay Hospital, Torquay. Mr Kearns and Amanda Thompson were taken by lifeboat to Exmouth Docks and transferred to a waiting ambulance.

The Honorary Secretary's note in the Return of Service reads:

'*A very tricky operation carried out in difficult conditions. At one time the Coxswain felt they were going to capsize. This is a particularly treacherous area – it was in this vicinity that our 'D' class L/B capsized last year – as the sea becomes very confused in the shallows.*'

For this outstanding service, the Royal National Lifeboat Institution awarded the Thanks of the Institution, inscribed on Vellum, to Lifeboat-man Geoffrey Ingram, who was also awarded a Service of Merit Badge, in recognition of his meritorious action. The RNLIs' Vellum Service Certificate was awarded to Coxswain Keith Graham, Second Coxswain/Motor Mechanic Tim mock and Lifeboat-man Bert Thomas, for their respective actions in this rescue. The official presentations took place at Exmouth Town Hall on Tuesday 28 January 1986 with the awards being presented by Exmouth Town Committee Chairman, Mr Bernard Hughes.

Throughout the spring of 1985 the *Caroline Finch* responded to a string of distress calls, all of which culminated in the rescue of wind-surfers who had found themselves in difficulties off the Exe estuary and Pole Sands.

At 10.40 hours on Friday 21 June 1985 the Brixham Coastguard requested the immediate launch of the Exmouth lifeboat to assist a sailing vessel which was in difficulty one mile off Sidmouth. Exmouth Deputy Launch Authority Sleeman assembled the crew and the *Caroline Finch* slipped her mooring, just six minutes later, at

10.46 hours. The lifeboat was under the command of 2nd Coxswain Tim Mock, his crew being Tom Chandler (A.M.M.), Geoff Ingram and A. Lockyear. Battling a Force 7-8 southerly wind, and a very rough sea with an eight foot swell, the lifeboat reached the casualty, ¼ mile off shore, at 11.18 hours; she was found to be the 40-foot ketch *Vamoss II*. Due to water having entered her fuel, the vessel was unable to use her auxiliary engine and pointing-up as high as she could, the *Vamoss II* was unable to sail against the strong onshore wind; in very rough seas and a heavy swell she was slowly but surely being driven ashore.

The *Vamoss II* was a steel-hulled vessel with protrusions from the gunwales on both sides and Coxswain Tim Mock immediately realised that any attempt to go alongside the casualty would risk severe damage being cause to the lifeboat, and place his crew in danger. Making a truly professional judgement, Tim Mock undertook to take the *Caroline Finch* in under the bow of the casualty in an attempt to establish a tow line. Timing his action to perfection, the Tim Mock made his run and a line was successfully passed to the *Vamoss II*, at the first attempt, and a tow secured. At 11.35 hours, the lifeboat informed Brixham Coastguard that the casualty was under tow to Exmouth Dock. The tow was painfully slow as the *Caroline Finch* continued to battle against the gale-force winds and heavy seas and swell. At 12.03 hours the lifeboat radioed Brixham Coastguard to inform them that the towline had parted and that the crew were endeavouring to re-establish the tow. At this time the lifeboat and casualty were 2 miles South-southeast of Sidmouth. By using a heaving line, a secure tow was re-established and at 12.13 hours the tow was once again underway.

At 13.10 hours the lifeboat and her casualty were off the Exe Fairway Buoy. Tim Mock assessed the sea conditions as the waves pounded over the notorious Exmouth Bar which, out of necessity, he needed to cross. Tim assessed that it would not be possible to cross the bar and continue in to Exmouth, without putting both the lifeboat and casualty at undue risk. He therefore decided to continue the tow by heading for Teignmouth, before turning south for Brixham. This course, as opposed to the more direct course across Torbay, would offer greater protection to the lifeboat and casualty as they continued their battle with the heavy seas; even so, on more than one occasion, it was reported that the bilge keel of the *Vamoss II* was clearly visible to the lifeboat crew.

At 13.44 hours the *Caroline Finch* gave her position as 2 miles East of Teignmouth; at 13.58 hours she gave her E.T.A. Brixham as 15.00 hours.

As the master of the *Vamoss II*, Mr D Hyde of Plymouth, and his crewmate, were both suffering from exhaustion, hyperthermia and sea-sickness, Tim Mock signalled the Brixham Coastguard to arrange for medical assistance to standby at Brixham. AT 14.53 hours the lifeboat was 2 miles off Brixham breakwater, berthing at Brixham at 15.20 hours. The Brixham lifeboat station provided refreshment for Tim and his crew while the *Caroline Finch* was re-fuelled for her return journey to Exmouth. At 16.25 hours the Exmouth crew received information, from their Station Hon. Secretary, that rough conditions continued to prevail on the Exmouth Bar and he advised that a further one hour of flood tide should be allowed before the lifeboat should attempt to return to station. With the crew refreshed and the boat refuelled, the *Caroline Finch* departed Brixham at 16.45 hours, arriving off the Exe Fairway Buoy at 17.23 hours and mooring alongside Exmouth Docks at 17.33 hours.

Having completed an arduous 7 hour rescue, the *Caroline Finch* was hosed-down, refuelled back on her mooring and her crew ready for service at 17.49 hours.

Second Coxswain/Motor Mechanic Tim Mock and his crew subsequently received a Letter of Appreciation from the Royal National Lifeboat Institution's Head of Operations for this outstanding service.

When Coxswain Keith Graham, 2nd Cox'n/Motor Mechanic Tim Mock, Assistant Motor Mechanic Tom Chandler and crewman D Perkin were called out on Sunday 24 March 1986, the muster could not be designated either 'Service' or 'Assembly.' The call-out was made by the Station Honorary Secretary, Derek Sargeant, following his receipt of a report, at 00.25 hours from the Brixham Coastguard, which advised: '*Storm Force 10 imminent – possible Hurricane 12 soon.*' Although confident that the *Caroline Finch's* moorings would hold, he was concerned that those of other vessels in the vicinity might be suspect and that, should they drag or break from their moorings, damage could be caused to the lifeboat by drifting vessels. Keith Graham and his

crew took the *Caroline Finch* off her mooring and entered Exmouth Dock. For the next 24 hours the near hurricane-force winds blew unabated, eventually abating some twenty-nine hours later. When the winds eased on Monday morning, the lifeboat was returned to her moorings and was ready for service at 06.30.

Coxswain Keith Graham and his crew launched the *Caroline Finch* at 18.46 hours on Saturday 3 May 1986 following a report being received from the Brixham Coastguard that a number of Cadet sailing dinghies, which were taking part in an Exe Sailing Club event, had capsized between No.1 Buoy and East of Orcombe Point. The Brede Class lifeboat launched into a South-easterly wind of force 6-7 and a rough sea with a three-foot swell.

The lifeboat was 'on scene' within ten minutes of lunch; her crew initially located three capsized dinghies but the crews were not to be seen. There were several small craft in the area and a search pattern was quickly established. Realising the potential seriousness of the situation, Coxswain Graham requested the assistance of Search and Rescue helicopter 169. The helicopter arrived at the scene at 19.34 hours. Confusion prevailed throughout the remaining dinghy fleet and indeed some of the rescue craft when, at 19.35 hours, a signal was received from the Exe Sailing Club which read '*all accounted for but two boys still not signed in*', the signal appearing contradictory.

The Brixham Coastguard requested further confirmation of the safety of the two boys before calling off the search. The required confirmation came from Exmouth Coastguard at 19.47 hours when the lifeboat was instructed to 'Return To Station' with the signal '*all accounted for and signed in*'.

As the *Caroline Finch* was returning to her Exmouth Station, at 19.53 hours the Brixham Coastguard requested Coxswain Graham to proceed to Teignmouth, to a suspected sunken vessel, as Helo 169 had reported sighting oil bubbling to the surface. The lifeboat was alongside the oil patch at 20.24 hours and reported oil continuing to bubble to the surface. The lifeboat was searching the immediate area when, at 20.32 hours, Helo 169 was diverted to Orcombe Point Exmouth, to investigate an 'object' that had been reported floating in the sea. The 'object' proved to be a wooden crate.

At 20.53 hours, with darkness falling and the emergency authorities not having received notification of any missing persons, the search was abandoned with the Coastguard instructing the helicopter and lifeboat to return to their respective station. Having spent three hectic hours at sea the crew of the *Caroline Finch* returned to Exmouth, the Return of Service report being endorsed '*No Service.*'

The rescue carried out by members of the Exmouth station, on Monday 25 August 1986, clearly demonstrated the outstanding capabilities of RNLI crews when working the All-Weather Lifeboat (ALB) in conjunction with the Inshore Lifeboat (ILB). An initial call, received from Brixham Coastguard at 15.05 hours, indicated that a yacht, with three persons onboard, was stranded on the seaward side of the Pole Sands. As the lifeboat crew were on station, having returned from service to a small dinghy, the *Caroline Finch* was immediately readied, and together with the ILB *D-255* was launched at 15.08 hours. Unfortunately as it was dead low-water the Brede Class ALB found great difficulty in crossing the Exmouth Bar. For their part, the three-man crew of the ILB were to attempt a rescue from the River Exe side of the Pole Sands. The two lifeboats had launched into a moderate to choppy sea and a Force 7 South-easterly wind. As they approached the Pole Sands the wind had increased to Gale Force 8 and the sea had increased to Sea State 5/6, rough to very rough. Both lifeboats were 'on scene' at by 15.20 hours albeit neither lifeboat could directly approach the casualty which was identified as a 25-foot sailing yacht, *Lynx* of Topsham. In order to reach the stranded yacht, Life-boatman Bert Thomas entered the water, from the *Caroline Finch*, and waded across the sands in the direction of the casualty. Whilst Keith Graham held the lifeboat steady in the main channel, the Helmsman of the ILB, John Walpole, manoeuvred the *D-255* into a position from where she could be beached and then dragged by her crew across the sands towards the *Lynx*. Peter Denfold, a member of the ILB's crew, also entered the water and with Bert Thomas reached the stranded vessel. Chest-deep in water, the two lifeboat-men were able to guide the crew of three, from the yacht, to the relative safety of a sand bank. John Walpole once again took the *D-255* into the shallows of the Pole Sands and succeeded in taking off the three casualties and the two lifeboat-men. The five men were transferred to the waiting *Caroline Finch* and landed at Exmouth Docks at 15.52 hours.

The Honorary Secretary endorsed the Service Record:

'*This service was carried out successfully and intelligently in atrocious conditions with the ALB and ILB working well together and, in my opinion, deserves consideration for some form of recognition.*'

The recommendation was heeded by the Institution with Mr Sargeant subsequently receiving a 'Letter of Thanks', signed by the RNLI's Chief of Operations, congratulating the crews of both the ALB and the ILB for their respective roles in this excellent service. Special reference was made to the local knowledge and navigational skills of Coxswain Keith Graham and Helmsman John Walpole.

Under the command of 2nd Coxswain / Motor Mechanic Tim Mock, O.N. 1088, the *Caroline Finch* slipped her moorings at 19.36 hours on Thursday 20 November 1986 to go to the assistance 55-foot commercial fishing vessel RX32 *Brigg*, Master Derek Eastwood of Portsmouth. Initial information received from Brixham Coastguard indicated that the vessel had suffered engine failure and was drifting 3½ miles East of Otter Point, her anchor cable having parted. The *Caroline Finch* launched into a Westerly wind of Force 4-5, and a slight sea with 1-foot of swell. Once away from her mooring, the lifeboat crew experienced a deterioration in both weather and sea conditions; at the position of the casualty the wind was gusting Force 6 and the sea state had increased to a 5/6, rough to very rough, with a 6 to 8-foot swell.

When the lifeboat reached the casualty, at 20.05 hours, Tim Mock found her position to be less than 2 miles from the shore and perilously drifting towards rocks. Despite the heavy swell, Tim Mock manoeuvred the lifeboat up to the casualty and a tow-line was quickly established. The drift of the *Brigg* towards the rocks was halted and at 20.25 hours the *Caroline Finch* commenced a long and eventful tow back to Exmouth Docks. During the tow through heavy seas and swell, the tow-line parted on no less than five occasions, one parting resulting in injury being received by lifeboat-man Simon Turl. The crew of Graham Ingram, C Harris and Simon Turl worked relentlessly, reconnecting the tow on each occasion. Thanks to the skilful seamanship of Coxswain Tim Mock, at 22.26 hours the lifeboat reported that, with the tow intact, she had cleared the Exmouth Bar. At 22.50 hours the *Brigg* was secured at Exmouth Docks and her crew of three were safely ashore.

The Station Return of Service records:

'This service was skilfully performed in very poor conditions. The casualty would undoubtedly have been swept ashore had it not been for L/B intervention. The persistence shown by the 2nd Cox/ Mech. and those on deck during the long and difficult tow, including five partings, is commendable.'

For this excellent service, a 'Letter of Thanks' was received from the Director of the Royal National Lifeboat Institution, acknowledging the actions of Acting Coxswain Mock and his crew.

In 1869 the Royal National Lifeboat Institution stationed the first of two lifeboats at a boathouse in Sidmouth; however, due to a decline in water based activities in the area, the station was closed in 1912. Since 1972 the town of Sidmouth has operated an independent lifeboat service (see 'Rimmington'.)

On the evening of Tuesday 17 January 1989 ON 1088 *Caroline Finch* was launched in response to information received, from Brixham Coastguard, that a member of the crew of the Sidmouth Rescue boat had been lost overboard. Coxswain Keith Graham and five members of his crew, slipped the moorings at 21.28 hours; additional crew was carried in anticipation of the need for a visual search. At the request of the Coastguard, the Exmouth Inshore Lifeboat was also launched. The lifeboats launched into a calm sea, light airs and good visibility. Both lifeboats entered in to a co-ordinated search pattern and at 01.17 hours the *Caroline Finch* reported that a torch belonging to the casualty had been found. Five minutes later, at 01.22 hours, the Coastguard received notification that the lifeboat had located and recovered a body. It was evident that the deceased had been in the water for a considerable time and that resuscitation was not an option.

The Lifeboat landed the deceased Alex Squance (18) of Sidmouth, at Ferry Steps, Exmouth, at 01.50 hours.

The *Caroline Finch* was taken 'off station' in the autumn of 1989, her replacement being the Relief Fleet lifeboat O.N. *1090 Foresters Future*. The Brede Class lifeboat, built in 1984, had served in the Channel Islands as the Alderney lifeboat (1984–1986), and in the Relief Fleet (1986-2002). Sold by the RNLI, the lifeboat was shipped to South Africa on Wednesday 26 February 2003. *Foresters Fortune* was the third Relief Fleet Brede class lifeboat to serve on the Exmouth Station, previous boats being O.N. *1105 Amateur Swimming Associations*; built in 1985 she was allocated to the Relief Fleet (1985-1989) and served as the Girvan Station Boat (1989-1993). When sold from RNLI Fleet in 1993, she was renamed *Sealord Rescue* and is known to have been in service as a Coastguard rescue boat at Port Nelson, New Zealand. The third relief Brede was the aforementioned O.N. *1087 Merchant Navy.*

The summer of 1989 saw the crew of the Exmouth Lifeboat respond to numerous local 'shouts'. On several occasions the lifeboat crew assisted small pleasure craft that had experienced either engine failure or had simply run out of fuel. Numerous calls to which either the *Caroline Finch* or the *Foresters Future* responded were to assist sail-boarders who were apparently experiencing difficulty. Thankfully, the majority of these calls received the classification *'Gave Assistance'* or *'No Service.'*

However, the launch that took place on Tuesday 23 January 1990 was of a quite different nature. It was at 03.12 hours that Brixham Coastguard requested the launch of the Exmouth lifeboat. The Honorary Secretary, Mr Sargeant, was informed that at 18.30 hours the previous evening a man had left Cockwood in a small dinghy, which was fitted with an outboard motor, to remove a water pump on the stern trawler *Albatross*. The man had failed to return home, his E.T.A. being 23.00 hours.

Coxswain Keith Graham and his crew T. Mock, T. Chandler and S. Turl, slipped the mooring of the Foresters Future at 03.29, reaching the *Albatross*, at 03.39 hours.

At 03.46 hours the lifeboat signalled the Coastguard that a check had been made of the trawler but there were no signs of the water pump having been removed. An initial search had failed to locate either the man or the dinghy. At 03.39 hours Keith Graham informed Brixham Coastguard that he intended to search the River Exe towards Cockwood. Coxswain Graham was informed that a shoreline search was to be

conducted by the Teignmouth and Exmouth Auxiliary Coastguard. The search by the lifeboat proved negative and at 04.16 hours the *Foresters Future* moved to a search area between Exmouth Docks and the I.L.B. Station. At 05.30 hours the Lee-on-Solent (HMS Daedalus) based Search & Rescue helicopter, Rescue 174, reached the scene and commenced a search in the area of Straight Point. Again the search proved negative.

As the search continued weather conditions deteriorated. The South by West wind had increased from Force 5-6 to Force 7-8 and the sea state had risen from a moderate/choppy 4 to a very rough 6. The tide had been on the ebb for some two-and-a-half hours when at 06.03 hours the lifeboat signalled

'We have searched up as far as Starcross Yacht Club. It's getting a bit dodgy as regards water. We are proceeding towards Dawlish Warren.'

Hopes were raised just three minutes later when the Auxiliary Coastguard unit Teignmouth 'Tango' reported

'Small white boat located by railway line near Dawlish Warren. Suggest helo investigates' but the hopes were dashed at 06.17 hours when *Rescue 174* reported *'It's an old catamaran sunk in the mud.'*

The Exmouth Boarding Boat, crewed by lifeboatmen G. Ingram and B. Thomas, was launched at 06.20 hours and searched the shallow waters accompanied by the lifeboat. Coxswain Keith Graham received a devastating signal from Brixham Coastguard at 07.40 hours confirming that, not just one, but two men were in fact missing.

At 08.03 hours the helicopter reported that she was hovering over a dinghy answering the description of the missing craft. The *Foresters Future* reached the casualty at 08.21 hours as *Rescue 174* withdrew from the search to refuel at Exeter Airport and was replaced on scene by the Portland bases Royal Navy helicopter *Rescue 172*. The *Foresters Future* recovered the dinghy and engine and passed a full description of the craft, and the engine number, to the Coastguard. It was particularly noted that the outboard engine was in gear and in the tilted position. At the request of the Coastguard, the dinghy and engine were conveyed to the Teignmouth mobile unit at

Starcross pier, for the purpose of identification, whist the Boarding Boat check nearby craft for the occupants of the dinghy. At 08.53 hours the Exmouth Inshore Lifeboat joined the search.

At 09.37 hours the Coastguard signalled the lifeboat positively confirming that the dinghy was indeed the missing craft. Rescue 172 returned to Portland at 10.13 hours and having searched the River Exe up as far as Turf Locks, at 10.54 hours the Coastguard instructed all RNLI and Coastguard units to discontinue the search and return to station.

The *Foresters Future* was on station, refuelled and ready for service at 11.17 hours.

Having resumed duty as the Exmouth Station lifeboat O.N. 1088 *Caroline Finch* slipped her moorings at 16.30 hours on Wednesday 27 June 1990 to go to the assistance of the skipper of the small fishing vessel *Serenity*. Initial information, received from the Brixham Coastguard, indicated that the man had severed fingers having caught his hand in a winch. It was known that there were three persons onboard the vessel which was off Straight Point. Due to the nature of the injuries, the attendance of a Doctor was requested. At 16.40 hours Dr. C. Stubbings boarded the lifeboat at Ferry Steps and Coxswain Graham set course for the casualty. The lifeboat reached the *Serenity* within 15 minutes and the injured man was transferred to the lifeboat where he immediately received medical attention.

It was found that the two anglers on board the *Serenity* were both physically disabled. Lifeboat crewman B. Thomas was put onboard the fishing vessel to assist the craft and the two anglers back to Exmouth Docks.

Escorted by the *Caroline Finch*, the *Serenity* was alongside Ferry Steps at 17.09 hours when the injured man was transferred to a waiting ambulance.

Both the *Caroline Finch* and the *I.L.B.* launched, in the early morning of Tuesday 31 July 1990, to go to the assistance of a male person who had received serious injuries having fallen from cliffs at Sandy Bay, Exmouth. Both lifeboats reached the casualty within 10 minutes. Coxswain Keith Graham stood-off with the lifeboat as the crew of the I.L.B. went in to the base of the cliffs to recover the casualty. The man had stopped breathing and resuscitation was carried out by Ambulance, Police and Auxiliary Coastguard personnel.

It is not common place for the crew of a RNLI lifeboat to have to respond to a vessel on fire, but the Exmouth crew of the *Caroline Finch* has to respond to two such calls within a matter of three days in September 1990. The first launch took place at 11.21 hours on Friday 14 September, following a report that a speedboat was on fire one-and-a half miles East of the Parson and Clerk Rock. The Station Honorary Secretary was informed that the F/V *Wild One* was standing-by the stricken craft and that Rescue Helicopter 172 was en-route. Having slipped her moorings the *Caroline Finch* was alongside the casualty in twenty minutes. The two male occupants of the speedboat, *Good Looking*, were taken onboard the lifeboat and the fire extinguished. The cause of the fire was established as being a faulty carburettor in the Mercury out-board engine. The *Good Looking* was taken in tow by the lifeboat, the casualties being landed at the Teignmouth Fish Quay at 12.50 hours.

Three days later, on Monday 17 September, The Second Coxswain /Mechanic, Tim Mock, contacted the Deputy Launch Authority, reporting a vessel on fire off Orcombe Point. Initial reports were that *'there was nobody in the water'* indicating that the crew of the stricken vessel were still onboard. In view of the urgency of the situation, Coxswain Keith Graham put to sea with a crew of four, a pump and five Fire Service personnel. The *Caroline Finch* slipped from her mooring at 13.59 hours and, just six minutes later, located the casualty, the 23-foot Shetland cabin cruiser *Pro-Tem,* off the seaward side of Pole Sands, opposite Orcombe Point. It was quickly established that the single occupant of the cabin cruiser had infact jumped into the sea and had been picked up by windsurfer who had, in turn, transferred the man to the pleasure vessel *Gorgeous Gussie*. As the *Pro-Tem* was known to have approximately 20 gallons of petrol on board and there was a real risk of an explosion, the fire was tackled by the Fire Service personnel. Having extinguished the fire, the resultant damage to the *Pro-Tem* was such that she sank.

Second Coxswain Tim Mock was putting the *Caroline Finch* through her paces whilst undertaking a Radar Exercise when he was alerted to a *'Pan–Pan'* distress call transmitted from the Wellington Sub-aqua Club's dive boat at 12.00 hours on Sunday 11 November 1990. The dive boat had suffered engine failure and was unable to recover surfacing divers. Thankfully the lifeboat was in the vicinity of the Exe Fairway Buoy and was quickly alongside the casualty. It was known that there were seven divers in the water and at 12.17 hours the lifeboat reported that all divers had been accounted for and recovered from the sea. The dive boat and divers were returned to the Exmouth Inshore Lifeboat slipway at 12.27 hours.

On Monday 30 September 1991 the former Alderney lifeboat, the Brede Class O.N. 1090 *Foresters Future* was on temporary duty at Exmouth when she was launched following a report of persons flashing a torch and shouting for help on the River Exe. At the same time a report was received of an overdue sailing dinghy. Coxswain Graham, with a crew of three, slipped the mooring at 21.57 hours; at the same time the Boarding Boat, also with a crew of three, slipped her mooring. It was intended that the crew of the Boarding Boat would search the shallow shoreline whilst the area of the search was illuminated by the lifeboat. The sky was overcast and there was a drizzle in the air but the sea remained calm. At 22.28 hours a 13ft. 6in. Mayfly sailing dinghy, with one person onboard, was located on a mud-bank, known locally as Bull Hill. To assist with the illumination of the scene, the Exmouth Inshore lifeboat was launched to convey additional para-flares to Coxswain Graham on the *Foresters Future*.

The sailing dinghy appeared to be stuck fast on the mud-bank, albeit the sails remain hoisted. Two of the crew of the Boarding Boat, B. Thomas and T. Wilkin, entered the water up to their armpits and waded across the mud towards the casualty. Unfortunately for the lifeboatmen, as they approached the dinghy the sails filled and the craft moved away from them. The crew returned to the Boarding Boat which, together with the life boat relocated to the far side of the mud-bank. At 22.45 hours the ILB and the Boarding Boat were alongside the casualty. The lone crewman, Mr. Rigby of Exeter, was taken onboard the ILB and transported to Exmouth Docks whilst the Boarding Boat towed the Mayfly dinghy to Shelly Beach. The *Foresters Future* was back on its mooring and ready for service at 23.45 hours.

Throughout her remaining time as the Exmouth Station Lifeboat, the *Caroline Finch* was launched on numerous occasions, most of which were to assist vessels which were stranded on the Pole Sands, had suffered steering failure or who had been reported as being 'overdue.' Thankfully that majority of the latter had reached land safely but had failed to report their arrival. It is apparent from the Returns of Service that the lifeboat crew responded to an increasing number of 'false alarms.'

In July 1994 the Brede Class lifeboat was withdrawn from the Exmouth Station and allocated to the Relief Fleet. Later that year the RNLI sold the *Caroline Finch* from the fleet. Renamed *South Star*, the former Exmouth lifeboat is known to have continued to perform duties as a lifeboat in Hermanus, South Africa.

13
The Louis Marchesi of Round Table
8 July 1994 – 6 July 1996

Class: Waveney   *Propulsion:* Twin 'Caterpillar' D3208T diesel engines   *Crew:* 5
Official Number: 1045   *Operational Number:* 44-019   *Speed:* 15 knots
Length: 44' 10"   *Beam:* Displacement: *Built:* 1977
Builder: Bideford Shipyard Ltd.   *Launches:* 39   *Lives Saved:* 5
Coxswain: Keith Graham   *Mechanic:* Tim Mock

On Friday 8 July 1994 the *Caroline Finch* was temporarily replaced by the Waveney Class lifeboat, O.N.1045, *Louis Marchesi of Round Table*. The steel-hulled lifeboat, which had been built in 1977, had initially served as the Newhaven lifeboat (1977-1985) before being transferred to the Relief Fleet (1985-1986). She was subsequently placed on service as the Alderney lifeboat (1986-

1994). Fitted with twin Caterpillar D3208T diesel engines, she had a top speed of 15 knots.

The *Louis Marchesi of Round Table* was presented to the Royal National Lifeboat Institution by the National Association of Round Tables of Great Britain and Ireland, in honour of its founder, on the occasion of the Golden Jubilee of the Association in 1977. The Waveney Class of

The Waveney Class lifeboat *44-019 Louis Marchesi of Round Table ON1045.* Melanie Mock

lifeboats were based on the proven design of the United States of America's Coastguard cutters.

The first recorded service launch undertaken by the *Louis Marchesi* took place at 17.50 hours on Monday 25 July 1994. On this occasion she was launched, by Coxswain Keith Graham, to assist in refloating the sailing yacht *March Hare* which had become stranded on the Pole Sands, near the No.8 buoy. The Exmouth ILB also attended the scene. A member of the lifeboat crew, Dave Perkin, entered the water and waded to the stricken vessel. Once onboard the yacht he established a tow and the yacht and crew were recovered to Exmouth Dock.

The assistance of Coxswain Keith Graham and the crew of the Exmouth lifeboat were requested, at 0606 hours on Friday 26 August 1994, to assist in the search for three missing divers. The divers, who had set out in a 5 meter inflatable boat fitted with an outboard engine, had been missing since 14.30 hours the previous day. Directed by the Portland Coastguard, the *Louis Marchesi* proceeded to a point in Lyme Bay, near the Empress of India creek, some seven to eight miles from the Exmouth Station. As the Exmouth lifeboat arrived on the scene, at 07.15 hours, to join a search team which included two

Search and Rescue helicopters and two lifeboats, the missing dive boat was located by the Lyme Regis lifeboat and towed in to port.

At 08.35 hours the three missing divers were located by the fishing vessel the *Provider*. The casualties having been air-lifted to Weymouth Hospital, by 'Helo167', the *Louis Marchesi* was released from the search at 09.00 hours. Coxswain Keith Graham nursed the lifeboat back to Exmouth under reduced power, due to the port engine overheating, arriving alongside Exmouth Dock at 10.35 hours.

Between Sunday 21 August 1994 and Sunday 6 November 1994, Keith Graham and his crew launched the *Louis Marchesi* on a total of eleven occasions. These launches were to assist vessels with engine failure and to search for persons who had been reported missing; all the latter were located, the majority having safely returned to their respective homes.

It was just after 17.00 hours on Sunday 4 September 1994 that the Brixham Coastguard received a 'MAYDAY' call from the 20-foot fishing boat *Don Pedro*. The vessel had reportedly suffered engine failure and was taking in water.

Waveney crew undergoing Crew Training at Poole. (l-r): Pete Denford, Clive Harris, Matt Graham, Dave Richards, Tim Mock, Keith Graham.

The Waveney Class lifeboat *Louis Marchesi of Round Table ON1045* on exercise with Search and Rescue helicopter. Shamus McCaffrey

44-019 Louis Marchesi of Round Table
ON1045 undergoing exercise Shamus McCaffrey

The crew of the stricken vessel reported their position as being one-mile off Straight Point, Exmouth. Authority was given for the launch of both the Exmouth *ILB* and the *Louis Marchesi*; the boats being launched at 17.08 hours and 17.14 hours respectively.

The casualty was infact located, at 17.30 hours, one-mile south of Ladram Bay by the crew of the ILB. At the location of the casualty the weather was overcast and a Force 5 south-westerly wind was accompanying a rough sea and four-foot swell. Initially the fishing vessel was taken in tow by the ILB, the tow subsequently being transferred to the lifeboat. With two RNLI personnel being placed onboard the *Don Pedro*, with a portable pump to ease the ingress of water, the casualty and crew were towed to the safety of Exmouth Dock, arriving at 19.27 hours.

The *Louis Marchesi* was launched, at 15.55 hours on Tuesday 8 November 1994, to search for a local man reported missing in the River Exe. The man was last seen at 08.30 hours that day, boarding his tender in order to make his way out to his launch, moored approximately one-quarter-mile from the boathouse. In the River Exe the weather was stormy with rain, visibility fair, at times, with a strong south-easterly wind and rough sea.

Coxswain Graham immediately commenced a systematic search of the surrounding area of the river, in conjunction with Police and coastguard units, before extending the search offshore between Langstone and Straight Point. As a search of this area proved negative, the lifeboat returned to concentrate the search in the River Exe.

With deteriorating weather conditions, the search was terminated at 18.45 hours and the *Louis Marchesi* returned to station. The Station Return of Service records that the missing person was not found.

An ever increasing number of launches undertaken by the Exmouth lifeboat were in response to 'missing person' reports. Unfortunately not all have a happy ending.

Whilst out on exercise on Sunday 20 November 1994, the Exmouth lifeboat was tasked, by Brixham Coastguard, to search the estuary of the River Exe for a 35 year-old man who had been reported missing; the man having been last seen in the area of Exmouth Docks. Coxswain Keith Graham commenced his search at 10.45 hours, in

an area between Straight Point and Langstone Rock. The Exmouth Boarding Boat was manned and used to search the dock area. The boats were released from the search and returned to station at 13.00 hours.

The following day, Monday 21 November, the *Express and Echo* newspaper reported:

A body found in Exmouth docks last night is believed to be that of a vulnerable man who went missing from his Sidmouth home yesterday.

The 35-year-old was found in the water at 5.14pm after a massive search involving a helicopter, three lifeboats and frogmen.

Police are not treating the death as suspicious. They were not releasing the name of the man at the request of his relatives.

The *Louis Marchesi* slipped her mooring, at 12.53 hours on Saturday 15 April 1995, to go to the assistance of a commercial pleasure craft which had become stranded in the River Exe. The launch was supported by the launch of the ILB and Boarding Boat. The 40-foot *Exonia*, owned by the Stuart Line of Exmouth, had reportedly run aground near the Maer Rocks, approximately one half-of-a-mile from the lifeboat station and was located by Coxswain Graham and his crew between the No.6 and No.8 buoy. The pleasure craft carried 24 passengers and two crew men.

Due to the lack of water, (high water 18.46 hours), the lifeboat had to 'stand-off', being unable to go alongside the casualty. The evacuation of the *Exonia* has to be undertaken by the ILB and the Boarding Boat, the passengers being transferred on to the *Louis Marchesi*.

The lifeboat then checked on four other craft that had also run aground. None of these craft were in danger and in each case the crew elected to stay onboard and wait for the flood tide.

The passengers and crew of the *Exonia* were landed at Exmouth Dock at 13.35 hours.

Keith Graham and the crew of the Exmouth lifeboat were engaged in a dramatic and tragic rescue on Friday 26 May 1995. Initial information, received from Brixham Coastguard at 09.56 hours, indicated that a vessel had sunk off Langstone Rock, Dawlish Warren and that five persons were in the water. The assembly signal was made at 09.57 hours and the *Louis Marchesi* slipped her mooring at 10.07 hours. The casualty was the fishing vessel *Blue Fin*, out of Teignmouth; the fishing party being Trevor Hall (29) skipper, David Bayliss (30), Jeremy Jones (48), John Vince (24) and Mark Stainer (32).

The ill-fated *Blue Fin* left Teignmouth at approximately 06.30 hours and within one hour started to take in water. Mr Bayliss told a reported for the *Western Morning News*:

'It didn't seem to be a major problem initially. We started to steam ashore but the bilge pumps weren't keeping up with the influx of water. I started to look for flares, but a wave came and the boat sank within 20 seconds.'

The Exmouth lifeboat reached the search area, a half-mile off Langstone Rock, at 10.30 hours and joined the Teignmouth *ILB*, the Atlantic 21, *B-588 Frank and Dorothy*, a Royal Navy Search and Rescue helicopter from Portland, the Devon Air Ambulance and the Dawlish Warren Rescue Boat in a systematic search of the area. At the scene there was partial cloud cover, visibility was very good and a fresh breeze blew from the south-west. The sea state was moderate to choppy with a one metre swell.

Three persons, David Bayliss, Trevor Hall and Jeremy Jones, managed to reach the shore, just before 10.30 hours, having spent two hour in the sea. Beach users assisted the men to a nearby amusement arcade and alerted the emergency services. Suffering from shock, trauma and hypothermia the three men were conveyed by ambulance to Wonford Hospital, Exeter. Mr Bayliss:

'We were about two miles offshore. We got ourselves around the life ring and we were all working together. We were kicking our legs and swinging our arms, and we were talking all the time. If we saw somebody's spirits flagging, someone would gee them up.

But as time went on and we started getting towards the shore, Mark began to suffer from hyperthermia. Trevor pulled him up, but it was obvious that he was in a much worse state than we realised. He died there, and we had our arms around him. He slowly slipped off the life ring.

The other chap (John) disappeared. We were so exhausted and we realised that if we went to

look for them we would all be risking our lives.

I wondered if it was worth going on. I thought "I don't believe this – we are 100 yards away from safety and they've gone."'.

Police Sergeant Colin Dawe, Constable Rob Henford, and Devon Air Ambulance paramedic, Paul Gerry, spotted Mr Stainer in the sea, some 100 yards from the beach, and waded out and pulled him ashore. Another flight paramedic, David Hartland battled to resuscitate Mr Strainer but his life had already ebbed away. Mr Vince also lost his life.

The helicopter search was called of in the early afternoon but the lifeboats remained on scene to continue the search. The search was terminated at 15.00 hours, the lifeboat being instructed to 'return to station'.

The *Louis Marchesi of Round Table* was temporarily 'off station' during the summer of 1995, her replacement being the 44-foot Waveney Class lifeboat, *44-001*.

Built at the United States Coast Guard (USCG) boatyard, Curtis Bay, Maryland, in 1964, as boat No. 44328, she entered the RNLI's Relief Fleet as an 'experimental' boat for evaluation.

44-001 was un-named and an Operational Number was not allocated by the RNLI.

Between Friday 9 June and Friday 1 September, *44-001* undertook nine service launches.

The first launch, on Friday 9 June, was at the request of the Brixham Coast Guard, following the report of a vessel on fire in the River Exe, on a mooring, near No27 buoy. It was reported that one person from the casualty was already ashore and seeking medical attention. Coxswain Graham, and his crew, launched at 09.36 hours. Initially the lifeboat proceeded to Starcross Pier where she picked up five Fire Brigade personnel. The Exmouth Boarding Boat was also launched to assist in conveying a portable pump and to assist generally in shallow waters. On reaching the casualty, at 10.00 hours, she was found to be the sail yacht *Bussy Lizzie*, owned by a Mr Riley of Bantry Bay, Ireland. It was established that the casualty, who was now receiving medical attention ashore, was the sole occupant of the yacht. The fire was quickly extinguished by the Fire Brigade who removed cans of fuel and gas canisters to render the vessel safe. Having returned the Fire Brigade personnel to Starcross, the *44001* was refuelled and ready for service at 11.15 hours.

At 05.25 hours on Monday 12 June 1995, *44-001* was launched, at the request of the Portland Coast Guard, to assist in a search for a 14-foot powerboat which had been reported overdue from a fishing trip. The vessel, *Flash*, had left Lyme Regis at 09.00 hours the previous day, since that time the vessel had not been sighted and no contact had been made by her crew of three.

Keith Graham and his crew set out for the search area in fine weather; visibility was very good (10-30 miles), a light breeze blew from the North-east, giving rise to a slight sea and swell. Having joined other vessels and air support in the search pattern, *44-001* was initially tasked to search an area between Seaton and Lyme Regis. With this area producing a negative result, the search area was extended further offshore, along a line from Lyme Regis to Berry Head, Brixham. Once again the search made by the Exmouth lifeboat proved negative and at 15.06 hours, Coxswain Graham received the signal '*Return to Station.*'

The Exmouth crew were not notified of the final outcome of the incident and assume that the *Flash* and her crew of three were lost.

The *Louis Marchesi of Round Table* slipped her moorings into near gale force winds, squally rain, a rough sea with a 2 – 3 metre swell and visibility of less than one mile, at 18.56 hours on Friday 6 October 1995. The lifeboat was launched at the request of Portland Coast Guard, to search for a missing sailboarder. The search area was in Lyme Bay, some eleven miles from the Exmouth Lifeboat Station, and 200 yards south of the Cobb, Lyme Regis.

The lifeboat reached the designated area at 19.43 hours and joined helicopters, Police and Coast Guard units in searching an area between Charmouth and Lyme Regis. The sailboarder was not located and in deteriorating weather conditions, the search was abandoned at 23.30 hours.

The following day, the Western Morning News reported:

'Fruitless hunt for surfer.'
'*Coastguard cliff teams, two rescue helicopters, Dorset police and Exmouth lifeboat carried out a massive search last night after a member of the public reported seeing a windsurfer in trouble off Lyme Regis.*

Despite rough seas, the team searched five miles of coastline and a mile out to sea in a three-and-a-half hour operation co-ordinated by Portland coastguard. Nothing was found and the coastguard will make further inquiries tomorrow.'

From 11.45 hours on Wednesday 22 May 1996, Coast Guard units commenced to monitor the progress of the 65-foot Stuart Line pleasure boat *Tudor Rose*, with four crew and ninety-six passengers on board, which had apparently lost power near No.22 buoy, between Topsham and Turf, on the River Exe. The Tudor Rose dropped anchor and arrangements were made for the vessel *Southern Angler* to tow the pleasure craft down river to Exmouth Dock.

Concern grew for the safety of the vessel and passengers as, throughout the time that the craft was under observation, weather condition deteriorated. By 13.40 hours it was raining heavily, visibility was less than one mile, and the wind, blowing from the South-southwest, was Force 6 gusting Force 8. These conditions combined to produce a rough sea with a five-foot swell.

As it became apparent that the *Tudor Rose* would require further assistance to dock, both the *Louis Marchesi* and the Boarding Boat were launched at 13.45 hours. The lifeboat was manned by Keith Graham, Tim Mock, Tom Chandler, Dave Perkin and Mark Chandler; the boarding boat was manned by Bert Thomas, Geoff Ingram and Matt Graham.

In atrocious weather, the crew of the boarding boat managed to get a line to the casualty; one end of the line was secured to the stern of the *Tudor Rose* whilst the other was secured to the lifeboat. In this manner Keith Graham used the lifeboat as a sea-anchor and assisted in stopping the *Tudor Rose* at the entrance to the dock.

This short, but important service proved successful, the *Tudor Rose* was secured at Exmouth dock pontoon with all passengers and crew being landed safely.

At 14.00 hours the *Louis Marchesi* was re-fuelled and once again ready for service.

The last recorded task undertaken at the Exmouth station by the *Louis Marchesi*, was performed on Saturday 29 June 1996. The lifeboat was on exercise, under the command of Tim Mock, when, at 19.40 hours, she was requested to assist a yacht, the *Lilly Lang*, that had gone aground at the Axmouth entrance. Before the lifeboat reached the casualty Portland Coastguard aborted the task.

Having returned to Exmouth, and refuelled, the *Louis Marchesi of Round Table,* O.N.1045, was back on her mooring at 21.00 hours without having provided a service.

Having served the Exmouth Station for two years, in 1996 The *Louis Marchesi of Round Table* was re-allocated to the Relief Fleet, before being subsequently sold by the RNLI.

During her 19 years of service with the RNLI, she performed 506 service call-outs and saved 264 lives.

In 1999, re-named the *P & O Nedlloyd Rescue,* she was being operated as a rescue boat by Waiheke Volunteer Coast Guard, New Zealand. By December 2009 she had been converted into a Houseboat/ cruiser based at Whangarei, New Zealand.

The Waveney Class Lifeboat *44-019 Louis Marchesi of Round Table.*

14
The Forward Birmingham
6 July 1996 – 20 May 2008

Type: Trent   Propulsion: Twin 800hp MAN diesels   Crew: 6/7
Official Number: 1210   Operational Number: 14-12
Length: 14.26m   Beam: 4.9m   Speed: 25 knots   Range: 250 n.miles
Displacement: 26 tonnes   Draft: Built: 1995
Builder: Green Marine (Lymington) Ltd.   Launches: 233   Lives Saved: 210
Coxswain: Keith Graham (1996-98)   Coxswain / Mechanic: Tim Mock (1998-2008)

There was much excitement in Exmouth on Sunday 23 June 1996, when the station took delivery of a new lifeboat. The boat was the Trent Class 14-12 *Forward Birmingham*. The lifeboat was escorted in to Exmouth, at 17.00 hours, by the *Louis Marchesi of Round Table*, accompanied by the Exmouth Inshore Lifeboat the *Clubs of the River Exe*, the station's boarding boat, the R.N.L.I. Teignmouth station's Atlantic 21 class I.L.B. *B-588 Frank and Dorothy*, together with a flotilla of pleasure boats and yachts.

The 14.26m (46ft 9in) Fibre Reinforced Composite hulled Trent Class lifeboat was introduced into the RNLI's Fleet in the mid 1990's and was designed to lie afloat. With a fuel capacity of 4,100 litres, (approximately 900 gallons), the twin MAN D2840LXE diesel engines, each producing 808hp, the lifeboat can reach speeds of 25 knots and operate in the worst of weathers and sea conditions. The keel is designed to totally enclose the propellers to protect them from any grounding damage.

The *Forward Birmingham* had been constructed by Green Marine (Lymington) Ltd. and fitted-out by Souter Marine Ltd., Cowes, Isle of Wight.

Several hundred people lined the beach and dockside to witness the arrival of the new hi-tech lifeboat which had twice been delayed, due to technical problems that had been discovered during testing. On the day, the *Forward Birmingham* arrived at Exmouth precisely on time; her six man crew having completed a two-day training run to the Channel Island and return via Salcombe.

Bill Sleeman, the Exmouth Lifeboat Station's Honorary Secretary said:

"There were boats everywhere. It was a lovely procession and the conditions were perfect. Everything that could make a noise was used to make a noise.

The crew are very pleased. It is very upmarket and everything we were told it would be in terms of handling. Everything is done by the press of a button."

The Trent Class *14-12 Forward Birmingham ON1210* arrives at Exmouth. Iain Grant

The new station Trent class lifeboat ON1210 *Forward Birmingham* was placed on service, at Exmouth, on Saturday 6 July 1996.

The first recorded service launch of the *Forward Birmingham* took place on Tuesday 16 July 1996 following a 'May Day' call transmitted from the yacht '*Rose Catacea*'. The call, which had been monitored by the Brixham Coast Guard, indicated that the vessel, with one person on board, was being driven ashore at the eastern end of Sandy Bay.

Slipping the moorings at 03.17 hours, Coxswain Keith Graham took the lifeboat out into fine weather, very good visibility and light airs. The sea state was smooth.

The Exmouth ILB, *Clubs of the River Exe*, had also been tasked to this service and locating the Ballerina Class yacht, succeeded in establishing a towline. Upon the arrival of the ALB, the line was transferred from the ILB and the *Rose Catacea* was towed to Exmouth Dock. This service baptism for the *Forward Birmingham* lasted for just fifty-three minutes.

Coxswain Keith Graham and the crew of the Exmouth lifeboat were out on a routine exercise, and still familiarising themselves with the new Trent Class lifeboat, on the evening of Wednesday 24 July 1966, when they received a radio communication reporting that a 11metre fishing vessel had suffered machinery failure. The position of the casualty was reported by Portland Coast Guard as being on a bearing of 170°, in Lyme Bay. The signal was received by the lifeboat at 21.10 hours. In fine weather, very good visibility, and a calm sea with a light breeze blowing from the southwest, the *Forward Birmingham* located the workboat at 22.06 hours. The cause of the machinery failure was quickly established as being a fuel problem. The weather and sea conditions were quite fortuitous as it was noted that the casualty had a faulty VHF radio, and carried neither lifejackets nor flares.

With her crew of two on board, the workboat was towed, by the lifeboat, to Lyme Regis harbour. The *Forward Birmingham* returned to Exmouth, refuelled, and was ready for service at 01.30 hours.

Coxswain Keith Graham and his crew slipped moorings at 12.40 hours on Sunday 4 August 1996, and headed the *Forward Birmingham* towards Budleigh Bay, a point some 4 miles from the Exmouth Station. The launch was in response to a request, made by the Brixham Coast Guard, for the lifeboat to join a sea and air search which was attempting to locate two missing skin divers. The location at which the two male divers had become separated from their diving support boat, an 18-foot RIB, belonging to the Exeter Divers Club, was approximately 1 mile south of Otterton Ledge. The *Forward Birmingham* arrived on the scene at 13.00 hours, and joined the Exmouth ILB, a SAR Helicopter, and other vessels in the search.

The weather was fine, visibility very good and a moderate to fresh breeze blew from the east. The sea produced moderate waves, taking a pronounced long form; white horses cresting the waves were forming.

The lifeboat had no sooner commenced a search pattern than the two missing divers were located and recovered by the helicopter, some one mile from their last reported location, having apparently been swept away from their support vessel by a sudden change in the weather.

Not all services provided by the crew of a lifeboat necessitate direct, physical assistance or intervention. Such was the service provided, on Tuesday 6 August 1996, to the 34-foot Sadler Class sail yacht *Stardust*.

Initial reports received from the Brixham Coast Guard, was of a yacht experiencing difficulty in the area of Straight Point, Exmouth. At the time of the reported incident the sea was rough, with a one metre swell, visibility, which at times was fair, was constantly reduced dramatically by heavy squalls. Coxswain Graham slipped the moorings of the *Forward Birmingham* at 11.50 hours and by 11.59 hours had located the casualty, which was on passage from Brixham to Exmouth, near the Fairway Buoy. During a temporary lull in the weather, with the crew of three remaining on board the yacht, Coxswain Graham decided to escort the casualty to her mooring in the River Exe. By 12.20 hours the *Stardust* had regained her mooring and, with no further assistance required, the Exmouth lifeboat regained her mooring at 13.00 hours.

The Naming Ceremony and Service of Dedication of the new self-righting Trent Class lifeboat took place at Exmouth Docks at 2.30pm on Friday 20 September 1996.

The naming of the lifeboat was performed by HRH The Duke of Kent, President of the Royal National Lifeboat Institution, who was formally welcomed by Mr Charles Tate, Chairman of the Exmouth Branch of the RNLI.

The Naming and Dedication Ceremony of the Trent, *14-12 Forward Birmingham ON1210*, 20 September 1996.

In the presence of Councillor David Roy, Deputy Lord Mayor of Birmingham, Mr Crocker, Chairman of the Forward Birmingham Lifeboat Campaign, formally handed-over the lifeboat to Mr David Ackland, Chairman of the RNLI. Mr Ackland, in turn, delivered the lifeboat into the keeping of the Exmouth Lifeboat Station. The lifeboat was received by Mr W. Sleeman, the Honorary Secretary of the station.

The Service of Dedication was conducted by Reverend A MacDonald, Rector, The United Benefice of Silverton, Butterleigh, Bickleigh and Cadleigh, and former Chaplain to the Exmouth Lifeboat Station.

Following the service, HRH The Duke of Kent formally named the Exmouth Lifeboat *Forward Birmingham*. In naming the lifeboat, The Duke of Kent, for the second time, cemented the tie between the great city of Birmingham and the seaside resort of Exmouth. The name of the lifeboat was derived from the name of the great West Midlands city, combined with the motto '*Forward*' which is carried on the city's Coat of Arms.

Funding for this lifeboat was raised by the citizens of Birmingham, and surrounding areas, who generously contributed to the *Forward Birmingham* lifeboat campaign. Donations in memory of W R (Bill) Bulpitt, together with his bequest, started the campaign. Other legacies towards the cost of the lifeboat included those received from Arthur Frank Buffin, Norah Kathleen Buffin, Barbara Buffin, John William Ingram, Juliet Meaking, Cissie Miller, Margaret Rose Nicholls, Albert Shaw and Robert William Howard Tett. Gifts included the support of the Belsize Charitable Trust No 1.

The generous subscriptions, which included a donation of £2,000 from the Exmouth Lions Club, when combined with other generous gifts and legacies, provided the £1,025,000 that was required to build this Tent class lifeboat.

Vic Crocker, Chairman of the Forward Birmingham Lifeboat Campaign, said:

'*The previous boat cost £65,000 about twenty-five years ago, so when we as a group of Birmingham businessmen were asked to raise £1million, we thought inflation had risen.*

Then we saw how advanced this boat is, and we wanted more than anything to achieve the target to provide this boat.'

A visitor from Birmingham, Chris Clifford commented: '*No one would pass you by without putting money in my box when I was fundraising for the Exmouth lifeboat.*'

To mark this very special occasion, over tree-hundred R.N.L.I. supporters, from Birmingham chartered a special high–speed train to travel to Devon. Prior to setting off from Birmingham, a ceremony took place at New Street Station, where the Mayor of Birmingham officially named the Class 43 unit, 43 071, *Forward Birmingham*.

The lifeboat crew were obviously delighted with the new station boat. Tim Mock, the Station Mechanic said: '*We could not wish for anything better. It is a fine boat, much more advanced than the one before.*'

Tim Mock, Coxswain / Mechanic 1998 to date.

Tim's colleague Chris Sims added: '*It's a lot more comfortable for us and those who we rescue.*'

The RNLI's spokesperson for Devon, Mary Jenner, said: '*In Devon we could not manage without the help of cities like Birmingham because we have nine lifeboats to support.*'

Among the oldest guests of honour were veteran crewmen from the first motor-powered lifeboat in Exmouth, the *Catherine Harriet Eaton*, which was placed on station in 1933.

The programme commemorating the Ceremony recorded the Officers and Crew of the Exmouth Lifeboat station as:

President: Vice Admiral Sir Ronald Brockman KCB CSI CIE CVO CBE DL
Chairman: Mr C A Tate
Vice Chairman & Hon. Secretary: Mr W Sleeman.
Hon. Treasurer: Mr L J Stapley.
Station Administration Officer: Mr B R Cole.
Committee: Mr M Green, Mr G Legg, Mr A Rodgers, Mr J Harvey, Mr R Carter.
Hon. Medical Advisors: Dr J A Davis, Dr C Stubbings
Coxswain: Keith Graham.
2nd Coxswain/Mechanic: Tim Mock.
Asst. Mechanic: Dave Perkin
Crew Members: Glen Smith, Geoff Ingram, Pete Denford, Dave Stuart, Mark Chandler, Simon Turl, Terry Wilkin, Dave Richards, Matt Graham, Steve Thompson, Mike Graham, Clive Harris, Bert Thomas, Dave Jeeves, Chris Sims, Giles White.
Deputy Launching Authorities: Andy Herbert, Ian Grant.

Hon. Secretary and Deputy Launch Authorities 2003. (l-r): Iain Grant (DLA), Mike Fagan (DLA), Frank Doyle (Hon. Secretary) and Andy Herbert (DLA). Haydn Jones

Crew member Carey Wreford. Haydn Jones

In 1996 the RNLI's dockside office building was demolished and replaced by 'temporary' cabins; these remained in used until 2009.

On her 18th birthday, in 1996, Cary Wreford's childhood ambition came to fruition when she was accepted as a member of the Exmouth lifeboat crew – the first female crew in the station's 193-year history. Since the age of 11, Cary's admiration of the lifeboat crew and fascination with the boats had drawn her closer and closer towards the lifeboat service. On several occasions Cary would take part in RNLI exercises, often offering herself as a 'casualty.' On more than one occasion she was found in the thick of things, being aboard the lifeboat when the crew responded to a 'shout.' She tried to join the crew at the age of 17 years but was told to '*try again.*' Her mother told the *Exmouth Journal*:

'*The maroons have gone off at midnight and Carey gets her bike out and pedals down there to help. She might not come back till 3.30 or 4. She's just so keen, it's incredible.*'

RNLI Dockside office buildings. Melanie Mock

Cabin office accommodation. Melanie Mock

The relief Tyne Class *47-021 The Famous Grouse ON1133.*

The relief Trent Class *14-37 Betty Huntbatch ON1274.*

The relief Trent Class *14-24 Dora Foster McDougall ON1228* and Jurassic Coastline.
Mike Rice

Carey's ambition? *'I love all of them really, but I want to be Coxswain; I think I will be one day!'*

The *Forward Birmingham* was launched on the morning of Sunday 22 December 1996, in response to a 'May Day' broadcast which had been monitored by the Portland Coastguard. As they slipped the mooring at 08.03hrs, Coxswain Keith Graham and his crew were about to engage the lifeboat on a major air and sea search.

The distress call, which had been received at 07.50 hours, appeared to have originated from the sailing vessel *Ventura*; her position being given as three-quarters of a mile from the shore, South of Budleigh Salterton. The Portland Coastguard helicopter was scrambled to the scene, together with Coastguard vessels from Sidmouth, Beer, Exmouth, Teignmouth, Lyme Regis and Torbay. Additionally the Lyme Regis RNLI lifeboat was launched together with the Sidmouth Rescue Boat.

After the initial search had failed to locate the casualty, the emergency services broadened the search area with the helicopter sweeping the area from Lyme Regis to Torbay, whilst the *Forward Birmingham* searched from Hope's Nose, Torquay to Chesil Beach, Dorset. As after four hours of searching the *Ventura* had not been traced the search was called off.

Peter Baker, Acting District Manager for Portland Coastguard estimated the cost of the helicopter search alone at more than £20,000. Mr Baker said:

'We can find no record of a yacht of that name in the whole of the South West. There was no indication of anybody in distress or any wreckage. The longer it goes on, the more likely it would seem that it was not a genuine call.'

The *Forward Birmingham* returned to station at 13.03 hours, and was refuelled and ready for service at 13.45 hours.

September 1998 saw the retirement of four crewmembers who, between them, had given nearly 60 years of service to the Exmouth lifeboat. The four men were the former Exmouth lifeboat Coxswain, Keith Graham, and crewmen Geoff Ingram, Dave Richards and Dave Stuart. Keith Graham and Geoff Ingram had both served for 18 years, during which time the Exmouth lifeboats is credited with saving 98 lives. Dave Richards had

served the station for 12 years and Dave Stuart 11 years.

In presenting their respective Service Certificates in March 1999, the RNLI's Deputy Divisional Inspector, Paul Jennings, paid tribute to the courage and professionalism of the men, when he told the assembled Exmouth lifeboat crew and Branch members,

'Anyone putting in as much time as they have done ought to be honoured as much as possible. On behalf of the RNLI and those they saved thank you very much.

I have been very impressed with the professionalism of the crew, which comes about by three things, hard work, time put in and experience generated by a station.

Those who have gone before you gained the experience and passed it down, so the ability you show is a direct reflection on these four chaps and the people who went before. It's a direct contribution to the station, so thank you very much, again.'

On Wednesday 15 September 1998, the former Second Coxswain/Mechanic of the Exmouth Station, Tim Mock, was appointed Coxswain of the Exmouth lifeboat.

The assembly signal was sounded at 21.05hrs on Thursday 20 January 2000 following a request having been received from the MRSC at Brixham to assist with the search for a missing person. The *Forward Birmingham* slipped her mooring, under the command of Coxswain Tim Mock, at 21.22hrs, and was 'on scene' in just five minutes. The 'D' Class ILB also launched.

Tim Mock and his crew were tasked to assist mobile Coast Guard Units in a shoreline search for the missing person, a 60 year old man who at 1400hrs had gone for a walk which routinely took him approximately one hour. In good visibility and a slight sea, the search was divided into two 'walk' areas, the first from Exmouth seafront to Budleigh Salterton, which was undertaken by the ALB and Coast Guard units; the second from Exmouth Rail Station to Lympstone Which was undertaken by the ILB. Portland MRSC co-ordinated the search.

The missing person was not located and the search units were stood-down at 2325hrs.

At 13.30hrs the following day, in poor misty

conditions and with a moderate sea, the *Forward Birmingham*, ILB and Boarding Boat were launched to join the Police, Royal Marines, Dartmoor Rescue Group and various volunteer groups in a combined shoreline search for a missing person. The *Forward Birmingham* returned to station at 17.00hrs.

On Wednesday 30 January 2002 the relief fleet Tyne Class lifeboat, 47-002 *Sam and Joan Woods (O.N. 1075)*, the Exmouth 'D' Class ILB, and the station's Boarding Boat were launched to assist the emergency services in locating a male person who had allegedly fallen from the sea-wall, in the vicinity of the Exmouth clock tower. The Brixham MRSC requested the assistance of the lifeboat at 21.22hrs, the assembly signal was made at 21.27 hrs and the boat slipped her mooring at 21.38hrs. The lifeboat was on scene within 3 minutes of the launch. In good visibility and a moderate sea state, the RNLI crews and two helicopters made an extensive search of the whole seafront and surf-line between Mamhead Slip and Orcombe Point but the casualty was not found. The lifeboat returned to station at 00.10hrs on Thursday 31 January.

The search for the missing man was resumed at 12.30hrs on Thursday 31 January 2002, at the request of MRSC Brixham, with the re-launch of the *Sam and Joan Woods* and the ILB. The lifeboats, Coast Guard and a helicopter unit once again methodically searched the area between Mamhead Slip and Orcombe Point but unfortunately the casualty was not found. Coxswain Tim Mock and his crew were released from the search area at 16.45hrs; by 17.00hrs the lifeboat was refuelled, on station and ready for service.

The *Sam and Joan Woods* was launched for service at 19.04hrs on Monday 4 February 2002 following a call for assistance being received, by MRSC Brixham from a Plymouth registered, 12 metre 'Sunsail 40' sailing yacht, with auxiliary engine, which had experienced engine failure 12 miles south-east of Straight Point. At the point of launch, at the location of the casualty, visibility was 20 miles; a Force 5 wind blew from the south-west and the sea was moderate with a swell height of 2 metres. A gale was forecasted as 'imminent.'

The yacht was on passage from the Solent to Plymouth, with a crew of two onboard, who having ripped the sail resorted to using the auxiliary engine. The engine had run well for a time but gradually lost power and died. The lifeboat reached the casualty at 19.04hrs, having located the yacht by radar, when the cause of the engine failure was diagnosed as being a blocked fuel filter. Due to the imminent gale forecasted, the *Sam and Joan Woods* took the 'Sunsail' in tow to Exmouth where the yacht was moored on the spare lifeboat mooring to await a mechanic. The lifeboat was once again ready for service at 22.50hrs.

The relief Tyne Class lifeboat *47-002 Sam and Joan Woods ON1075* Rick Tomlinson

The Exmouth Station Boat, the *Forward Birmingham*, responded to an emergency on Sunday 24 February 2002, which involved a response by two lifeboats and a Search and Rescue helicopter. On this occasion the *Forward Birmingham* was under the command of 2nd Coxswain Peter Denford.

The Exmouth lifeboat launched, at 12.10hrs, following the receipt of a 'Pan-Pan' alert, received by the Brixham MRSC; the broadcast had been made by the 10 meter motor fishing vessel, the *Flourish*. The sole crewman on the *Flourish* reported that, due to a broken engine cooling pipe, the vessel was taking water into the engine-room and that he anticipated that the vessel would sink within an hour. Whilst en- route to the casualty Peter Denford was made aware that Coxswain Mark Criddle and the crew of the Torbay ALB, the Severn Class *17-28 Alec and Christina Dykes (O.N.1255)* who were on exercise, had also been tasked to the casualty. The co-ordination of the rescue was passed to the Portland Coast Guard who authorised the launch of a SAR helicopter unit.

On reaching the casualty she was experiencing a moderate sea with a 2.5 metre swell. The wind was Force 5-6 blowing from the West. The vessel's fishing gear remained down. The crew of the Coastguard helicopter, *Whisky Bravo*, lowered a pump to the skipper of the *Flourish* which lowered the water level in the engine-room and enabled the skipper to affect a repair to the fractured cooling pipe. Having stood-by whilst the repair was carried out, Peter Denford put a crewman aboard and assisted in raising the fishing gear. The lifeboat escorted the *Flourish* back to Exmouth arriving at 16.35 hours. The *Forward Birmingham* was refuelled and ready for service at 17.00 hours.

Monday 7 July 2003 was a fairly typical summer day in Exmouth; at sea visibility was good and the sea state calm. Even in these tranquil conditions, the services of the men and women of the Royal National Lifeboat Institution are often called upon.

It was just after 10.30 hours that the Lifeboat Operations Manager at Exmouth received a message from the Brixham Coastguard requesting the launch of the *Forward Birmingham* to assist a passenger vessel that was in distress. The assembly signal was made at 10.36 hours and the lifeboat slipped her moorings, with Coxswain Tim Mock at the helm, and a crew of four, at 10.41 hours.

The launch of the ALB was accompanied by that of the ILB *D516 Spirit of the Exe*, with Carey Wreford as helm and Simon Turl as crew.

Alarms onboard the casualty had sounded indicating flooding of the bilge space. The 18 metre passenger vessel *Tudor Rose* had forty-four persons onboard who as precautionary measure, were reported to be donning lifejackets.

With the two lifboats standing-by, the water egress was halted and the bilges pumped out. The Tudor Rose was then escorted back to Exmouth without further incident.

A day set aside for a public relations visit resulted in a service launch when, on Monday 28 July 2003, Coxswain Tim Mock and the crew of the *Forward Birmingham* took the lifeboat along the coast to an 'open day' at Lyme Regis, Dorset Whilst alongside at Lyme Regis the lifeboat was tasked by Portland Coastguard to assis the yacht *Hoina* that, due to heavy weather, had been forced to abort an attempt to enter Axemouth Harbour.

The two person crew of the 8 metre sail yacht, with auxilary motor, had contacted Portland Coastguard by radio indicating that they were proceeding slowly towards Lme Regis harbour. The casualty was encountering squally weather with visibility reduced to one mile. A southwesterly Force 6/7 wind was producing a moderate to rough sea and a 2 meter swell. Expressing concern for the safety of the crew of the *Hoina*, the Lyme Regis Harbour Master requested the assistance of the lifeboat. The *Forward Birmingham* cast-off at 19.53 hours, located the casualty at 20.05 hours and ecorted the *Hoina* in to Lyme Regis at 20.25 hours. Having returned to Exmouth the lifeboat was on station, refuelled and ready for service at 22.50 hours.

The *Forward Birmingham*, was launched at 11.54 hours on Saturday 8 November 2003. On this occasion the launch was requested by the Portland Coastguard following a report being made by a Pilot of a Light Aircraft to Exeter Air Traffic Control of the sighting of a yellow coloured life-raft 1 mile ESE of Straigh Point, Exmouth. The lifeboat was launched to search an area East-southeast of Staight Point and to give support to the relief inshore lifeboat, *D429 RJM*, which had also been launched.

On arrival at the scene the two lifeboats undertook a methodical search, albeit nothing was found. There were Northern and Southern DZ buoys within the search area and it was believed that one of these buoys, which are yellow in colour, may have been mistaken as life-raft.

In December 2005 trials were undertaken at Exmouth, to evaluate beach conditions, near the ILB station, for launching and indeed to assess the station for its suitability to house a Mersey class lifeboat. These trials involved personnel and crew from other carriage stations around the country and involved the RNLI's relief fleet Mersey Class lifeboat, *12-004 Royal Shipwright (ON1162),* and Talus tractor, 'T97'.

The Mersey Class lifeboat can either lie afloat or be launched from a slipway, being the RNLI's first 'fast' carriage lifeboat, making the Class ideal for operating in shallower waters.

RNLI records show that in 2005 the Exmouth station was the busiest lifeboat station in Devon, launching 132 times and rescuing 110 people. From January 2000 to December 2005 the

Exmouth all weather and inshore lifeboats undertook a total of 545 service launches. The station is credited with rescuing 437 persons during that period, and recovering boats and equipment to the value of £1.7M.

On Wednesday 28 June 2006, the Royal National Lifeboat Institution revealed their initial plans for a new Exmouth boathouse to representatives of the Town Council. The proposed new building would bring both the station's lifeboats together under one roof and

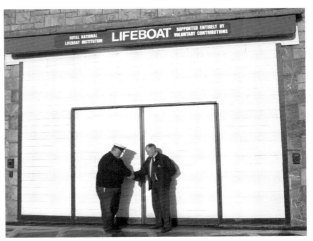

Right: Tim Mock (Coxswain) and Kevin Riley (Lifeboat Operations Manager) finally lock up the ILB boathouse to move to the new boathouse.

Below: Inside the new boathouse.   Melanie Mock

ensure the RNLI volunteer crews could react to incidents 24 hours a day. At that time the Trent class all weather lifeboat, *Forward Birmingham*, was tidally restricted by it's moorings at Exmouth Docks which meant that it could not launched for service across the bar at low water.

Simon Pryce, RNLI Divisional Inspector, explained that the new building would bring Exmouth RNLI into the 21st century:

'Our biggest difficulty has been the tidal restriction on the all weather lifeboat. This new boathouse at Maer Rocks would initially house a Mersey class, which is an all weather carriage lifeboat that can be launched from a special trailer at any state of the tide. Both it and the inshore lifeboat would be stationed together and all the necessary facilities needed to support the lifeboats and the volunteer crews would be available on one site.'

2007 saw the Exmouth coxswain and crew carrying out further carriage trials, this time with the Mersey Class lifeboat *12-11 Lifetime Care (ON 1148)* and Talus tractor 'T91'. These trials were carried out at the site of the proposed new lifeboat station. The trials proved a success and established the site of the new lifeboat station at Queens Drive, Exmouth.

ON1210 slipped her mooring at 05.33 hours on Sunday 13th April 2008, to assist police in the search for a missing/distressed female who was thought to be in the Exmouth to Straight Point area. The ILB, *D-669 George Bearman*, was also launched.

Within a few minute of the launch the missing person telephoned the police to report that she was safe and well. Both boats returned to station.

This proved to be the last operational service undertaken at Exmouth by the Trent Class lifeboat, *Forward Birmingham*. The Forward Birmingham, which had served as the Exmouth station boat for just under twelve years, had undertaken 233 operational launches and saved a total of 210 lives.

A new era in the history of the Exmouth lifeboat station was marked, on Wednesday 23 April 2008, with the arrival of the all-weather lifeboat, the Mersey Class *12-21 Margaret Jean (ON 1178)*. Ultimately, the *Margaret Jean* was to replace the *Forward Birmingham*. During the following week crew members were engaged on training to familiarise themselves with the layout, systems, stowage, machinery, equipment, and capabilities of the lifeboat.

14-12 Forward Birmingham *ON1210*.
16 May 2008. Mike Rice

Cox'n and crew of 2007, (l-r): David Preece, Roy Stott, Lee Comley, Dr Colin May (Lifeboat Medical Advisor), Andrew Stott, Andy Smith and Tim Mock (Coxswain/Mechanic).

The Exmouth station was visited by the Divisional Inspector and Engineer, on Thursday 1 May 2008, when both the lifeboat and crew were passed for operational service.

With the arrival of the *Margaret Jean* the end of years of negotiations, trials and fund-raising was in sight. The combined efforts and hard work of all concerned were rewarded on Tuesday 6 May 2008 with the 'tarmac breaking' ceremony which marked the start of the building of the new Exmouth Lifeboat Station. Members of the Exmouth RNLI were joined by representatives of East Devon District Council, Exmouth Town Council and the constructors company, Dawnus Construction. Guests of Honour at the ceremony were Mrs Gill Smith (niece of the late crew member William Carder) and Henry Mock (the son of Coxswain Tim Mock), who took turns on the excavator to remove the first scoops of tarmac.

On the evening of Monday 19 May 2008, the *Forward Birmingham* was opened to the public before, after twelve years of service, on Tuesday 20 May 2008, the Trent class lifeboat gracefully bowed out from being the Exmouth station lifeboat and was allocated to the RNLI's Relief Fleet.

During her time on the Exmouth station, the *Forward Birmingham* was launched on 233 occasions, rescuing 210 people and recovering craft to the value of £182,200. The lifeboat also carried out one rescue while 'on passage', assisting three persons.

The Trent class lifeboat was replaced by a Mersey class boat which would prove to be more suited to the shallow conditions in the Swashway channel.

Tim Mock, RNLI Coxswain at Exmouth, said that although the station was delighted with the new Mersey class lifeboat, it was sad to see their former lifeboat leave for the last time:

'Forward Birmingham has served us well over the last 12 years and her departure will mark

the end of another RNLI era in Exmouth. When thinking back over the years it is important not to forget that during her service here we completed many successful rescues but were also involved in incidents with loss of life. Whilst not wishing to dwell on such tragic events, they were difficult times for the crew who acted in a professional and capable manner with the best boat the RNLI could provide.'

Operational status declared at the new Lifeboat Station: 20th November 2009.
(l-r aboard lifeboat) Dave Perkin (Asst Mech), Tim Mock (Cox/Mechanic), Mark Sansom (Asst Mech), Adrian Carey (Divisional Inspector South), Scott Ranft (Dep Cox), Steve Hockings-Thompson (Dep Cox) and Giles White (Dep Cox) kneeling.   (l-r) Nigel Pearce, Mark Cockman, Steve Satchell, Andy Smith, Andrew Stott, Roger Jackson (Stn Training Co-ordinator), Richard Vine, Ian Taylor, Guy Munnings, Tom Angell, Dr Colin May, Kevin Riley (Lifeboat Operations Manager), Pete Thomas (DLA), Dave Jackman (Deputy Divisional Engeneer South), Chris Sims, Neil Hurlock (DLA), David Page (Divisional Engineer South), Pete Renouf, Don Hodgkinson (DLA), Dave Preece, Hedley Saunders, Tommo Thompson, Tiny Haynes, Dave Ashman, Rob Kathro, and Mark Newton. Mike Powell

15
The Margaret Jean
20 May 2008 –

Type: Mersey   *Propulsion:* 2 x Caterpillar 3208T diesels   *Crew:* 6
Official Number: 1178   *Operational Number:* 12-21
Length: 12.00m   *Beam:* 3.8m   *Speed:* 16 knots   *Range:* 140n.miles
Weight: 14 tons   *Draft:* 1m   *Built:* 1991   *Builder:* FBM Marine Ltd. Cowes.
Launches: ??   *Lives Saved:* ??   *Coxswain/Mechanic:* Tim Mock

The Mersey class lifeboat, which was introduced in to the RNLI's fleet in 1988, was designed as the Institutions first 'fast' carriage lifeboat. The design allowed primarily for the boat to be launched from a carriage but the class could equally lie afloat or be launched from a slipway. The propellers are fully protected by partial tunnels and substantial bilge keels allowing the boat to take the ground without damage. Each boat is equipped with a comprehensive range of electronics including full MF and VHF DSC radio equipment, DGPS Navigator and electronic chart system, VHF/DF, Radar and weather sensors.

In common with her predecessors the boat, destined for the Exmouth station, was to be moored afloat, on the River Exe.

The first Mersey Class lifeboat, the unnamed *ON 1119*, was built in 1987, undergoing sea trials during 1987-88. The first lifeboat of the class to enter the RNLI's operational fleet became the Bridlington lifeboat in 1988; she was the *12-001 Peggy and Alex Caird, (ON1124)*.

With the withdrawal of the Trent Class lifeboat, *Forward Birmingham*, from the Exmouth Station, on 20 May 2008 the Mersey Class lifeboat *12-21 Margaret Jean, (ON1178)* was designated the station's 'temporary' lifeboat.

Construction of the lifeboat had been carried out at the yard of FBM Marine Ltd. Cowes, between 1 June 1989 and 2 December 1991.

Whilst under construction, on 9 April 1990, the *Margaret Jean* was allocated to the Relief Fleet, where she remained until 1998. The lifeboat carries a brass Donor Plate, on a timber backing, bearing the words:

"RNLB Margaret Jean. This lifeboat was the gift of Peter and Jean Bath of Cambridgeshire".

The Naming and Dedication Ceremony was held at the yard of FBM Marine Ltd, Cowes, on Tuesday 12 November 1991. The *Margaret Jean* was named in memory of the late Mrs Bath. Whilst on trials at Exmouth the *Margaret Jean* proved her worth in a low-water rescue on Thursday 8 May 2008 when she successfully negotiated the

Trent *14-12 Forward Birmingham* with *Mersey 12-21 Margaret Jean.* Melanie Mock

Swashway channel to assist a yachtsman who had run aground. The stations former Trent class lifeboat would not have been able to launch due to the state of the tide.

Tim Mock, the RNLI Coxswain at Exmouth, saw the 22-foot yacht grounding in broken seas on the seaward side of the Pole Sands and launched the *Margaret Jean* together with the inshore lifeboat, the *George Bearman,* to assist the stranded vessel. Within half an hour, on the rising tide, the sailing boat had been towed clear of the sand.

The Mersey Class boat made all the difference to the rescue, as Kevin Riley, RNLI Lifeboat Operations Manager at Exmouth, explained:

'The Trent class lifeboat was tidally restricted and couldn't leave her moorings for around two hours each side of low tide. We wouldn't have been able to use her today. But the Mersey with its shallower draft was able to negotiate the channel successfully allowing both lifeboats to work together in assisting the yacht. It's proof that the Mersey is the ideal lifeboat for Exmouth, especially with the

channel changing and silting up so quickly.'

Once the yacht had been taken off the sand, a member of the lifeboat crew navigated the yacht into Exmouth docks as both lifeboats had been further tasked to assist three kite surfers who were experiencing difficulties off Exmouth's main beach.

In July 2008 the *12-21 Margaret Jean,* was officially designated the Exmouth station lifeboat.

With the anticipated date of occupancy of the new station boathouse approaching, 2009 saw the practical commencement of operational planning to house the Mersey Class ALB and 'D' Class ILB within the same building. On Tuesday 14 April 2009 the station took delivery of the 19 tonne Talus tractor 'T108', and carriage, which would facilitate the slipway launch of the Mersey Class lifeboat. Final slipway trials were completed whilst the *Margaret Jean* was in refit; the relief boat used in the trials being *12-33 Fisherman's Friend* ON1192.

Dave Page, RNLI Divisional Engineer commented:

Mersey *12-21 Margaret Jean ON 1178* entering boathouse.
Melanie Mock

Above: Arrival in Exmouth of Mersey Class *12-21 Margaret Jean ON1178.* Melanie Mock

Left: Dedication of RNLI Memorial, Poole, 3 September 2009. (l-r James Seed (Portsmouth RNLI), Hilary Seed (Great Granddaughter of Coxswain Henry Squire who died whilst launching the lifeboat in 1907) and Coxswain Tim Mock. Melanie Mock

Below left: RNLI's National Memorial, Poole, Dorset. RNLI/Tony Roddam

Below right: The station takes delivery of the Talus Tractor 14 April 2009 Melanie Mock

"It's going very well. The equipments been working really well, the volunteers have given up their time and put their heart and soul into this and have worked really hard to have achieved the standard they have got to."

"The boat remained operational at all times throughout the training, and is put back on the mooring each night. This week the boat has been launched and recovered many times and attracted quite a lot of interest by people visiting the beach."

With the development of the new lifeboat station nearing completion, debate and speculation continued in respect of the future use of the 'old lifeboat station', the lease on which was due to expire in May 2010. The speculation was put to rest when it was announced that the RNLI's beach lifeguards would take over the building as a support centre for its East Devon units.

Steve Instance, RNLI Lifeguard Inspector, explained that the old building would provide back-up for the new boathouse near Maer Rocks; he said:

'This building will provide a key support base for the four extremely busy beaches in East Devon. Spare RNLI lifeguard equipment will be based here as will the two RNLI lifeguard supervisors for the area who need office space. We will also use the old boathouse as a base for lifeguard training before and during the season.'

The Royal National Lifeboat Institution's Annual Rescue Statistics, released on Friday, 30 January 2009, revealed that in 2008 Poole, Dorset, was busiest lifeboat station in the South-west region where the crews launched 156 times, rescuing 213 people. Exmouth was second busiest station with 125 launches being followed by Falmouth, Cornwall.

At 12.20 hours on Thursday 3 September 2009, a one-minute silence was observed by lifeboat crew and supporters at lifeboat stations throughout the United Kingdom and Republic of Ireland in remembrance, and as a mark of respect, to the many brave people, connected with the charity, who have lost their lives helping to save others at sea. The period of silence coincided with that observed during the Ceremony of Dedication for the first official Royal National Lifeboat Institution Memorial, which was unveiled by HRH The Duke of Kent at RNLI Headquarters, Poole, Dorset.

The RNLI Memorial, designed by Sam Holland ARBS, stands more than 4.5m in height and depicts a person in a boat saving another from the water, symbolising the history, and future, of the RNLI in its most basic and humanitarian form. It also bears the names of those who gave their lives for the benefit of others.

The Exmouth lifeboat crew and families remembered, in particular, Coxswain Henry Squire who died in 1907 whilst launching the *Joseph Somes* and William Carder who was tragically lost from the *Maria Noble* on Christmas Day, 25 December 1956.

RNLI Chief Executive Andrew Freemantle, CBE, explained:

'The RNLI Memorial is a tribute to the many hundreds of people who have given their lives selflessly to save others over the last two hundred years. Its location, in front of The Lifeboat College here in Poole, is truly fitting and will inspire generations of lifesavers from all over the British Isles who will train here in the years to come.'

There were celebrations at the Exmouth lifeboat station on Friday 21st November 2009 when Adrian Carey, RNLI Divisional Inspector (South) announced that, following rigorous inspection, the new lifeboat station had been passed as being *'Fully Operational.'* Mr. Carey commented:

'It was clear to me that all was going smoothly on Friday. The lifeboat crew and shore-helpers are fully trained and confident in launch and recovery procedures and it was a pleasure to inform them of the good news. The main operational change at Exmouth involves launching and recovering the all-weather lifeboat over the beach using a tractor and carriage. This is a procedure that requires the crew to follow safe and rehearsed procedures which I am pleased to say I was able to witness on Friday. I am also now fully satisfied that the excellent new facility at Exmouth lifeboat station is ready to be used operationally by both the inshore and all-weather lifeboats. My thanks go to all who have made this possible and the local support for the volunteers who keep the station going is very much

The New Exmouth Lifeboat Station (2009). Bill Davies

appreciated. The future of our 24 hour availability at Exmouth is now secure."

Tim Mock, Coxswain/Mechanic of the Exmouth lifeboat said:

"It is a very proud moment in my career to be involved in a new state-of-the-art boathouse. To have been involved with the concept, design and build phase was challenging but equally rewarding."

Kevin Riley, the Exmouth Lifeboat Operations Manager commented:

"The first phone call I made after Adrian declared we were operational in the new

station was to Brixham Coastguard. This was a call I had been looking forward to making. I know we have one of the best boathouses in the country and one the crew and town needed to allow us to be operational 24 hours a day - and provide the service of saving lives at sea 24/7 every week of the year. To have our volunteer crews out of those cabins and into these new facilities is such an asset. All this would not have been possible without the generous donations from the public, whether that be pennies in the tin or tens of thousands of pounds, we should all be very proud of what has been achieved."

The *Margaret Jean* was launched on her first 'shout' from the new lifeboat station at 17.54

hours on Wednesday 17th March 2010. The launch was made as the result of the Brixham Coast Guard monitoring the words *'May Day'* broadcasted on VHF Channel 16; no other transmission was received. Coordinates obtained and plotted by the Coast Guard indicated that the call had originated somewhere between Torbay and Orcombe Point, Exmouth, a 13 mile stretch of coastline. Visibility, in fog, was near zero.

In support of the *Margaret Jean*, at 18.10 hours Second Coxswain Roger Good lunched the Torbay lifeboat, the Severn Class *17-28 Alec and Christina Dykes ON1255*, to search a line 018 deg. from Berry Head, Brixham.

In near zero visibility, both lifeboat crews carried out a visual and radar search but with nothing untoward being found, the search was called off at 20.30 hours; the lifeboats returning to their respective stations.

Kevin Riley, RNLI Lifeboat Operations Manager, Exmouth, explained:

'A diligent search was carried out in adverse conditions with zero visibility. There was good coordination carried out by Brixham Coastguards and RNLI lifeboats. The crew here at Exmouth were carriage launched in ten minutes and on scene by fifteen. Compared to the Trent, I would estimate launch time was cut down by 40 per cent.'

Tim Mock, Coxswain of the Margaret Jean added:

'We were more than ready for our first launch as we have been training intensively by the RNLI charity for the last few months. The whole process went very well and a great credit to all our volunteers on the lifeboat crew and new launching crew. The search was quite intensive with virtually no visibility requiring high levels on concentration on chart work, radar and the navigation plotter.'

16
The Inshore Lifeboats

The 1960's were the golden years for the tourist industry of South Devon, with the traditional family seaside holidays being at their peak. These popular family holidays, together with an ever-growing number of foreign visitors and students visiting our resorts, saw a vast increase in the number of persons using the coastline for recreational purposes. Persons, with little or no knowledge of seafaring took to the water in small fishing craft, dinghies, cruisers and yachts. Many of the more adventurous needed rescuing from the cliffs and rocks as they became cut off by the tide. Being acutely aware of these problems, together with the increasing and varying demands upon the service, the RNLI readily identified the need for a small, fast, shallow draft craft that could be launched, and manned, by the minimum number of crew in a matter of minutes.

With these factors in mind, in May 1963, the RNLI introduced the first of its fleet of high-speed, inflatable, Inshore Rescue Boats, (IRB's), later to develop into the 'D' Class lifeboats, or ILB's (Inshore Lifeboats). The hull of the first IRB's was constructed of neoprene/nylon; the craft were 15'6" in length, driven at 20 knots by a 40 h.p. outboard-engine. These small, agile, craft, manned by a crew of two or three, depending upon the service required, met the design and operational requirements admirably. They proved to be able to operate in shallow water or confined space, into which the larger lifeboats could not manoeuvre, and in other circumstances when the full service of the All Weather Lifeboat, (ALB) was not necessarily required. Such was the case at Exmouth where the launch of the lifeboat was often hindered by tidal restrictions. It was later to be proven that the service provided by the crew of an ILB regularly complimented the operation of the station's lifeboat thus providing a flexible and formidable resource.

D-89 (Unnamed)
1966–1972

The first Inshore Rescue Boat to be placed at Exmouth, the 'D89', arrived on station in May 1966, the boat being kept at the Lifeboat Display Centre, the former lifeboat house. To launch the ILB it was necessary to cross the sea road and launch from the beach.

The I.R.B. was instrumental in saving four lives within four hours of being commissioned on Whit-Sunday, 29 May 1966. It was at 15.35 hours that the Hon. Secretary of the Exmouth Lifeboat station, Mr C.E. Chown, received information from the police that a number bathers were in

Exmouth's first *IRB, No. 89*, is prepared for launch.

difficulty about two miles south-west of Exmouth, off Dawlish Warren. The crew of the Inshore Rescue Boat responded immediately and after battling their way through Bank Holiday crowds and traffic, helmsman Peter Rowsell and his brother Brian Rowsell, Coxswain of the lifeboat, launched the boat within 10 minutes of the alert. Throughout the morning a strong wind, gusting to gale force, had been blowing from the east, but at the time of launch had diminished to a force 4 – 5 and veered to the east-south-east.

Although visibility was good, it was half an hour after high water, on a neap tide, and the crew of the IRB found that they had to contend with a difficult swell. The state of the tide however allowed the IRB to take a course through the Western way, inshore of the Monster Sand but as the boat left the shelter of the Monster Sand, the crew found a heavy swell breaking. Without warning, the IRB was struck, on the port-side, by a heavy sea which stood her up on to her starboard sponson. Both Peter and Brian Rowsell were thrown from their craft into the water. Miraculously both men regained the safety of the lifeboat, restarted the engine and continued on course reaching the casualties within 10 minutes of the launch. Peter Rowsell engaged the engine neutral and the two brothers used oars to manoeuvre the boat up to the bathers. Three swimmers were taken onboard the lifeboat, one of whom was in need of urgent medical attention.

The casualties were landed immediately and a male person was immediately transferred to the Devon & Exeter Hospital.

Whilst the lifeboat was ashore, disembarking the casualties, it was learnt that one swimmer was unaccounted for. Peter and Brian Rowsell launched their lifeboat and once again battled their way out through the breaking surf to search for the missing swimmer. Again the IRB was struck by a freak wave, throwing the lifeboat crew into the sea for a second time. At 17.25 hours the Exmouth lifeboat, was launch, as was a helicopter from R.A.F. Chivenor. When the Exmouth lifeboat reached the scene, Peter and Brian Rowsell were relieved by a fresh crew. The crew was change on two further occasions before the search for the missing swimmer was abandoned. The lifeboat and the IRB returned to their respecting stations at 21.00 hours. The missing casualty was not found.

For the outstanding courage displayed throughout this rescue, the RNLI awarded Peter and Brian Rowsell the Institute's Certificate on Vellum. The Vellums were presented by Cllr. T.C. Buckingham at a meeting of the Exmouth Urban Council. Amid great applause, Cllr. Buckingham said:

'*We are very proud of you indeed and very pleased to have you here tonight. What you did was equal to anything in the annuls of Exmouth.*'

At 11.30 hours on Friday 4 April, 1969, the Hon. Secretary of the Exmouth station received notification from Coastguard that a small boat, with two persons onboard, had capsized near the Western Way outside Pole Sands. Within 10 minutes a crew had been mustered and the IRB launched in to a light south-easterly breeze with a corresponding sea. It was three hours after high water that the crew of the IRB found the casualties clinging to the hull of their upturned boat. The two persons were take onboard the IRB and were landed safely at Exmouth where they were transferred to Hospital by ambulance. Both casualties were treated for exposure and shock.

The IRB returned to her station at 12.30 hours.

Between 1966 and 1973, the 'D89' was credited with 24 Service Launches and 13 Lives Saved.

D-214 (Unnamed)
1972–1977

Exmouth's new 'Zodiac 3', Inshore Lifeboat, '*D214*', was the centre of attraction, on Sunday 10 June 1973 when, in a ceremony held on the slipway opposite the Display Centre, Mr Ricky Wheeler, President of the local Rotarians, presented a cheque for £500 to Admiral Sir Wilfred Wood, the late Chairman of the Royal National Lifeboat Institution. In his opening address, the Admiral referred to '*the excellent record of Exmouth in supporting its own lifeboats.*' The Rotarians, he said, had decided to make the local branch of the RNLI its main fund-raising object for the year.

Colonel G.A. Haward, Chairman of the Local Branch, presented a cheque for £300, on behalf of the Branch, the sum having been raised by donations in memory of Col. Haward's son-in-law who had died in a boating accident the previous year. Together the cheques paid fully for the new lifeboat and her equipment.

After the formal presentations, the Rev. R.T. Urwin, Rector of Littleham-cum-Exmouth blessed the boat and wished God's speed to her and her crew. The boat was then launched and gave a demonstration of rescuing swimmer 'in trouble' from the sea.

Typical of the type of service undertaken by the ILB's was that carried out on Monday 9 September 1974 when the D-214 was launched, at 19.03 hours, in response to a report of a youth stranded on cliffs near Straight Point. Having reached the distress youth within ten minutes, the crew of the D-214 were confronted by a heavy sea and swell rebounding from the face of the cliff. A member of the crew was put ashore; he scrambled up the 30-foot cliff and assisted the 14 year-old boy to the safety of the lifeboat. They boy was the conveyed to the nearby beach were he was reunited with his parents. D-214 regained the boathouse at 19.37 hours.

During her time on station as the Exmouth ILB, the D214 was credited with 122 Service Launches and saving 51 lives.

D-255 (Unnamed)
1977~1988

On Saturday 14 May 1977 members of the RNLI's Birmingham Area Lifeboat Guild travelled to Exmouth for the Handing-over Ceremony of the new Inshore Lifeboat, the 'D' Class boat, the D-255. Once again Exmouth had been provided with a lifeboat courtesy of the people of Birmingham. On this occasion the appeal had been launched by the boat *Birmingham Evening Mail*.

The boat was formally handed over by the Assistant Editor of the *Birmingham Evening Mail*, Mr Clem Lewis.

Sunday 23 May 1982 saw the crew of the D-255, Tim Mock, Kipper Sargeant and Chris Douglas, engaged on a marathon three-hour rescue mission. That afternoon members of canoe clubs were holding a race from Dawlish Warren to Exmouth. The boat was launched at 15.15 hours when, in deteriorating weather conditions, competitors were reported to be getting in to difficulty. Upon reaching an up-turned canoe, at the southern most point of the Pole Sands, the occupant was found slumped across her canoe in a

Rescue by *D-225* of Simon Hill, cut off by tide at Orcombe Point. Helm Clive Harris, crew Chris Douglas. 12 June 1983. Courtesy Colin Lee

state of total exhaustion. She was recovered into the ILB and rendered First Aid. The ILB crew then located two more exhausted female competitors who, having suffered capsize, were unable to up-right their canoe. The girls were also recovered into the lifeboat.

Whilst returning to the shore the lifeboat crew found two male canoeists who, although apparently in some difficulty, declined assistance. The men eventually made their own way ashore.

The three rescued girls, Sandra Davies, Kathryn Edge and Justine Clark were landed back at Dawlish and placed into the care of the race organisers.

The D-255 was immediately tasked to search for a further three male competitors, who had been reported missing. The men, all from the Serpentine Club, London, later reached land safely at Dawlish Warren and Exmouth.

Whilst returning to station, the ILB crew were tasked yet again, this time to assist two children who, on a rising tide, had been cut-off and stranded on rocks at Orcombe Point, Exmouth. Whilst en-route to Orcombe, the engine of the inshore lifeboat failed and the radio aerial snapped. Tim Mock successfully restarted the engine, only to be informed that the two children had made their own way to safety.

Commenting on the whole operation, to a reporter from the *'Herald'*, Mr Derek Sargeant, Deputy Launching Authority for the station said:

'During the three hour operation, the crew displayed great persistence in the face of deteriorating weather and mechanical conditions.'

On the evening of Sunday 12 June 1983, helmsman Clive, Harris and crewman Christopher Douglas launched the *D255* to go to the assistance of a local 14-year-old boy who had become trapped below the cliffs at Orcombe Point. A Coastguard cliff-rescue team had also been alerted and was standing-by. The crew of the *D255* located the casualty beyond Maer Rocks, having been cut off by a swiftly rising tide. Clive Harris initially tried to anchor and veer down to the boy but in the confused sea the anchor would not hold. Clive Harris, and his crewman Christopher Douglas, made further attempts to approach the stranded youth but the breaking wave and back swell made control of the lifeboat extremely difficult. Finally Clive Harris made a 'running-pass' and judging the right moment, called to the casualty to jump from the rocks, into the lifeboat. This manoeuvre, which needed great skill and judgement, proved successful and the casualty was subsequently returned safely to the beach.

Mr Colin Lee, of Bideford, an eyewitness to the incident, told a local reporter:

'There was a strong current and a heavy swell. There was no way the lad could get around the rocks. It was quite a tricky manoeuvre for the lifeboat. They had to make two or three attempts to get into the rocks where the boy was trapped as there was a bit of a swell running.'

For this service Helmsman Clive Harris received a *'Letter of Thanks'* from the Royal National Lifeboat Institution.

D-364 *Clubs of the River Exe* 1988~1997

On Monday 23 May 1988 *D-364* was placed on station at Exmouth. The craft had an overall length of 15' 6", a beam of 6' 4", and weighed 550 lbs. She was powered by a single 40hp. outboard engine mounted on a wooden transom. The lifeboat had a top speed of over 20 knots and could

remain on service for at least two hours. The flexible hull and inflatable sponsons were divided into compartments. Being constructed of an exceptionally tough nylon, coated with neoprene/hypalon, the inflatable could come into contact with rocks, piers and other craft, usually without sustaining serious damage. The construction of the craft made her completely stable; the buoyancy tubes making her unsinkable. The 'D' class was equipped with a VHF radio, first aid kit, flares and a spare propeller.

The crew, which comprised a helmsman and one or two crewmen, knelt on a mattress which gave protection from the pounding and slamming in the waves. The RNLI declared that the lifeboat would be *'generally used in moderate seas. The 15' 6" 'D' Class with a single engine is only used during daylight other than in exceptional circumstances such as bright moonlight.'*

Donated by the Water Sports Clubs of the River Exe, the Handing-over Ceremony and Service of Dedication of the boat was held at the head of the slipway, opposite the Lifeboat Display centre, Exmouth, at 3pm on Saturday 10 September 1988. Mr C.A. Tate, Chairman of the Exmouth Station Branch, opened the proceedings. Captain A.G. McCrum RN, a member of the Committee of Management, presented the Institution's Silver badge to Mr. L.J. Stapley, Chairman of the Exmouth Guild, RNLI, and Honorary Treasurer, Exmouth Station Branch.

Mr Gordon Mortimer, President of the Starcross Fishing and Cruising Club handed over the lifeboat, on behalf of the River Exe Watersports Clubs, to Captain McCrum who accepted the boat on behalf of the Institution. Captain McCrum, in turn, handed the lifeboat into the safe keeping of Mr D.W.H. Sargeant, Honorary Secretary of the Exmouth Station Branch, who accepted it on behalf of the Branch.

The Service of Dedication was conducted by the Revered Mike Vincent, Honorary Chaplain of the Exmouth Lifeboat Station. Music was provided by the Band of the 4th (Volunteer) Battalion, Devon and Dorset Regiment, under the direction of WO1 (Bandmaster) Dyer, and the Choir of St. Peter's School, Lympstone.

The D-364 carried the name *'Clubs of the River Exe.'*

D-364 was launched on the afternoon of Friday 17 June 1988 to assist a number of children who

The Naming of ILB D-364 *Clubs of the River Exe* 10 September 1988.

had been cut off by an incoming tide, on rocks, at Straight Point, Exmouth. The lifeboat was launch at 17.00 hours and reached the casualties by 17.10 hours. Initially three children, all of who were suffering from hyperthermia and one whom had additionally suffered an arm injury, were taken aboard the ILB and conveyed to a waiting ambulance at Sandy Bay. Returning immediately to the scene the ILB crew took of a further six children, transferring the to the Exmouth Harbour Patrol boat. The rescue culminated in the ILB taking off s further five children, and their teacher, landing all safely before returning to station at 18.10 hours.

This rescue established the pattern of many rescues which were to be undertaken by *Clubs of the River Exe*, comprising the rescue of person stranded on rocks, windsurfers who were in difficulty, and those who suffered injury as the result of cliff falls.

D-*516 Spirit of the Exe* ### 1997~2006

On Friday 27 May 1997 the RNLI placed the second D Class lifeboat to be donated by the Water Sports Clubs of the River Exe, on station at Exmouth. The boat designed to carry a crew of 2/3, was 16' 3" (4.95m) in length and has a beam of 6' 7" (2.0m). Her weight was 745lbs (338kg) and she was fitted with a 40hp Mariner outboard engine that provided 3-hour endurance at 20 knots.

She was handed over to the Exmouth Station, at a Naming and Service of Dedication, held at the

Handing over & Dedication Ceremony programme, *Clubs of the River Exe.*

head of the slipway opposite the Lifeboat Display Centre, at 2pm on Saturday 9 August 1997.

The proceedings, having been opened by Mr Bill Sleeman, Vice-Chairman of the Exmouth Station Branch, continued with Mr Rodney Turner, Chairman of the River Exe Combined Water Sports Clubs, handing over the 'D' Class boat to the Royal National Lifeboat Institution. Mr Richard Barclay FCIB, A Member of the RNLI's Committee of Management accepted the boat on behalf of the Institution and delivered it into the car of the Exmouth Station. The boat was accepted by Mr Bill Sleeman.

The Service of Dedication was conducted by the Reverend Graham Dench, Superintendent of the Royal National Mission to Deep Sea Fishermen. Music was provided by the Lympstone Band, Musical Director Mr Charlie Fleming and, following an address by Mr Les Vipond, Divisional Inspector of Lifeboat, on the development of the 'D' Class lifeboat, Mr Gordon Mortimer, founder

The Handing-over Ceremony and Service of Dedication of *D-364 Clubs of the River Exe*, 10 September 1988.

The Exmouth ILB *D-516 Spirit of the Exe* with the relief Trent *14-01 Earl and Countess Mountbatten ON 1180*. ILB: (l-r) David Preece, Ian Taylor and Roger Jackson   Aboard Trent (l-r): Lee Comley, Scott Ranft (Dep Cox), Tim Mock (Cox/Mech), Carey Wreford, Steve Hockings-Thompson (Dep Mech) and Roy Stott.

of the River Exe Combined Water Sports Clubs, named the lifeboat the *D-516 Spirit of the Exe*.

On the evening of Thursday 25 June 1998, a local youth Andrew Collins, aged 11, spotted a young couple stranded on rocks at Straight Point, Exmouth. The alarm was raised and both the all-weather lifeboat, *Forward Birmingham*, and the Inshore Lifeboat, *Spirit of the Exe* were launch.

On their arrival at the scene, the boats encountered a heavy swell and confused sea; waves were breaking on rocks and, on a rising tide, they had to endure a ferocious back swell where waves broke at the foot of the cliff.

Showing exceptional seamanship, the helmsman of the ILB, Mark Chandler took the 'D' Class boat into the swell, between the rocks, to reach the stranded casualties.

Two runs were made to rescue the trapped couple. The first run necessitated crewman David Jeeves entering the water to entice a young girl from the rocks, and into the ILB, before transferring her to the *Forward Birmingham*. The ILB crew then re-entered the breaking seas and back-swell to rescue the youth. The youth was also transferred to the *Forward Birmingham*.

Speaking after the rescue Keith Graham, the Exmouth lifeboat coxswain, in describing the rescue said:

'*Mark did well. Because of the position of those youngsters, on a ledge in a rocky cove, he had to manoeuvre the boat bows in. He held the boat there while a crewman helped one of the youngsters over the bows, then went astern to transfer her to the big boat, before going in for the second casualty.*

There was a three foot swell running – quite big for a small boat – and the rescue called for skill and seamanship. Mark manoeuvred the boat very well.

The *Forward Birmingham* landed the young couple, from Stoke-on-Trent, at Exmouth Docks, cold and wet but none the worse for their experience.

The *D-516 Spirit of the Exe* was launched, at 15.17 hours on Friday 17 September 1999, to assist the occupants of a dinghy which had been reported in trouble off Straight Point, Exmouth. The dinghy had been swamped by seas, whipped up by south-westerly winds of force 4–5; the engine had failed and the craft was in imminent danger of being driven onto rocks. The ILB's crew was Mark Chandler and the brothers Roy and Karl Stott. The inshore boat reached the casualty within ten minutes of launch but the dinghy had already been driven into a cove and onto rocks.

Initially helmsman Mark Chandler attempted a direct approach to the dinghy, which had two men onboard, but in heavy surf, shallow water and with very little space to manoeuvre between rocks, he was forced to abandon the approach, causing slight damage to the ILB's propeller as he did so.

The next approach was made by the ILB crew

D-516 Spirit of the River Exe and Trent 14-24 Dora Foster McDougall ON12-28 30 June 2006. Mike Rice

dropping their anchor and, once it held carrying out the process of 'veering-down' on to the casualty. Unfortunately due to submerged rocks, heavy surf and further damaged being caused by the grounding of the propeller, this attempt also had to be abandoned.

Finding all avenues of direct approach impractical, Mark Chandler took the *D-516* some little distance along the coast where he safely beached the lifeboat. The brothers Roy and Karl Stott made their way along the shoreline, and assisted the two occupants of the dinghy back to the safety of the ILB. During their absence Mark Chandler carried out maintenance to the lifeboat. With the casualties rescued and the damaged propeller replaced, the lifeboat landed the men, at the ILB station, at 16.45 hours.

In appreciation of this service, a Letter of Thanks was sent by the Royal National Lifeboat Institution's Chief of Operations to helmsman Mark Chandler and crewmen Karl & Roy Stott, in which each was thanked *'for your contribution to the successful outcome of this service.'*

Exmouth RNLI's D class inshore lifeboat, *Spirit of the Exe*, was launched on Monday 30 January 2006 following reports of four capsized canoes in the entrance to the River Exe. After finding one empty canoe, the volunteer lifeboat crew were directed to another person who was in a canoe with a girl in the water beside it. The lifeboat crew rescued both before transferring them to the coastguard helicopter.

RNLI volunteers David Preece, Justin Adkin and Roger Jackson launched the Exmouth inshore lifeboat into rough conditions and were directed to the two casualties by lookouts at Straight Point Firing Range whose precise information led them straight to the couple. At this stage they requested that the Teignmouth Atlantic 21 inshore lifeboat, *B588 Frank and Dorothy*, be put on stand by. The Teignmouth RNLI volunteer crew of Kevin Clifton, Alan Edwards and Peter Shillabeer, then launched. While the Exmouth crew rescued the two canoeists, the Teignmouth lifeboat volunteers assisted in bringing the empty canoes and equipment back to Exmouth Beach. The coastguard helicopter, Whiskey Bravo, also airlifted a third casualty from the beach.

All three canoeists were taken to the Royal Devon and Exeter Hospital for treatment, including the woman who was rescued from the

Yacht *Ambition* grounded Exmouth 20 September 2006.
Melanie Mock

water by the Exmouth lifeboat. She was suffering from severe hypothermia.

Tim Mock, RNLI Coxswain at Exmouth, said:

'We could see the two casualties rescued by the inshore lifeboat, from the boathouse, including the girl who was in the water. It was vital that the lifeboat crew got to them quickly because the water is very cold at this time of year. The volunteer crew did a marvellous job and worked w ell with the coastguard helicopter to transfer the casualties. We train regularly for this kind of situation and that crew training definitely paid off.'

On Wednesday 20 September 2006, the Trent, *Forward Birmingham Exe* was launched to assist a 40-foot Ferro cement sail yacht, with auxiliary engine, which had dragged its anchor and was being driven aground near Maer Rocks, Exmouth. At the scene of the incident visibility was poor, with a force 5-6 south to south-westerly wind stirring up a choppy to rough sea with one to two meters of swell. The Staff Coxswain of the ALB, Ian Firman, had also requested the launch of the ILB, *Spirit of the Exe*. Both lifeboats were launched at 01.44 hours. The Helm of the ILB was Dave Preece; his crew were Steve Hockings-Thompson and Lee Comley.

The ILB crew located the casualty, the *Ambition*, with three people on board, floundering in heavy surf with waves crashing over the vessel. The lifeboat took up station as close to the casualty as safety would allow and flood-lit the scene with white 'Para-flares'.

Following consultation it was agreed that the crew of three would be taken off the yacht by the ILB. The crew of the ILB picked their way between the treacherous rocks and through the heavy swell and surf that continued to run. At this stage the vessel was starting to go ashore and hitting the bottom. One by one the ILB crew managed to pluck the sailors from their boat, and transfer them to the *Forward Birmingham*. The men were landed safely at Exmouth but the *Ambition,* which had been on passage from the Hamble to Cardiff, was driven aground. Attempts were made to set an anchor to prevent the yacht being driven further ashore. The attempts were unsuccessful.

Following the return of the casualties to shore, both lifeboats returned to the scene in order to attempt a recovery of the vessel. This attempt was also unsuccessful

At the time, Dave Preece, explained what happened:

'By the time we went in, the water was very shallow and we were having to pick our way through the rocks and surf, which isn't easy when there's a large swell running. It was also dark though the casualty vessel did have her lights on. We managed to get alongside and take the three men off the vessel, which was at this stage aground, but we had to do it in three separate approaches taking them off one by one. It was a difficult and demanding task, but this is when all our RNLI crew training pays off and we put all we practise into ensuring we can save the lives of those who get into trouble at sea.'

In his Letter of Commendation, Michael Vlasto, RNLI Operations Director, said of Dave Preece:

'You demonstrated first class seamanship and leadership during this service and both lifeboats worked well together. Well done!'

Later attempts to refloat the *Ambition* also failed and she broke up in storms a few days later.

When the *Spirit of the Exe,* was withdrawn from the Exmouth, she had served the station for 9 years. Her volunteer crews had responded to more than 450 emergency call outs. They had launched to 62

large sailing craft, 32 large powerboats, 53 small powerboats, 32 rubber dinghies, 52 windsurfers, 9 kayaks, 7 jet skis, 6 divers, 18 kite boards, 1 water skier and a single aircraft. These 'shouts' had led to the successful rescue of 323 people, directly saving 36 lives.

D-669 George Bearman
2006-to date

Exmouth RNLI officially welcomed the station's new 'D' class inshore lifeboat at a special naming ceremony on Saturday 30 September 2006. The IB1 is the latest version of this class of inshore lifeboat that was first introduced into the RNLI fleet in 1963. The *George Bearman* is faster than the *Spirit of the Exe* boasting improved manoeuvrability and equipment, specifically:

Length: 4.95m (16ft)
No. of crew: 3 or 4
Propulsion: Mariner 50hp outboard
Max. Speed: 25 knots
Endurance: 3 hours at full speed
Displacement: 338 kg.

The new lifeboat was named by Mrs Pauline Smith, granddaughter of George Bearman during a special ceremony on Exmouth seafront opposite the inshore lifeboat station.

Tim Mock, RNLI Coxswain at Exmouth, says the lifeboat represents the bravery shown by all volunteers who aim to save lives at sea, as she is named after a coastguard who lost his life on the east coast of England back in 1898.

'We are delighted to receive this new inshore lifeboat and would like to thank Mrs Pauline Smith for her generosity. As a charity, the RNLI relies on public support and as crew we rely on the best training, equipment and lifeboats to carry out our work saving lives at sea.'

A party of jet skiers had a lucky escape, near Exmouth, on Sunday 16 March 2008 when the two craft they were using broke down shortly after two of their group had fallen in to the water.

The party of five were a mile off Orcombe Point, in relatively calm seas and a northerly wind of force 4, when two of their number fell from a jet ski. Shortly after this both vessels broke down.

ILB *D-669 George Bearman* on exercise 30 June 2006. Mike Rice

Roger Jackson and Ian Taylor land injured dog 5 April 2009. RNLI/Giles White

Kerys and Adam Nash rescued 25 August 2009.
D Perkin

Relocating ILB to new boathouse. Melanie Mock

ILB Boathouse. Melanie Mock

The group were not equipped with either radio or mobile phone but, fortunately the incident had been observed from the shore by a member of the public who immediately alerted the coastguard.

The Exmouth RNLI 'D' class inshore lifeboat, *George Bearman*, was launched in record time, at 11.40am, thanks to the vital team of RNLI volunteer shore helpers, and recovered the group extremely quickly to shore. The two adults and three children, all from Somerset, were very cold and near hypothermic; two being found some distance way away from the jet skis.

The volunteer lifeboat crew, Dave Preece (Helmsman), Ian Taylor and Andy Stott, all of whom had undergone professional first aid training with the RNLI, immediately transferred the children, aged between 11 and 14, to an ambulance at Orcombe Point, which took them to the local hospital. They were released after treatment.

Bob Paterson, RNLI Deputy Launching Authority at Exmouth lifeboat station, said that, in his opinion, the group were not well equipped for going to sea on a cold day in March:

'One of the adults had a dry-suit on and the other was wearing a wet suit, but the youngsters were not dressed in suitable clothing. The sea is still very cold at this time of year and you need to protect yourself against the wind chill and the sea temperature. Thick wet suits or dry suits are ideal in case

It is not only stranded person or distressed sailors who call upon the services of the RNLI; at 13.58 hours on Sunday 5 April 2009, the Exmouth ILB launched to assist a dog which had fallen down cliffs at Orcombe Point, Exmouth. A local coastguard team initially tended the dog, but due to a rising tide, it was decided to task the Exmouth RNLI Inshore Lifeboat. The volunteer crew of Roger Jackson, Carey Wreford and Ian Taylor were quickly on the scene and transported the boarder collie to the ILB station where it was reunited with its anxious owner and was subsequently taken to a local vet's for a thorough-check up.

The Portland Coastguard tasked the *D669 George Bearman* to rescue an eight year old girl and her father when they got into difficulties in the sea off Otterton Ledge, Budleigh Salterton on Tuesday 25th August 2009

The young girl, Kerys Nash, had been boogie boarding in the River Otter when she was swept out to sea.

Family members, who had been watching Kerys from the beach, raised the alarm as her father rushed in to the sea to help his daughter but, caught by the strong outgoing tide both father and daughter were swept further out to sea. On the falling tide Mr Nash and Kerys found, and desperately clung to a partially exposed rock to await the arrival of the lifeboat.

The *George Bearman* was launched at 12.26 hours and reached the casualties within ten minutes.

On seeing the ILB approaching, Mr Nash used the white underside of his daughter's boogie-board to signal to the approaching craft. Both casualties were taken onboard the *George Bearman* but, due to heavy surf they were unable to be landed on the beach at Budleigh Salterton. The Exmouth all-weather lifeboat, the *Margaret Jean* launched, rendezvoused with the ILB, transferred the casualties and returned them safely to Exmouth. Mr Adams later commented:

"I was relieved my sister-in-law is level headed enough to have contacted the Coastguards when she did. The response time was quick and it's great to see that the system works so well. We thank everyone involved."

With the Exmouth ALB now housed in her new boathouse, it was the turn of the ILB, the *George Bearman*, to leave the old boathouse, which had house an Exmouth lifeboat for 106 years, and take up her accommodation in the new station. The ILB was about to be recovered to the boathouse when the crew spotted a kite-surfer in difficulties; they diverted and assisted the kite-surfer back to shore. This proved to be their first rescue from the new boathouse

Bibliography

Express & Echo (Exeter) Various

The Birmingham Post Various

The Exmouth Journal Various

The Western Morning News Various

Trewins Exeter Flying Post Various

Chown, C E, *A Short History of the Exmouth Lifeboat Station and its Lifeboats*

Farr, Grahame, *Wreck and Rescue on the Coast of Devon* 1968

Morris, Jeff, *Exmouth Lifeboats 1803 – 2003*. 4th Ed. 2003

RNLI The Story of the Exmouth Lifeboats c 1974

RNLI Exmouth Lifeboat Station – Returns of Service Various

Denton, Tony, *Lifeboat Enthusiasts' Society Handbook* 2009